ROGER PROTZ

The Real
Ale
Drinker's
Almanac

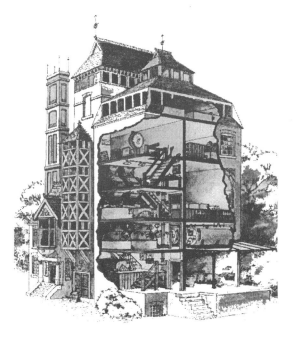

Neil Wilson Publishing Ltd Glasgow Scotland
in association with the Campaign for Real Ale

Published by Neil Wilson Publishing Ltd
Suite 309 The Pentagon Centre, 36 Washington
Street, GLASGOW G3 8AZ

A catalogue record for this book is available from
the British Library

ISBN 1-897784-17-1

Typeset in 8 on 8.5pt AvantGarde by Face to Face
Design Services, Glasgow

Printed in Musselburgh by Scotprint Ltd

Overleaf: A typical British ale brewery with liquor
tanks and malt and hop stores on the top floor, malt
mills below leading to mash tuns. Below the mash
tuns are the coppers and one floor down is the
hopback. The hopped wort is then pumped up to
the fermenting vessels and the raw beer then flows
down to conditioning tanks. Finally the beer is
racked into casks prior to delivery to the pubs.
Illustration by Trevor Hatchett.

CONTENTS

INTRODUCTION

The real ale revolution continues its onward march. It is the drink of the 1990s. As sales of standard lagers slip, despite the massive amounts of money thrown at them, and even stronger 'premium' lagers feel the pinch, cask-conditioned beer, like Topsy, just goes on growing. The national giant brewers, who turned their backs on the country's unique contribution to the world of beer in their helter-skelter rush to lagerise Britain, are now hurrying to join a trend that is fuelled by genuine consumer demand. Press and TV advertisements now proclaim the joys and pleasures of cask beer.

The turnaround is caused by a major change in beer drinkers' habits and perceptions. The British are now concerned with quality, tradition and healthier living. Real ale meets such demands. It is brewed in the main from the finest ingredients and does not need the cheap adjuncts or chemical pit-props used in keg and lager production.

The regeneration of real ale results, too, from the determination of regional brewers to keep the cask beer flag flying. In the dog days of the 1970s it would have been easy for them to have hauled the flag down and either gone over to keg and lager production or to have sold their pubs to the national brewers and retired on the proceeds. Instead they went on brewing what they knew and liked best. Their dedication has had a knock-on effect, encouraging a new breed of micro-brewers to set up mash tuns and coppers and add to the joys of British beer.

Once again the country is awash with a remarkable choice of rich-tasting beers. It is not only bitter that is enjoying a renaissance: milds, porters, stouts, old ales, winter warmers and barley wines are also pouring from an ever-growing number of breweries.

Interest in beer is heightened by knowledge. Other countries produce some of their beer by the method of warm or top fermentation but most of it is found in bottled form. In Britain we drink the greater proportion of our beer on draught and real ale, uniquely, comes to fruition through a secondary fermentation in the cask, rather as Champagne reaches maturity in the bottle. It is that conditioning in the cask that gives the beer its ripeness of flavour and depth of character, with aromas and palates sharply different to lager beers produced by cold or bottom fermentation

Beer of great quality, produced by craftsmen, is as deserving of consideration as fine wine. Enormous attention is given to the product of the grape while the fruit of the barley tends to be tipped indiscriminately down the throat. But it takes more skill to make good beer than wine and the end result deserves just as much respect and admiration. The variety of malt and the blend of hops give each beer its own character and charm. As well as good 'beery tastes' in the mouth, there are a myriad bouquets and aromas redolent of the harvest and the hop field. This book is a contribution to unlocking and appreciating those tastes and flavours.

THE LANGUAGE OF BEER

Brewing beer is like making tea. Both are the result of a simple infusion of basic ingredient and hot water. The analogy can be extended: the finished taste of the product depends crucially on the variety of tea or malt used. A Lapsang Souchong is smoky and intense, an Earl Grey light, quenching and aromatic. Similarly, an ale brewed from pale malt will have a bouquet and palate radically different from a beer made from darker malt with a dash of roasted barley.

In the brewery the mash tun is the tea pot. The malt that comes pouring into the vessel from a grain hopper has been carefully nurtured by specialist maltsters. Only a small proportion of the barley grown in Britain is suitable for brewing. It must be high in starch and low in nitrogen so that the sugars can be easily extracted, and it must sprout quickly. In the maltings the grain is immersed in tanks of water and encouraged to germinate by soaking up the liquid. The wet grain is then spread on malting floors in warm, dry rooms and within a few days shoots break through the husks. The cells of the barley are broken down by germination, making the conversion of starch to sugar possible.

When the maltster judges that partial germination has taken place, he moves the malt to a kiln where it is heated by hot air to stop further germination. The heat is gradually increased to produce the type of malt needed by the brewer: a pale, golden beer requires a lightly kilned malt; tawny ales will have a proportion of crystal malt that has been heated to a higher temperature; dark beers — milds, porters and stouts — will have chocolate or black malts that have been kilned to the point where there is little fermentable sugar content left but which are vital for both colour and flavour. Roasted but unmalted barley, which has the aroma and palate of coffee beans, is another favourite grain for both colour and bitter flavours.

In the brewery the malt is crushed in a mill to produce a coarse powder known as grist. Brewers may use just one type of malt in the mash tuns or they may blend pale and crystal with a dash of chocolate according to the recipe. Many brewers use small amounts of wheat flour, torrefied wheat or barley (similar to popcorn), and maize to counter protein haze and to encourage a lively head on the finished beer.

The stronger the beer, the greater the amount of grist that is used. It is mixed in the mash tun with pure hot water, called 'liquor', either from the public supply or from the brewery's own wells. Many brewers add salts to the liquor to reproduce the hardness found in the water of Burton-on-Trent, which is considered ideal for brewing pale ale.

The thick porridge lies in the tun for an hour or two. During this time the sugars are released from the malt and dissolve into the liquor. Temperature in the tun and the length of time the grist lies in the vessel have to be carefully judged in order to extract the maximum amount of sugar. When the brewer is satisfied, the sweet liquid, called 'wort', is run out of the bottom of the mash tun through a slotted base. The thick slurry of grain is then sprayed or 'sparged' with more hot liquor to wash out any remaining sugars. An individual brew is known as a 'gyle'; by adjusting the amount of liquor, some brewers make more than one beer from a brew or, by adding different amounts of priming sugars and hops, will produce several beers of the same strength. The system is known as 'parti-gyling'.

The wort is pumped to a copper where it is boiled vigorously with hops. The rise of European lager in Britain has led to a fall in demand for English hop varieties but the brewers who have listed their hops for this book still have a great attachment to such traditional strains as Fuggles and Goldings from Kent and Worcestershire. The hop is a climbing plant with remarkable properties. Its blossom — the cone — contains tannins, resins and oils that not only add classic bitterness to beer but also help clarify the wort, kill bacteria and reduce protein haze. The hops used in a particular brew may be a blend of several varieties. The brewer will not necessarily tip in all the hops at the start of the boil.

The classic recipe often entails Fuggles, with their tangy bitterness, added at the start of the boil, and Goldings, renowned for their resiny aroma, added later. If the whole flower of the hop is used, they settle on the base of the copper and act as a filter when the boil is finished. If the hops have been compressed into pellets, the hopped wort will be filtered in a whirlpool centrifuge. While the wort is in the copper, many brewers add special brewing sugars to encourage a strong fermentation. Too much sugar will lead to a thin beer and purists prefer not to use it.

The hopped wort is cooled and then pumped to fermenting vessels in preparation for the violent confrontation with yeast. It is this stage that marks the great divide between ale and lager. Ales are produced by a top-fermenting yeast strain that works quickly and vigorously at a warm temperature (59-77°F/15-25°C). Breweries cultivate their own yeast strains and guard them with enormous care for they retain vital flavours and pass them on to each brew. Remove a yeast from one brewery and transfer it to another and within weeks it will have added new dimensions to the palate of the beer.

Yeast is 'pitched' or mixed with the wort. Slowly a thin slick appears on top of the liquid. Bubbles burst to the surface, the slick becomes a foam and within twenty-four hours it has transformed itself in a white-yellow-brown heaving crust. Above the fermenters the air is heady with the aromas of raw alcohol and carbon dioxide. The head of the yeast is skimmed and the remainder slowly sinks to the bottom of the vessel as the sugars are converted to alcohol.

Brewers control the amount of sugar left in the beer. No beer has all the sugar fermented out, for the finished brew would be uncomfortably dry. Higher gravity beers tend to be sweeter than lower gravity ones. The amount of sugar left is known as the 'degree of attenuation'.

Warm fermentation takes about a week. The raw or green beer is run into conditioning tanks and left to mature for a few days. Conditioning allows the beer to purge itself of the rough, unpleasant flavours produced by fermentation. Finings — isinglass — a glutinous substance made from the sturgeon, is added to force the remaining yeast to settle, and priming sugar is also mixed in to encourage a strong secondary fermentation. Brown roasted sugar — caramel — is sometimes added to give colour. Many brewers add a handful of hops — dry hopping — to give a good floral or resiny aroma.

The beer that now leaves the brewery is not yet ready to be drunk. It is in the pub cellar that it undergoes its second fermentation in the cask. As the remaining yeast settles to the belly of the cask it continues to turn the last of the sugar into alcohol. The skill of the cellarman, using porous venting pegs in the bunghole on top of the cask to control the escape of gas, determines when conditioning is complete and the mature beer, redolent with good malt, hops and fruit aromas, is ready to be served.

THE TASTE OF BEER

The nose or bouquet of a beer and its flavour in the mouth are predominantly malty and hoppy. But there are other aromas and tastes produced by fermentation. As yeast turns sweet sugars into alcohol and carbon dioxide it produces what are known as esters. In a low gravity beer, where the predominant aroma is that of the hops, esters may be present in the form of a light citric fruitiness—though some brewers believe that character comes more from the hop than the malt. In stronger beers with a high malt content, fruitiness is apparent in a riper fashion and banana, apple, pear drops and gooseberry are common. Crystal and amber malts give a pleasing nut character while dark and black malts add a touch of chocolate, coffee, burnt toast and liquorice. In barley wines there is often a powerful vinous aroma with strong hints of tannin, leather, dried fruit and pineapple.

This book encourages drinkers to use their noses as well as their tastebuds. The nose or bouquet of a top-fermented beer is often slow to develop. Beer should be kept at a cellar temperature of 55°F/12°C. The aromas begin to come out as the beer warms up in the glass. Drink some beer to leave room and then give the glass a good swirl to help release the nose. Then give a good sniff.

As the temperature of the beer rises the predominant malt and hops character will be joined by other aromas produced by fermentation. Agitate the beer in the mouth to get the full flavour of the liquid and let it slowly trickle over the tongue. The tongue recognises sweetness at the front, saltiness and sourness in the middle and bitterness at the back. 'Finish' refers to the aftertaste of the beer. Dryness is often wrongly associated with hops. In fact, dryness and even astringency come from the malt.

Beer tasting is a highly subjective assessment and the aroma and palate of a beer can change from one brew to another and from one year's crop of barley and hops — though careful blending of ingredients will remove any sharp differences.

Beer should be delivered from cellar to bar in the way described and preferred by the brewer. The success of Yorkshire beers, with their typical tight and creamy heads of foam, has encouraged many publicans to force all beers through 'tight sparklers' fitted to the spouts of beer engines. But sparklers push all the volatiles into the head, which is what a Yorkshire brewer wants in order to get the distinctive tart and tangy aromas. Southern beers are not brewed for such a method of delivery and the balance of aromas and flavours is upset by such treatment. Midlands and southern beers should be served with a loose collar of foam in order to enjoy the brewers' skills. In Scotland, though the English beer engine and handpump are spreading, the traditional method of serving cask beer is the tall fount primed by air pressure.

THE STRENGTH OF BEER

Two systems are used in the guide to indicate the strength of beer. Original gravity (OG) is a measure for duty purposes of the fermentable sugars present in the wort. Water has a gravity of 1000°. A beer with an OG of 1036° will have 36 parts of fermentable sugars present in the wort. OG is now being replaced by Alcohol by Volume, a measure of the alcohol present in the finished beer.

In June 1993 all beer duty will levied at the 'factory gate' and will be based on the ABV. Original gravity will cease to be used. When a beer is 'highly attenuated' or brewed out there can be a substantial difference between OG and ABV and the use of both systems is useful. Boddingtons Bitter, for example, has a modest OG of 1035° but is brewed out to 3.8% ABV, which means it is higher in alcohol than the gravity suggests.

Units of Colour and Units of Bitterness are registered on a European scale and give a useful indication of a beer's appearance and bitterness. Not all brewers have the equipment to measure colour or bitterness.

Nearly all the brewers in this new addition now give substantial information about recipes. The handful who keep their recipes secret should be reminded that drinkers have a right to know what goes into their beers and may draw the wrong conclusions about such reticence.

My thanks to the brewers who have once again

cooperated in the production of the book. I hope that between now and the next edition they will all give thought to their recipes and ask whether it is not time to cut back on or eradicate high levels of adjuncts such as sugars and unmalted ingredients in order further to improve the quality and appreciation of British beer.

JOIN CAMRA

Membership of the Campaign for Real Ale is currently £10 a year. It will rise to £12 in January 1994. Membership entitles you to attend meetings, brewery visits and beer tastings, with free entry to beer festivals. You will receive a monthly newspaper, What's Brewing, and get generous discounts on the price of the Good Beer Guide and other books.

Send a cheque, made out to 'CAMRA Ltd' to CAMRA, 34 Alma Road, St Albans AL1 3BW. For further information phone 0727 867201.

AUTHOR'S NOTE

On June 1, 1993, a new system of collecting beer duty, known as End Point Duty, was introduced by the Government. This is based on the Alcohol by Volume (ABV) ratings of beer, rather than Original Gravity (OG). Several brewers said they would reduce the ABVs of their beers in order to avoid paying higher rates of duty.

As a result, some of the ABVs listed in the Almanac may be lower than stated. For example, Ruddles Best Bitter will be 3.7% rather than 3.8%, Ruddles County 4.9% (5%), Websters Yorkshire Bitter 3.5% (3.8%) and Worthington Best Bitter 3.6% (3.8%). The brewers say they will compensate for any decrease in body in the beers by increasing the original gravity.

Roger Protz
St Albans
June, 1993

KEY TO SYMBOLS

- ▭ Address
- ① Telephone number
- ▥ Reception centre
- ⋔ Availability of tours
- *i* Status of brewery

SCOTLAND

With the exception of the small Borve and Orkney breweries, Scotland's beer producers are based in the Lowlands. The concentration of breweries around Alloa, Edinburgh and Glasgow was encouraged by the fact that the best barley for malting grew in the Borders and North-east England. Further north, barley that survives the hard climate is best suited for distilling.

Scotland has a rich beer heritage and its ales are distinctively different to those from England and are brewed to withstand the rigours of a cold climate. Roasted barley or dark and chocolate malts give a darker, nut-sweet appeal to beer. The lack of an indigenous hop industry means the imported plant is used sparingly. Beer terms are different, too. Low gravity ale is called 'light' even when it is dark or walnut brown in colour, medium strength ale is 'heavy' while stronger 'export' ales recall the pioneering days of Scottish brewing when the likes of Younger refreshed the colonies.

The terms 60/-, 70/-, 80/- and 90/- refer to a 19th-century system of invoicing beers according to strength. The traditional method of serving cask beer is the tall fount primed by air pressure, though the English hand pump and beer engine are also in widespread use.

Scotland was once difficult territory for cask ale, with keg beers and lager dominant. But cask is undergoing a dramatic revival thanks to the efforts of small brewers and English exporters. The revival may shake Scottish & Newcastle out of its lethargy. At least it brews cask ale while Tennent Caledonian's only contribution is to market Draught Bass for its English owner.

Alloa Brewery Company Ltd

🖃 **Whins Road, Alloa, Clackmannanshire FK10 3RB**
① **0259 723539**
🏛 **No.**
🕴 **Yes.**
i **Subsidiary of Carlsberg-Tetley**

ARCHIBALD ARROL'S 80/-
OG 1041˚ ABV 4.2%
Ingredients: pale malt (90%), crystal malt (10%), maltose syrup plus cane sugar for priming in cask. British hop varieties (pellets). Dry hopped. 23 units of bitterness.

TASTING NOTES

Nose	Rich fruit aroma with hint of butterscotch and hop resin
Palate	Sweet malt in the mouth, dry finish with light hop character
Comments	Heavy fruity beer

Belhaven Brewery Company Ltd

🖃 **Dunbar, East Lothian EH42 1RS**
① **0368 62734**
🏛 **Yes.**
🕴 **by arrangement.**
i **Independent, owned by Control Securities**

BELHAVEN 60/-
OG 1030.5˚ ABV 3%
Ingredients: Pipkin pale malt (89%), black malt (2%), crystal malt (2%), liquid sugar (7%). 43 units of colour. Whitbread Goldings Variety hops for bitterness, Fuggles and Goldings for aroma. All pellets. 21 units of bitterness.

TASTING NOTES

Nose	Light hop and dark malt aromas
Palate	Pronounced malt in the mouth with delicate dry finish
Comments	Delicious dark mild with appealing walnut brown colour.

BELHAVEN 70/-
OG 1035.5° ABV 3.5%

Ingredients: Pipkin pale malt (92%), black malt (1%), crystal malt (2%), liquid sugar (5%). 23 units of colour. Whitbread Goldings Variety for bitterness, Fuggles and Goldings for aroma. All pellets. 23 units of bitterness.

TASTING NOTES

Nose	Hop resin and dry fruit aromas
Palate	Nutty on the tongue with light, sweet finish
Comments	Delectable honey-coloured session beer.

BELHAVEN 80/-
OG 1041.5° ABV 4.1%

Ingredients: Pipkin pale malt (86%), black malt (1.5%), crystal malt (2.5%), liquid sugar (10%). 33 units of colour. Whitbread Goldings Variety for bitterness, Fuggles and Goldings for aroma. All pellets. 29 units of bitterness.

TASTING NOTES

Nose	Stunning aromas of rich grain, gooseberry, hops and toast
Palate	Mouth-filling balance of malt and tart fruit with intense dry finish
Comments	Memorably rounded ale, a complex balance of fruit and hop.

ST ANDREW'S ALE
OG 1046° ABV 4.5%

Ingredients: Pipkin pale ale malt (86%), black malt (1.5%), crystal malt (2.5%), liquid sugar (10%). 35 units of colour. Whitbread Goldings Variety hops for bitterness, Fuggles and Goldings for aroma. All pellets. Dry hopped. 36 units of bitterness.

TASTING NOTES

Nose	Rich and peppery hop aroma with fruit notes
Palate	Full malt and nut in the mouth, bitter-sweet finish with good hop character
Comments	A fine addition to the range, the only beer to be dry hopped which shows in aroma and palate.

BELHAVEN 90/-
OG 1070° ABV 7.5%
Ingredients: Pipkin pale ale malt (84%), black malt (4%), liquid sugar (12%). 75 units of colour. Whitbread Goldings Variety for bitterness, Fuggles and Goldings for aroma. All pellets. 34 units of bitterness.

TASTING NOTES

Nose	Light hop aroma, hints of pineapple
Palate	Rich malt in the mouth with powerful hop finish and dark chocolate notes
Comments	Rich, warming old ale, to be sipped and savoured.

■■■■■■■■■

Borve Brew House
- ✉ **Ruthven by Huntly, Aberdeenshire AB54 4SR**
- ☎ **046687 343.**
- 🏛 **in public house attached.**
- 术 **Yes.**
- *i* **Independent.**

BORVE ALE
OG 1040° ABV 3.7%
Ingredients: pale malt (97%), crystal malt (1.5%), chocolate malt (0.5%), roast barley (1%). Target hops for bitterness, Omega for bitterness and aroma. All pellets. 26 units of bitterness.

TASTING NOTES

Nose	Delicate hop aroma with aromas of light citric fruit and hop resins
Palate	Bitter-sweet in the mouth, long, quenching finish with balance of malt and hops
Comments	A light-coloured beer using 'palest pale malt' with complex balance of malt, tart fruit and hops.

Broughton Brewery Ltd

▱ **Broughton, Biggar, Lanarkshire ML12 6HQ.**
① **08994 345**
▥ **No.**
☘ **by arrangement.**
i **Independent**

GREENMANTLE ALE
OG 1038˚ ABV 3.9%
Ingredients: pale ale malt with small percentage of flaked maize and roasted barley. 34 units of colour. Fuggles and Goldings hop pellets primarily for bitterness. 24 units of bitterness.

TASTING NOTES
Nose	Pronounced orange and lemon fruit aromas
Palate	Rich malt in the mouth with beautifully balanced bitter-sweet finish.
Comments	A copper-coloured brew with a ripe fruity appeal. Broughton Special Bitter is Greenmantle Ale dry hopped for the English market.

SCOTTISH OATMEAL STOUT
OG 1040˚ ABV 3.8%
Ingredients: pale ale malt, pinhead oatmeal, roasted barley. 130 units of colour. Fuggles and Goldings hop pellets primarily for bitterness. 28 units of bitterness.

TASTING NOTES
Nose	Dominant aromas of roasted grain and oatmeal
Palate	Creamy sweetness from the oatmeal and roasted coffee beans in the mouth, dry and grainy finish
Comments	A superb stout with a pronounced Scottish character.

OLD JOCK
OG 1070˚ ABV 6.7%
Ingredients: pale ale malt with small percentage of roasted barley. 48 units of colour. Fuggles and Goldings hop pellets primarily for bitterness. 32 units of bitterness.

TASTING NOTES

Nose	Spicy and vinous aromas
Palate	Rounded malt, fruit and butterscotch dominate the mouth, long bitter-sweet finish
Comments	Powerful and complex dark ale packed with fruit flavours.

Caledonian Brewing Company Ltd

▭ **Slateford Road, Edinburgh EH11 1PH**
① **031-337 1286**
🏛 **Yes.**
⍟ **Yes.**
i **Independent.**

CALEDONIAN 70/-
OG 1036° ABV 3.3%
Ingredients: Golden Promise barley malt, crystal malt, amber malt, chocolate malt, black malt, wheat malt and enzymic malt. Fuggles and Goldings whole hops. 28-30 units of bitterness.

TASTING NOTES

Nose	Light hints of Ovaltine and hop resin
Palate	Good balance of malt and hops with bitter-sweet finish
Comments	Fine, refreshing amber session brew.

R&D DEUCHARS IPA
OG 1038° ABV 3.9%
Ingredients: Golden Promise barley malt and crystal malt, small percentage of wheat malt. Whole Fuggles hops for bitterness, Goldings for aroma. 34-36 units of bitterness.

TASTING NOTES

Nose	Distinctive peppery Goldings aroma with citric fruit notes
Palate	Quenching balance of malt and hops in mouth, lingering hoppy finish
Comments	Superb golden beer named after a defunct Edinburgh brewery.

CALEDONIAN PORTER
OG 1042° ABV 4%

Ingredients: Golden Promise barley malt, crystal malt, amber malt, chocolate malt, black malt, wheat malt. Fuggles and Goldings whole hops. 34-36 units of bitterness.

TASTING NOTES

Nose	Rich aromas of roast barley and black chocolate
Palate	Biscuity in the mouth, dry complex finish with good hop character and dark chocolate and coffee
Comments	A delectable dark brew, a fine member of the new stout breed.

EDINBURGH REAL ALE
OG 1042° ABV 4%

Ingredients: Pipkin pale malt, crystal malt, chocolate malt, wheat malt and roasted barley. Fuggles and Goldings whole hops. 36-38 units of bitterness.

TASTING NOTES

Nose	Roast barley dominates, with hints of dark chocolate and hop resins
Palate	Rich, velvety texture in the mouth with complex finish of roast grain, dark chocolate and coffee
Comments	A traditional dark Scottish Heavy first brewed for the Bow Bar in Edinburgh but now available in other outlets.

CALEDONIAN 80/-
OG 1043° ABV 4.1%

Ingredients: Golden Promise barley malt, crystal malt, amber malt, chocolate malt, wheat malt. Fuggles and Goldings whole hops. 34-36 units of bitterness.

TASTING NOTES

Nose	Rich aromas of malt and hops with citric fruit notes
Palate	Full malt in the mouth, deep, dry hoppy finish with hints of chocolate
Comments	Superbly balanced golden Heavy.

GOLDEN PROMISE
OG 1048° ABV 4.9%

Ingredients: 100% Atem organic malted barley. Progress organic English hops. 50-52 units of bitterness.

TASTING NOTES

Nose	Pronounced malt and hop flower aromas
Palate	Complex balance of malt, hops and orange fruit in the mouth, a deep, beautifully-balanced finish with hop and fruit notes
Comments	A pale golden beer using only organic materials. It has the seal of approval of the Soil Association.

MERMAN XXX
OG 1052° ABV 4.9%

Ingredients: Golden Promise malt, crystal malt, amber malt, chocolate malt, black malt, wheat malt. Fuggles whole hops. 48-50 units of bitterness.

TASTING NOTES

Nose	Deep bouquet of hop resins, chocolate and ripe fruit
Palate	Malt, biscuit, fruit and hop bitterness in the mouth, long, dry finish with chocolate notes
Comments	Warming, rounded and complex dark beer based on a late 19th-century recipe.

CALEDONIAN STRONG ALE
OG 1078° ABV 7.6%

Ingredients: Golden Promise pale malt, crystal malt, amber malt, chocolate malt, black malt, wheat malt. Fuggles and Goldings whole hops. 62-64 units of bitterness.

TASTING NOTES

Nose	Massive assault of hop resins, malt, fruit, nut and apple
Palate	Mouth-filling grain and hops with intense dry, vinous finish

Comments	Rich old ale, fermented for 10-12 days to remove any tendency towards cloying on palate. Sold in the US as MacAndrew's Strong Ale.

Harviestoun Brewery Ltd
⌨ **Dollar, Clackmannanshire FK14 7LX**
☎ **025942141**
🏛 **Yes.**
🜩 **by arrangement.**
i **Independent**

WAVERLEY 70/-
OG 1037˚ ABV 3.7%
Ingredients: Halcycon pale malt, crystal malt, roasted barley (2%), soft brown sugar (5%). Progress hops for bitterness, Goldings for aroma. All pellets. Dry hopped with hop oil. 24 units of bitterness.

TASTING NOTES
Nose	Tempting Goldings hop aroma with hint of roast grain
Palate	Quenching yet full-flavoured; long, well-balanced finish with complex flavours of malt, fruit and hops
Comments	An easy-drinking, chestnut-coloured session bitter.

ORIGINAL 80/-
OG 1041˚ ABV 4.1%
Ingredients: Halcyon pale malt (92%), crystal malt (8%), soft brown sugar. Fuggles hops for bitterness, Goldings for aroma. All pellets. Dry hopped with hop oil. 22 units of bitterness.

TASTING NOTES
Nose	Spicy hop aroma
Palate	Fruit in the mouth with good balance of hops; long, dry finish
Comments	Golden quenching beer with pronounced hop character for a Scottish brew.

PTARMIGAN
OG 1045° ABV 4.5%
Ingredients: Halcyon pale malt (91%), crystal malt (3%), wheat (2%), white sugar (4%). Saaz hop pellets. Dry hopped with hop oil. 26 units of bitterness.

TASTING NOTES

Nose	Pungent floral hop aroma
Palate	Malt and hops finely balanced in mouth, bitter-sweet finish
Comments	Golden ale with great complexity; the brewer says it is reminiscent of a Pilsner.

OLD MANOR
OG 1050° ABV 5%
Ingredients: Halcyon pale malt (93%), crystal malt (6%), chocolate malt (1%), soft brown sugar. Northern Brewer hops for bitterness, Goldings for aroma. All hop pellets. Dry hopped with hop oil. 24 units of bitterness.

TASTING NOTES

Nose	Powerful Goldings aroma with rich fruit developing
Palate	Rich balance of malty sweetness and hop bitterness in the mouth; nuts and chocolate notes in long, dry finish
Comments	Rounded, complex beer of great character; fine end-of-session strong ale

Maclay & Company Ltd
⌨ **Thistle Brewery, Alloa, Clackmannanshire FK10 1ED**
① **0259 723387**
🏛 **Yes.**
⚔ **Trade only**
i **Independent.**

MACLAY 60/-
OG 1036° ABV 3.6%
Ingredients: Golden Promise pale malt (45%), Camargue pale malt (45%), crystal malt (5%) wheat malt (5%). 80 units of colour. Fuggles hops for bitterness, German Brewers Gold for aroma. All whole hops. 30 units of bitterness.

TASTING NOTES

Nose	Light hops and biscuit aromas
Palate	Rich malt and hops in mouth, vanilla notes in light, dry finish
Comments	Potable dark ale with chewy malt appeal

MURRAYS SUMMER ALE
OG 1036° ABV 3.6%

Ingredients: pale malt (90%), crystal malt (5%), wheat malt (5%). 15 units of colour. Fuggles hops for bitterness, German Brewers Gold for aroma. All whole hops. Dry hopped. 50 units of bitterness.

TASTING NOTES

Nose	Powerful fresh hop flowers aroma
Palate	Hops and light fruit in the mouth, spritzy, well-balanced finish
Comments	Quenching summer season beer with great hop appeal.

MACLAY 70/-
OG 1036° ABV 3.6%

Ingredients: 100% Scottish Golden Promise barley malt with caramel for colour. 30 units of colour. Whole Fuggles hops.

TASTING NOTES

Nose	Delicate hop aroma
Palate	Refreshing balance of malt and hops, with lingering dry finish
Comments	Refreshing copper-coloured ale

MACLAY 80/-
OG 1040° ABV 4%

Ingredients: 100% Scottish Golden Promise barley malt with caramel for colour. 25 units of colour. Whole Fuggles hops.

TASTING NOTES

Nose	Powerful hop bouquet with rich fruit developing
Palate	Full rounded malt offset by hops in mouth; long finish with creamy vanilla notes underlying dryness
Comments	Fine example of a rich Scottish Export.

KANE'S AMBER ALE
OG 1040˚ ABV 4%
Ingredients: Golden Promise pale malt (45%), Camargue pale malt (45%), crystal malt (5%), wheat malt (5%). 25 units of colour. Whole Fuggle hops. 30 units of bitterness.

TASTING NOTES
Nose	Delicate hops and nutty malt
Palate	Fine balance of malt and hops in mouth, long finish with sherry-like fruit and hops
Comments	Superb amber beer named in honour of Dan Kane, former Scottish organiser of CAMRA who died of leukaemia in 1992.

MACLAY PORTER
OG 1040˚ ABV 4%
Ingredients: pale ale malt (90%), wheat malt (5%), crystal malt (5%). 80 units of colour. Brewers Gold, Fuggles and Goldings whole hops.

TASTING NOTES
Nose	Light grain and hops aromas
Palate	Chewy malt in the mouth, dry hops-and-toast finish
Comments	Tasty dark ale.

MURRAYS AMBER HEAVY
OG 1040˚ ABV 4%
Ingredients: pale ale malt (90%), crystal (5%), wheat malt (5%). 35 units of colour. Brewers Gold, Fuggles and Goldings whole hops. Dry hopped.

TASTING NOTES
Nose	Powerful fresh hops aroma
Palate	Ripe malt in the mouth, bitter-sweet finish
Comments	Refreshing amber-coloured ale with great hop character.

OAT MALT STOUT
OG 1045˚ ABV 4.5%
Ingredients: Golden Promise pale ale malt (40%), Camargue pale malt (40%), malted oats (15%), roasted barley (4%), chocolate malt (1%). 50 units of colour. Fuggles whole hops. 35 units of bitterness.

TASTING NOTES

Nose	Enticing aromas of rich hops and roast grain
Palate	Subtle malty sweetness in mouth, bitter-sweet finish with hint of chocolate
Comments	Luscious stout based on an 1895 recipe.

MACLAY SCOTCH ALE
OG 1050˚ ABV 5%
Ingredients: Golden Promise pale ale malt (47.5%), Camargue pale malt (47.5%), caramalt (5%). 12 units of colour. Fuggles whole hops. 35 units of bitterness.

TASTING NOTES

Nose	Rich hops aroma
Palate	Rounded malt in the mouth balanced by hops, bitter-sweet finish with delicate fruit notes
Comments	Complex, fruity golden ale.

OLD ALLOA ALE
OG 1070˚ ABV 6.5%
Ingredients: 100% pale ale malt. 25 units of colour. Fuggles whole hops.

TASTING NOTES

Nose	Rich malt and hops aromas with delicate fruit notes
Palate	Massive malt and fruit in the mouth, long bitter-sweet finish with vinous notes
Comments	Robust Scottish strong ale. Maclays prides itself on using only malt in its ales, with no cereal adjuncts, plus well water and whole hops.

McEwan and Younger
⌨ **Fountain Brewery, Edinburgh EH3 9YY**
☎ **031-229 9377**
🏛 **Yes.**
🕴 **Yes.**
i **Trading names of Scottish and Newcastle Breweries With the exception of Younger No 3, McEwan and Younger cask beers are identical brews.**

McEWAN 70/-; YOUNGER SCOTCH in Scotland and NE England; YOUNGER BITTER in other areas of England
OG 1036.5˚ ABV 3.7%

Ingredients: Scotch ale malt, roast barley, maize, wheat and cane sugar. English and German Hallertau whole and pellet hops.

TASTING NOTES

Nose	Light malt notes with delicate fruit developing
Palate	Creamy on the tongue with short, dry finish and vanilla notes
Comments	A background beer without any strong characteristics.

McEWAN 80/-; YOUNGER IPA
OG 1043˚ ABV 4.5%

Ingredients: Scotch ale malt, roast barley, maize, wheat and cane sugar. English and German Hallertau whole and pellet hops.

TASTING NOTES

Nose	Strong malt character with citric fruit notes
Palate	Mouth-filling maltiness with dry, slightly fruity finish
Comments	A sweetish amber-coloured beer.

YOUNGER NO 3
OG 1043˚ ABV 4.5%

Ingredients: Scotch ale malt, roast barley, maize, wheat and cane sugar. English and German Hallertau whole and pellet hops.

TASTING NOTES

Nose	Rich hops and biscuit aromas
Palate	Complex mix of chewy maltiness and bitter hop character; intense dry finish with chocolate and nut notes
Comments	A distinctive malty dark Scottish ale.

◼◼◼◼◼

Orkney Brewery

⌧ **Quoyloo, Sandwick, Orkney KW16 3LT.**
☏ **0856 84 802**
🏛 **No.**
⚦ **Yes.**
i **Independent.**

RAVEN ALE
OG 1038˚ ABV 3.8%
Ingredients: Golden Promise Scottish malt (92%), crystal malt (3%), chocolate malt (1%), torrefied wheat (4%). Whitbread Goldings Variety hops for bitterness, Goldings for aroma. All hop pellets. 18 units of bitterness.

TASTING NOTES
Nose   Rich malt aroma with hints of plum jam
Palate   Stunning balance of malt, hops and fruit with complex finish of hoppy dryness and crystal malt nuttiness
Comments   Delectable rounded ale with a fruitiness that suggests greater strength

DRAGONHEAD STOUT
OG 1040˚ ABV 4.1%
Ingredients: Golden Promise Scottish malt (90%), crystal malt (2%), roasted barley (3%), black malt (1%), torrefied barley (3%). Omega hops for bitterness, Goldings for aroma. All hop pellets. 29 units of bitterness.

TASTING NOTES
Nose   Rich bouquet of dark malts and hops
Palate   Complex bitter-sweet balance in the mouth, dry finish with bitterness from hops and dark malts and chocolate notes
Comments   A dark stout with great depth of flavours.

DARK ISLAND
OG 1045˚ ABV 4.7%
Ingredients: Golden Promise Scottish malt (85%), crystal malt (3%), chocolate malt (3%), torrefied wheat (3%), cane sugar (6%). Omega hops for bitterness, Challenger for aroma. All hop pellets. 22 units of bitterness.

TASTING NOTES

Nose	Ripe, fruity aroma with hop notes developing
Palate	Rounded and refreshing in the mouth with good malt and hop balance; long dry finish with hop bitterness and fruit notes
Comments	Rich wine-coloured ale

SKULLSPLITTER
OG 1080° ABV 8.5

Ingredients: Golden Promise Scottish malt (88%), crystal malt (3%), chocolate malt (1%), torrefied wheat (3%), cane sugar (5%). Whitbread Goldings Variety hops for bitterness, Goldings for aroma. 20 units of bitterness.

TASTING NOTES

Nose	Deep vinous aroma
Palate	Satiny malt in the mouth; deceptively light; long dry finish with rich fruit notes
Comments	A reddish coloured ale with a smooth and dangerous drinkability.

Traquair House Brewery

✉ **Traquair House, Innerleithen, Peebles-shire EH44 6PW**
① **0896 831 370.**
🏛 **No.**
🕴 **by arrangement.**
i **Independent**

BEAR ALE
OG 1050° ABV 5%

Ingredients: pale ale malt (99%), black malt (1%). East Kent Goldings and Red Sell whole hops. 34 units of bitterness.

TASTING NOTES

Nose	Rich malt and hops aromas with powerful marmalade fruit developing
Palate	Warm fruit and nut on palate, bittersweet finish with roast notes
Comments	Rich and rounded traditional Scots Heavy.

TRAQUAIR HOUSE ALE
OG 1075˚ ABV 7%

Ingredients: pale ale malt (98.1%), black malt (1.9%). East Kent Goldings and Red Sell whole hops. 35 units of bitterness.

TASTING NOTES

Nose	Stunning aromas of malt, hops, dark chocolate, rich fruit and spices
Palate	Powerful vinous attack of malt and hops with intense bitter finish and strong hints of pineapple and chocolate
Comments	A dark, heady and potent brew produced in restored 18th-century brewhouse in grounds of stately house.

West Highland Brewery

⌑ **Old Station Brewery, Taynuilt, Argyllshire PA35 1JB.**
☏ **08662 246.**
🏛 **Yes (in station bar).**
🚶 **by arrangement.**
i **Independent**

HIGHLAND HEAVY
OG 1038˚

Ingredients: pale malt (88%), crystal malt (10%), wheat malt (2%). Fuggles and East Kent Goldings whole hops, dry hopped with Goldings.

TASTING NOTES

Nose	Massive Goldings hop bouquet with malt notes
Palate	Quenching bitter-sweet malt and hops in mouth, long, dry and bitter finish with hops and light fruit
Comments	Stunningly bitter beer by Scottish standards

OLD STATION PORTER
OG 1041˚

Ingredients: pale malt (80%), crystal (10%), black malt (5%), wheat malt (5%). Goldings whole hops.

TASTING NOTES

Nose	Hops, malt and dark coffee aromas
Palate	Malty in the mouth, dry, hoppy finish with hint of oatmeal
Comments	Dark, smooth ale with good balance of malt and hops.

HIGHLAND SEVERE
OG 1050˚

Ingredients: pale malt, crystal malt, chocolate malt, small percentage wheat malt. Fuggles and Goldings whole hops.

TASTING NOTES

Nose	Rich aromas of malt and dark fruit
Palate	Sweet malt and fruit in the mouth, deep finish with hop bitterness and ripe fruit
Comments	Dangerously quaffable amber-coloured ale with complex fruit character. The brewery is based in Taynuilt railway station with a bar created out of station waiting rooms. There is a growing free trade for the beers.

NORTH-EAST ENGLAND

The north-east is a beery buffer between Scotland and the rest of England. When Geordies call for a 'Scotch' they want a beer, not a whisky, and they mean a brew that is malty and lightly hopped. Vaux of Sunderland brews a specific beer to meet this demand, Lorimer's Best Scotch, based on an ale once brewed in Edinburgh. At the height of its popularity the bulk of Lorimer's production was drunk not in Edinburgh but in the north-east via the Caledonian railway.

Further south in Teesside drinkers demand powerful ales: Cameron's Strongarm, with a 4 per cent alcohol rating, is considered a supping 'session' beer. Camerons, now owned by the thrusting Wolverhampton and Dudley group, has a greater chance of survival and will continue to ferment its beers in two-storeyed 'dropping' vessels similar to Yorkshire 'squares'.

Whitbread's Castle Eden Brewery, a model of traditional methods, has also been given a new lease of life with a contract to brew a splendid Porter and is likely to pick up some of the pieces from the closure of the group's Sheffield plant. Butterknowle and Border bring new pleasures to the region with their well-crafted 'micro-brewery' beers.

████████████████

Big Lamp Brewers
- ☒ **1 Summerhill Street, Newcastle-upon-Tyne NE4 6EJ.**
- ☎ **091-261 4227.**
- 🏛 **No.**
- 👫 **No.**
- *i* **Independent.**

BIG LAMP BITTER
OG 1038˚ ABV 3.9-4%
Ingredients: best pale malt (95%), crystal malt (5%). Whole Fuggles hops for bitterness, Kent Goldings for aroma.

TASTING NOTES
Nose	Light aromas of malt and hops
Palate	Fine balance of malt and hops in mouth, dry, crisp finish with orange peel notes
Comments	Superb chestnut-coloured ale packed with malt, fruit and hops; antidote to mass-produced keg Geordie beers.

PRINCE BISHOP ALE
OG 1044˚ ABV 4.8-5%
Ingredients: 100% best pale malt. Whole Fuggles hops for bitterness, Kent Goldings for aroma.

TASTING NOTES
Nose	Rich aromas of malt, fruit and peppery Goldings
Palate	Mouth-filling malt and fruit with complex finish of powerful hop and tart fruit
Comments	Deceptively strong, Pilsner-coloured ale.

OLD GENIE
OG 1070˚ ABV 7.5-8%
Ingredients: best pale malt (93%), crystal malt (5%), chocolate malt (2%). Fuggles whole hops for bitterness, Kent Goldings for aroma.

TASTING NOTES
Nose	Ripe bouquet of malt, fruit and Goldings
Palate	Rich malt in the mouth, deep bitter-sweet finish with complex banana and gooseberry notes
Comments	Sumptuous dark beer with vinous appeal.

Border Brewery Company Ltd

☞ **The Old Kiln, Brewery Lane, Tweedmouth, Berwick-upon-Tweed TD15 2AH.**
① **0289 303 303.**
🏛 **Yes.**
🕴 **Yes.**
i **Independent.**

OLD KILN BITTER
OG 1036˚ ABV 3.8%
Ingredients: Camargue pale malt (94%), crystal malt (6%). Equal amounts of Fuggles and Goldings whole hops.

TASTING NOTES

Nose	Peppery, resiny hop aromas underpin the malt
Palate	Good balance of malt and hops in mouth, hops dominate the dry finish with some fruit notes
Comments	Complex and finely-balanced amber ale.

OLD KILN ALE
OG 1038˚ ABV 4%
Ingredients: Camargue pale malt (87%), crystal malt (13%). Equal amounts of Fuggles and Goldings whole hops.

TASTING NOTES

Nose	Malt, nut from the crystal and Goldings aromas
Palate	Malty in the mouth, bitter-sweet finish with good hop character
Comments	Sweeter than the bitter, brewed for the Borders' palate but with plenty of hop appeal.

Butterknowle Brewery

📠 **The Old School House, Lynesack, Butterknowle, Bishop Auckland DL13 5QF.**
① **0388 710109.**
🏛 **No.**
👥 **by arrangement.**
i **Independent.**

BUTTERKNOWLE BITTER
OG 1036° ABV 3.6%
Ingredients: Halcyon pale malt and crystal malt. 28 units of colour. Challenger whole hops. 40 units of bitterness.

TASTING NOTES

Nose	Rich hops aroma with malt notes
Palate	Bitter-sweet, refreshing malt in mouth, light hoppy finish with delicate fruit notes
Comments	Refreshing straw-coloured pale ale bouncing with hops.

CONCILIATION ALE
OG 1042° ABV 4.2%
Ingredients: Halcyon pale malt, crystal malt, chocolate malt. 34 units of colour. Challenger whole hops. 38 units of bitterness.

TASTING NOTES

Nose	Powerful smack of hops with fruit notes developing
Palate	Full flavours of malt, hops and fruit in mouth, deep fruit and hops finish
Comments	A rich and fruity tawny ale.

BLACK DIAMOND
OG 1050° ABV 4.8%
Ingredients: Halcyon pale malt, crystal malt, roast barley. 72 units of colour. Challenger whole hops. 41 units of bitterness.

TASTING NOTES

Nose	Rich nutty hop aroma with roast and hop notes
Palate	Chewy malt and nut in the mouth, big finish with massive hop and some fruit

Comments   A ruby-red ale named to commemorate the local coal-mining industry.

HIGH FORCE
OG 1060˚ ABV 6.2%
Ingredients: Halcyon pale malt, crystal malt, sugar (10%). 31 units of colour. Challenger whole hops. 36 units of bitterness.

TASTING NOTES
Nose	Massive spicy hops aroma with malt and citric fruit notes
Palate	Fine malt and hops balance in mouth, long bitter-sweet finish with quenching fruit notes
Comments	Dangerously drinkable pale gold brew.

OLD EBENEZER
OG 1080˚ ABV 8%
Ingredients: Halcyon pale malt, crystal malt, roast barley, sugar (10%). 82 units of colour. Challenger whole hops. 30 units of bitterness.

TASTING NOTES
Nose	Tempting roast grain and hops aromas
Palate	Rich malt in the mouth with chewy nut and roast, deep bitter-sweet finish with ripe fruit and hops
Comments	Tawny, fruity ale brewed for Christmas trade but now produced regularly to meet demand.

J W Cameron & Co Ltd

⌨ **Lion Brewery,**
Hartlepool TS24 7QS.
☏ **0429 266666.**
🏛 **Yes.**
⚐ **Yes.**
i **Subsidiary of Wolverhampton & Dudley Breweries.**

CAMERON'S BITTER
OG 1036˚ ABV 3.6%
Ingredients: Maris Otter pale malt (86%), crystal malt (6%), brewing sugars (6%). 27 units of colour. Challenger, Fuggles and Goldings hop pellets. 32 units of bitterness.

TASTING NOTES

Nose	Delicate hop and malt aromas with pronounced crystal nuttiness
Palate	Light balance of malt and hops in mouth, long dry finish with fruit notes
Comments	Fine Fuggles and Goldings character in a copper-coloured ale served with a Yorkshire creamy head.

CAMERON'S STRONGARM
OG 1042˚ ABV 4%
Ingredients: Maris Otter pale malt (79%), crystal malt (13%), brewing sugars (8%). 52 units of colour. Challenger, Fuggles and Goldings pellet hops. 32 units of colour.

TASTING NOTES

Nose	Rich malt and hops aromas with orange peel notes
Palate	Round malt and fruit in mouth, long dry finish with fruit, hops and roasted grain from crystal
Comments	Distinctive ruby-red ale, complex and deep-tasting.

Castle Eden Brewery
- ✉ **PO Box 13, Castle Eden, Hartlepool TS27 4SX.**
- ☏ **0429 836007.**
- ▥ **Yes.**
- ⅋ **Yes.**
- *i* Subsidiary of Whitbread PLC.

CASTLE EDEN ALE
OG 1040˚ ABV 4%
Ingredients: pale malt (70%), torrefied wheat (10%), sugar (20%). 23 units of colour. Hops: extract 50%, pellets 50%. Target for bitterness, Styrian Goldings for aroma. Dry hopped with whole Styrian Goldings. 23 units of bitterness.

TASTING NOTES

Nose	Strong Goldings aroma with distinct blackcurrant jam notes
Palate	Rich malt and fruit in mouth, delicate dry, hoppy finish
Comments	Ripe, fruity, tawny ale.

WHITBREAD PORTER
OG 1052° ABV 4.5%
Ingredients: pale malt (76%), brown malt (20%), chocolate malt (2%), black malt (2%). 290 units of colour. 100% English Goldings hop pellets, dry hopped with whole Styrian Goldings. 36 units of bitterness.

TASTING NOTES

Nose	Powerful Goldings aroma with hints of coffee and chocolate
Palate	Massive dark malt appeal in mouth, long, dry finish with bitter malt, hops and fruit
Comments	A superb new beer brewed with great bravado and based on a 1850s Whitbread London recipe. A significant contribution to the porter revival.

WINTER ROYAL
OG 1054° ABV 5.5%
Ingredients: pale malt (95%), crystal malt (5%). 36 units of colour. 100% Target pellet hops. 36 units of bitterness.

TASTING NOTES

Nose	Malt and fruit aromas with powerful hint of oranges
Palate	Fruity palate with a hint of pear drops and lingering bitter-sweet finish.
Comments	Deep ruby-red ale, formerly Wethered's Winter Royal now in a new home.

■■■■■■■■■

Hadrian Brewery Ltd
▭ **Unit 10, Hawick Crescent Industrial Estate, Newcastle-upon-Tyne NE6 1AS.**
① **091-276 5302.**
🏛 **No.**
🕴 **by arrangement.**
i **Independent.**

GLADIATOR BITTER
OG 1039° ABV 4%
Ingredients: pale malt (99%), coloured malt (1%). Fuggles and Target whole hops.

TASTING NOTES

Nose	Delicate fresh hop aroma

| Palate | Mellow balance of hops and malt with light dry finish |
| Comments | A quenching, copper-coloured bitter |

CENTURION BEST BITTER
OG 1045˚ ABV 4.5%
Ingredients: pale malt (99.5%), coloured malt (0.5%). Fuggles and Target whole hops.

TASTING NOTES

Nose	Ripe aromas of fruit and hops
Palate	Complex balance of malt and fruit in mouth, long dry and hoppy finish
Comments	Pale and characterful strong bitter

EMPEROR ALE
OG 1050˚ ABV 5%
Ingredients: pale malt (98%), coloured malt (2%). Fuggles and Target whole hops.

TASTING NOTES

Nose	Light hops aroma with hint of liquorice
Palate	Rounded fruit and malt in mouth with long dry finish and vanilla notes
Comments	A fine fireside old ale, deep red colour.

Newcastle Breweries Ltd

📠 **Tyne Brewery, Gallowgate, Newcastle-upon-Tyne NE99 1RA.**
① **091-232 5091.**
🏛 **Yes.**
⍤ **Yes.**
i **Subsidiary of Scottish & Newcastle Breweries**

THEAKSTON'S BEST BITTER
OG 1038˚ ABV 3.8%
Ingredients: pale and crystal malts, unmalted cereal, sugar. 15 units of colour. Fuggles and other whole and pelletised English hops; Fuggles for aroma. Dry hopped with whole hops. 24 units of bitterness.

TASTING NOTES

Nose	Delicate aromas of malt and hops
Palate	Clean and quenching balance of malt and hops with dry finish
Comments	Newcastle version of the famous Yorkshire bitter. It is believed the two brews are sometimes blended. See also Theakston entry in Yorkshire. CAMRA has protested to the Advertising Standards Authority about promotions suggesting the beer only comes from the Masham brewery in Yorkshire.

THEAKSTON'S XB
OG 1044˚ ABV 4.5%

Ingredients: pale and crystal malts, unmalted cereal, sugar. 26 units of colour. Fuggles and other whole and pelletised English hop varieties; Fuggles for aroma. Dry hopped. 26 units of bitterness.

TASTING NOTES

Nose	Rich nutty malt and peppery hops
Palate	Full malt in mouth, deep dry finish with hop and fruit notes
Comments	A ripe, rounded bitter, another refugee from the Masham brewery in Yorkshire. As with Best Bitter, may be blended with the Yorkshire beer.

Northern Clubs Federation Brewery Ltd

- ⌑ **Lancaster Road, Dunston NE11 9JR.**
- ☎ **091-460 9023.**
- 🏛 **No.**
- ⋔ **by arrangement.**
- *i* **Independent clubs co-operative.**

BEST BITTER
OG 1034˚ ABV 3.6%

Ingredients: English pale ale malt (76%), torrefied wheat (12%), glucose (12%). 27 units of colour. Bramling Cross, Challenger, East Kent Goldings and Target hops in whole, pellet and oil form; Goldings used for aroma. 21 units of bitterness.

TASTING NOTES

Nose	Delicate fresh hops and malt aromas
Palate	Good malt flavour on tongue, light bitter finish
Comments	Pleasant, easy-drinking session beer.

SPECIAL ALE
OG 1040° ABV 4%
Ingredients: English pale ale malt (76%), torrefied wheat (12%), glucose (12%). 17 units of colour. Bramling Cross, Challenger, East Kent Goldings and Target hops in whole and pellet form; Goldings for aroma. Dry hopped. 23 units of bitterness.

TASTING NOTES

Nose	Rich malt and fruit aromas
Palate	Chewy malt character with delicate hop finish
Comments	A sweetish, malty brew with light hop notes.

BUCHANANS ORIGINAL
OG 1042° ABV 4.4%
Ingredients: English pale ale malt (79%), torrefied wheat (11%), glucose (9%). 45 units of colour. Bramling Cross, Challenger, East Kent Goldings and Target hops in whole and pellet form. Dry hopped. 25 units of bitterness.

TASTING NOTES

Nose	Light hop and fruit aromas
Palate	Malt and grain in mouth, light bitter-sweet finish
Comments	Rich coloured and full-bodied beer. All the 'Fed' beers would improve with less torrefied wheat which gives a slightly sticky popcorn note to the beers.

North Yorkshire Brewing Company

⌨ **80-84 North Ormesby Road,
Middlesbrough TS4 2AG.**
☎ **0642 226224.**
🏛 **Yes.**
⚗ **Yes.**
i **Independent**

BEST BITTER
OG 1036˚
Ingredients: Maris Otter pale malt, crystal malt. Northdown whole hops.

TASTING NOTES

Nose	Fresh hops aroma
Palate	Smooth malt in mouth, bitter-sweet finish.
Comments	Pale beer, quenching and creamy.

YORKSHIRE BROWN
OG 1040˚
Ingredients: Maris Otter pale malt, crystal malt and chocolate malt. Northdown whole hops.

TASTING NOTES

Nose	Rich fruit and nuts aromas with good hop notes
Palate	Rounded malt and nut in mouth, long dry finish with vanilla notes
Comments	Superb copper-coloured ale.

YORKSHIRE PORTER
OG 1040˚
Ingredients: Maris Otter pale malt, roasted barley. Northdown whole hops.

TASTING NOTES

Nose	Rich malt and roast grain aromas
Palate	Smooth and dry malt in mouth, mellow bitter finish
Comments	Dark beer with pronounced creamy, roasted grain appeal.

ERIMUS DARK
OG 1046˚
Ingredients: Maris Otter pale malt, crystal malt, chocolate malt and roast barley. Northdown hops.

TASTING NOTES

Nose	Rich aromas of roast barley and hops
Palate	Mellow in mouth with creamy nut and light fruit; deep finish with fine balance of hop, fruit and malt
Comments	Fine ruby-coloured ale, smooth-drinking with a soft creamy head.

FLYING HERBERT
OG 1048˚
Ingredients: Maris Otter pale malt, crystal malt, chocolate malt. Northdown whole hops.

TASTING NOTES

Nose	Ripe plum jam aroma
Palate	Massive fruit and malt in mouth, long dry finish with pronounced fruitiness
Comments	Rounded and full-flavoured ruby-dark ale

DIZZY DICK
OG 1080˚
Ingredients: Maris Otter pale malt, crystal malt, chocolate malt. Northdown whole hops.

TASTING NOTES

Nose	Massive vinous fruit and spicy hops aromas
Palate	Ripe fruit and spices in mouth, deep finish with pronounced raisin and sultana fruit
Comments	Rich barley wine to be sipped and savoured; one for the armchair.

Vaux Breweries Ltd

- 🖃 **The Brewery, Sunderland SR1 3AN.**
- ① **091-567 6277.**
- 🏛 **Yes.**
- 👭 **Yes.**
- *i* **Independent**

LORIMER'S BEST SCOTCH
OG 1036° ABV 3.6%
Ingredients: blend of pale malts, roasted barley. Challenger and Fuggles hop pellets.

TASTING NOTES

Nose	Light hop aroma with toasted grain notes
Palate	Rich creamy malt in mouth, dry finish with coffee notes
Comments	A dark, creamy ale brewed to match the Scotch ales once produced in Scotland for the north-east.

VAUX BITTER
OG 1037° ABV 3.9%
Ingredients: best pale ale malt. Challenger, Fuggles and Target hops pellets.

TASTING NOTES

Nose	Delicate hop resin aroma
Palate	Good balance of malt and hops in mouth with light dry finish
Comments	A pale-coloured session beer.

VAUX SAMSON
OG 1042° ABV 4.1%
Ingredients: blend of pale malts. Challenger, Fuggles and Target hop pellets.

TASTING NOTES

Nose	Rich attack of hops and malt
Palate	Mouth-filling malt and hops; long dry finish with hops and banana and raisin fruit
Comments	Copper-coloured ale, ripe and deliciously fruity.

DOUBLE MAXIM
OG 1044˚ ABV 4.2%
Ingredients: blend of pale malts. Challenger, Fuggles and Target hop pellets.

TASTING NOTES

Nose	Spicy hops and rich malt aromas
Palate	Bitter-sweet balance of malt and hops in mouth, long finish with hop bitterness and light fruit notes
Comments	Draught version of a renowned north-east bottled beer, packed with earthy malt, hops and fruit flavours.

LATE ENTRY

Hexhamshire Brewery
⌧ **Leafield, Ordley, Hexham NE46 1SX.**
☏ **0434 673031.**
i **Independent. A new small brewery based at the Dipton Mill Inn but with several free trade accounts. It started brewing early in 1993 but the beers were not available for tasting when the Almanac went to press.**

LOW QUARTER ALE
OG 1035˚ ABV 3.5%
Ingredients: pale ale malt. Goldings hops.

SHIRE BITTER
OG 1037˚ ABV 3.75%
Ingredients: pale ale malt, small proportion of crystal malt. Goldings and Target hops.

DEVIL'S WATER
OG 1042˚ ABV 4.2%
Ingredients: pale ale malt, crystal malt, roast barley. Goldings and Target hops.

YORKSHIRE

Yorkshire beer lovers say their brews are the best. Certainly the label 'Yorkshire Bitter' acquired a cult status in the 1980s but not all the beers that acquired the title were worthy of the name. John Smith's has dropped the appendage from its title and some might think that Webster's determination to continue to use Yorkshire in the name of its main brand does the region few favours.

Yorkshire can certainly lay claim to a singular style of ale brewing, the 'Yorkshire stone square' system which originally used fermenting vessels made of local stone or slate. A Yorkshire square is made of two linked chambers. The lower section is filled with hopped wort. When fermentation begins the yeast rises into the top chamber through a central hole. The wort is pumped into the top chamber and vigorously mixed with the yeast. When fermentation is complete the beer runs back into the bottom chamber. The system gives a high level of natural carbonation to beer and the famous thick, creamy head.

There are still good tasty dark milds in the region while bitters range from the delicate hops aroma of Theakston's through the quenching citric acidity of Tetley's to the explosion of fruit in Timothy Taylor's renowned ales.

■■■■■■■■■■■■■■■■■■

Bass Brewing (Sheffield)

- 🖃 **Cannon Brewery, 43 Rutland Road, Sheffield S8 8BE.**
- ① **0942 349 433.**
- 🏛 **Yes**
- 🏃 **by arrangement.**
- *i* **Subsidiary of Bass.**

BASS LIGHT 5 STAR.
OG 1030˚ ABV 3.2%.
Ingredients: cask ale malt (83%), crystal malt (1.3%),
wheat flour (6%). 18 units of colour. Challenger and
Northdown whole hops. 23 units of bitterness.

TASTING NOTES
Nose	Light malt and hops bouquet.
Palate	Malt in the mouth with slight hop edge, short bitter-sweet finish.
Comments	Light quaffing beer.

BASS MILD XXXX.
OG 1031˚ ABV 3.2%.
Ingredients: cask ale malt (89%), crystal malt (4%), maltose syrup (7%). 66 units of colour. Challenger and
Northdown hops for bitterness, Goldings and Target for
aroma. All whole hops. 22 units of bitterness.

TASTING NOTES
Nose	Light malt and nut aromas.
Palate	Malt in the mouth, short dry finish with pronounced nut character.
Comments	Easy drinking dark mild.

BASS SPECIAL BITTER
OG 1034˚ ABV 3.5%.
Ingredients: cask ale malt (83%), crystal malt (1.3%),
wheat malt (6.1%). 21 units of colour. Challenger, Goldings, Northdown and Progress whole hops. 26 units of
bitterness. Dry hopped. 26 units of bitterness.

TASTING NOTES
Nose	Light malt aroma with delicate fruit notes.
Palate	Pronounced malt in the mouth, dry bitter-sweet bitter.
Comments	Malt-accented bitter.

NB The three beers above have been transferred from the Bass Tadcaster brewery, which now produces only keg beers.

STONES BEST BITTER
OG 1038° ABV 4.1%.

Ingredients: cask ale malt, high maltose syrup. 13 units of colour. Challenger and Northdown hops for bitterness, Goldings and Progress for aroma. All whole hops. 28 units of bitterness.

TASTING NOTES

Nose	Fragrant dry hop aroma with light fruit notes.
Palate	Delicate malt in mouth with mellow bitter finish.
Comments	A straw-coloured beer with a delicate balance of malt, hops and light fruitiness.

Bass Brewing (Sheffield)
⌨ **Hope Brewery, Claywheel Lane, Wadsley Bridge, Sheffield S6 1NB.**
① **0742 349433.**
🏛 **Yes.**
🜘 **by arrangement.**
i **Subsidiary of Bass**

WORTHINGTON WHITE SHIELD
(bottle conditioned)
ABV 5.6%

Ingredients: Halycon and Pipkin pale ale malt, black malt for colour. 20.5 units of colour. Challenger and Northdown hop pellets. 40 units of bitterness.

TASTING NOTES

Nose	Spices, peppery hops, light fruit and sulphur notes
Palate	Malt, hops and spices in mouth, deep nutty finish with hop character and light fruit notes, apple dominating

Comments   The classic, original India Pale Ale, formerly brewed in Burton-on-Trent. The beer was repackaged in 1992 and became available in off-licences and supermarkets as well as pubs. A new yeast strain was used as Bass considered the old strain to have become tired and too fruity. The new beer has a hoppier character. At the end of the brewing process the beer is sterile filtered and then bottled, primed with sugar to encourage a second fermentation and re-seeded with yeast.

NB The Hope Brewery is due to close and production of White Shield will move to Mitchells & Butlers in Birmingham.

Black Sheep Brewery PLC

☞ **Wellgarth, Masham, near Ripon HG4 4EN.**
① **0765 689 227.**
🏛 **Yes.**
🀫 **by appointment.**
i **Independent**

BLACK SHEEP BEST BITTER
OG 1038˚ ABV 3.8%
Ingredients: Maris Otter pale ale malt (85%), crystal malt (5%), torrefied wheat (10%) plus roast malt extract (0.005%). Fuggles, Goldings and Progress whole hops. Late copper hopped.

TASTING NOTES
Nose   Powerful attack of Fuggles with malt background
Palate   Peppery hop in mouth and in long, bitter finish
Comments   Pale gold ale with distinctive hop character.

BLACK SHEEP SPECIAL STRONG BITTER
OG 1044˚ ABV 4.4%
Ingredients: Maris Otter pale ale malt (83%), crystal malt (7%), torrefied wheat (10%) plus roast malt extract (0.005%). Fuggles, Goldings and Progress whole hops. Late copper hopped.

TASTING NOTES

Nose	Malt, hops, cobnuts and orange fruit aromas
Palate	Bitter-sweet in mouth with dry finish packed with fruit and Goldings hops
Comments	Superb premium bitter with robust malt, fruit and hops. The brewery was set up in 1992 by Paul Theakston, who left Theakstons in Masham following the Scottish & Newcastle takeover.

Clark's

📧 **H B Clark & Company Ltd, Westgate Brewery, Wakefield WF2 9SW.**

① **0924 373328.**

🏛 **Yes.**

🕴 **Yes.**

i **Independent**

CLARK'S TRADITIONAL BITTER
OG 1037˚ ABV 3.7%
Ingredients: pale malt, crystal malt (4%), chocolate malt (1%), priming sugar. Challenger hops.

TASTING NOTES

Nose	Rich hop resin bouquet with some light fruit notes
Palate	Good balance of malt and hops in mouth, dry finish full of hop character and some citric fruit
Comments	A fine-tasting and well-balanced beer.

WINTER WARMER
OG 1044˚ ABV 4.85%
Ingredients: pale malt, crystal malt, chocolate malt, priming sugar. Challenger hops.

TASTING NOTES

Nose	Vinous and malty aromas
Palate	Powerful malt and roast flavours in mouth, big bitter-sweet finish with fruit and hops notes
Comments	Dark brown, malt-accented beer.

RAM'S REVENGE
OG 1046˚ ABV 4.9%
Ingredients: pale malt, crystal malt, chocolate malt, roasted malt for colour. Challenger hops.

TASTING NOTES

Nose	Smooth malt and hops aromas with roast grain notes
Palate	Full, rich malt and hops in mouth, deep finish with dominant hops and roast malt notes
Comments	Ripe and rounded premium ale.

BURGLAR BILL
OG 1047˚ ABV 4.75%
Ingredients: pale malt, crystal malt (4%), chocolate malt (1%), priming sugar. Challenger hops. Dry hopped.

TASTING NOTES

Nose	Powerful bouquet of malt, ripe fruit and hop resins
Palate	Rich fruit and malt in mouth, deep and intense finish with good hops character and fruit notes
Comments	Mellow dark beer with complex malt, fruit and hops.

HAMMERHEAD
OG 1055˚ ABV 5.8%
Ingredients: pale malt, crystal malt (4%), chocolate malt (1%), priming sugar. Challenger hops.

TASTING NOTES

Nose	Massive attack of malt and fruit
Palate	Ripe malt in the mouth with good hops balance; deep and rounded fruit and hops finish
Comments	Powerful and vinous strong ale.

Commercial Brewing Co Ltd
☞ **Worth Brewery, Worth Way, Keighley BD21 5LP.**
☏ **0535 611914.**

KEIGHLIAN MILD
OG 1034˚ ABV 3.5%
Ingredients: two pale malts and crystal malt. 20-24 units
of colour. East Kent and Styrian Goldings whole hops.

TASTING NOTES
Nose	Light malt, nut and hops aromas
Palate	Delicate malt in the mouth, short finish
Comments	Easy-drinking supping bitter.

BECKSIDER
OG 1034˚ ABV 3.3%
Ingredients: pale malt (85%), chocolate malt (7%), crystal malt (8%). 100 units of colour. East Kent Goldings
(100%).

TASTING NOTES
Nose	Rich hint of chocolate with Goldings notes
Palate	Rich malt and chocolate in mouth, nutty finish with good smack of hops
Comments	A well-rounded beer for its strength, packed with malt and hops character.

KEIGHLIAN BITTER
OG 1036˚ ABV 3.7%
Ingredients: pale ale malt (97%), crystal malt (3%). 24-26
units of colour. East Kent Goldings hops (100%).

TASTING NOTES
Nose	Delicate balance of malt and hops
Palate	Clean, quenching malt in mouth, dry and hoppy finish with some fruit notes
Comments	Full-bodied and refreshing session bitter.

WORTH BITTER
OG 1045˚ ABV 4.5%
Ingredients: pale ale malt (100%). 12-14 units of colour.
East Kent and Styrian Goldings whole hops.

TASTING NOTES

Nose	Citric lemon fruit and Goldings hops aroma
Palate	Clean balance of malt and hops, dry finish with light fruit and hops finish
Comments	Pale golden bitter with great hop character.

WORTH
TRADITIONAL
PORTER
Dark and Delicious

1045 o.g.   4.61% A.B.V.

WORTH BREWERY • KEIGHLEY

PORTER
OG 1045˚ ABV 4.5%
Ingredients: pale ale malt (85%), chocolate malt (5%), crystal malt (10%). 100 units of colour. East Kent and Styrian Goldings whole hops.

TASTING NOTES

Nose	Rich malt, roasted grain, chocolate and hops bouquet
Palate	Full malt in mouth, bitter-sweet finish with chocolate and hops
Comments	Rounded, full-bodied and distinctive dark beer.

OLD TOSS
OG 1065˚ ABV 6.5%
Ingredients: pale ale malt (80%), chocolate malt (10%), crystal malt (10%). 100 units of colour. East Kent Goldings whole hops.

TASTING NOTES

Nose	Fruity, vinous aromas
Palate	Ripe malt and fruit in mouth, long bitter-sweet finish with complex balance of hops, ripe fruit and chocolate
Comments	Rich and winey strong dark ale.

Cropton Brewery Co

⌨ **New Inn, Cropton, Pickering YO18 8HH.**
① **07515 330.**
🏛 **Yes (in the pub).**
👭 **by arrangement.**
i **Independent: home-brew pub supplying the free trade.**

TWO PINTS BEST BITTER
OG 1040˚ ABV 4%
Ingredients: pale ale malt, crystal malt. Challenger and Goldings whole hops.

TASTING NOTES
Nose	Fresh inviting hop aromas
Palate	Delicate balance of fruit and hops with light dry finish
Comments	Fine refreshing bitter, so named because you won't be satisfied with just one pint.

SCORESBY STOUT
OG 1042˚ ABV 4.2%
Ingredients: Halcyon pale malt (75%), crystal (15%), roasted barley (10%). Challenger hops for bitterness, Goldings for aroma. All whole hops.

TASTING NOTES
Nose	Rich malt, roasted grain and Goldings hops aromas
Palate	Powerful roasted malt in the mouth, long dry finish
Comments	Distinctive dark beer with great malt character.

SPECIAL STRONG BITTER
OG 1060˚ ABV 6.3%
Ingredients: pale malt, crystal malt. Challenger and Goldings whole hops.

TASTING NOTES
Nose	Powerful smack of hops and fruit notes
Palate	Rich and rounded with fine balance of malt and hops in mouth and long finish with fruit notes

Comments	Dark, nutty and fruity strong beer with good hop character to counteract the malty sweetness.

Daleside Brewery

✉ **Camwal Road, Starbeck, Harrogate HG1 4PT.**
☎ **0423 880041.**
🏛 **No.**
🕴 **No.**
i **Independent (formerly Big End Brewery)**

DALESIDE BITTER
OG 1038˚
Ingredients: not revealed.

TASTING NOTES
Nose	Aromatic hop aroma
Palate	Quenching balance of malt and hops with light, delicate finish
Comments	Fine tasting and well-hopped ale.

DALESIDE OLD ALE
OG 1042˚ ABV 4%
Ingredients: not revealed.

TASTING NOTES
Nose	Rich hop and toast aroma
Palate	Fruit on tongue, deep bitter finish with chocolate hints
Comments	Dark, rich and fruity ale.

MONKEY WRENCH
OG 1056˚ ABV 5.3%
Ingredients: not revealed.

TASTING NOTES
Nose	Massive hop aroma with ripe fruit notes
Palate	Fruity, vinous malt in mouth, long bitter-sweet finish with hops predominating
Comments	Complex, rich and fruity ale.

Franklins

▱ **Bilton Lane, Bilton, Harrogate HG1 4DH.**
① **0423 322345.**
🏛 **No.**
🏃 **No.**
i **Independent**

FRANKLINS BITTER
OG 1038˚ ABV 3.9%
Ingredients: Maris Otter pale malt (95%), crystal malt (5%). Continental pellet hops.

TASTING NOTES

Nose	Inviting hops aroma with fruit notes developing
Palate	Complex balance of fruit and malt with dry, bitter finish
Comments	Distinctive copper-coloured ale.

FRANKLINS BLOTTO
OG 1050˚ ABV 6%
Ingredients: Maris Otter pale malt (90%), crystal malt (10%). Continental pellet hops.

TASTING NOTES

Nose	Ripe fruit aroma
Palate	Rich malt and nut in mouth, dry finish with some fruit and good hops balance
Comments	A fruity strong ale with fruit-and-nut notes from generous use of crystal and fine hops character.

Hambleton Ales

▱ **The Brewery, Holme on Swale, Thirsk YO7 4JE.**
① **0845 567 460.**
🏛 **No.**
🏃 **by arrangement.**
i **Independent**

BEST BITTER
OG 1036˚ ABV 3.7%
Ingredients: pale malt, crystal malt, pale chocolate malt. Northdown hops.

TASTING NOTES

Nose	Crisp hops aroma with malt and chocolate notes
Palate	Clean, quenching sweet malt and bitter hops flavours in mouth, dry bitter-sweet finish with chocolate hints
Comments	Tawny ale, rounded and full-bodied for the gravity.

PORTER
OG 1036˚ ABV 3.7%

Ingredients: Halcyon pale malt (84%), crystal malt (8%), pale chocolate malt (3%), roast barley (3%). Northdown whole hops. 25 units of bitterness.

TASTING NOTES

Nose	Chocolate and nuts from dark malts, good hops underpinning
Palate	Complex flavours of dark malt, hops and fruit in mouth, light, dry finish
Comments	Dark ruby-red just short of black; multi-flavoured 'in true Entire fashion' says brewer.

STALLION
OG 1042˚ ABV 4.4%

Ingredients: Halcyon pale malt (93%), crystal malt (6%), roast barley (0.75%). Northdown whole hops. 40 units of bitterness.

TASTING NOTES

Nose	Malt, roast grain and hops aromas
Palate	Rich malt in mouth, bitter-sweet finish with strong and creamy roast barley character
Comments	Full-bodied dark amber beer.

Kelham Island Brewery

🖃 **23 Alma Street, Sheffield S3 8SA.**
① **0742 781867.**
🏛 **No.**
🏃 **Yes.**
i **Independent**

HALLAMSHIRE BITTER
OG 1036° ABV 3.8%
Ingredients: Maris Otter pale malt (90%), crystal malt (5%), wheat malt (5%). Challenger whole hops.

TASTING NOTES

Nose	Flowery hops aroma
Palate	Dry and light in mouth with fruit notes developing; bitter finish
Comments	Pale and refreshing light bitter with great hops appeal.

KELHAM ISLAND BITTER
OG 1038° ABV 4%
Ingredients: Maris Otter pale malt (95%), crystal malt (5%). Challenger whole hops.

TASTING NOTES

Nose	Rich and earthy floral hops aroma
Palate	Grainy, nutty malt and hops in mouth, lilting bitter-sweet finish
Comments	Stunning pale bitter with complex aroma and flavour.

CELEBRATION ALE
OG 1046° ABV 4.7%
Ingredients: Maris Otter pale malt (91%), crystal malt (9%). Challenger whole hops.

TASTING NOTES

Nose	Ripe malt and hops bouquet
Palate	Malt dominates the mouth with fruit, hops and toffee notes in the finish
Comments	A beer full of rich fruit-and-nut character from generous use of crystal malt.

BÊTE NOIRE
OG 1055˚ ABV 5.5%
Ingredients: Maris Otter pale malt (83%), chocolate malt (7%), wheat malt (10%), plus small quantity of roast barley. Challenger whole hops.

TASTING NOTES

Nose	Rich chocolate and coffee aromas
Palate	Smooth malt in mouth, developing bitter chocolate with raisin and rich damson notes plus coffee in the finish
Comments	Enormously complex strong ale with dark malt and fruit dominating. The brewery lies behind the Fat Cat pub and has a growing free trade as far away as Hertfordshire.

Linfit

- ☞ **The Sair, Lane Top, Linthwaite, Huddersfield HD7 5SG.**
- ① **0484 842370.**
- 🏛 **No (beers available in Sair Inn).**
- 🕴 **Yes.**
- *i* **Independent**

LINFIT MILD
OG 1032˚ ABV 3%
Ingredients: pale ale malt (87%), roast barley (12%), flaked barley (1%). Challenger whole hops.

TASTING NOTES

Nose	Light malt aroma
Palate	Chewy malt in mouth, dry finish with roasted grain notes
Comments	Quaffable darkish mild.

LINFIT BITTER
OG 1035˚ ABV 3.5%
Ingredients: pale ale malt (87%), crystal malt (12%), flaked barley (1%). Challenger whole hops.

TASTING NOTES

Nose	Delicate malt and hops aromas
Palate	Clean, quenching hops and malt with dry, bitter finish

Comments   Refreshing session bitter.

LINFIT SPECIAL
OG 1041° ABV 4%
Ingredients: pale ale malt (88%), crystal malt (11%), flaked barley (1%). Challenger whole hops.

TASTING NOTES

Nose	Malt and hops aromas, fruit notes developing
Palate	Mouth-filling rounded malt, dry finish with vanilla notes
Comments	Rich copper-coloured ale.

ENGLISH GUINEAS STOUT
OG 1050° ABV 5%
Ingredients: pale ale malt (87%), roast barley (12%), flaked barley (1%). Challenger whole hops.

TASTING NOTES

Nose	Tempting aromas of hops and roast cereal
Palate	Rich nut and hops in mouth, dry chocolate finish
Comments	Tasty dark stout packed with roasted malt and hops.

OLD ELI
OG 1050° ABV 5%
Ingredients: pale ale malt (90%), crystal malt (9%), flaked barley (1%). Challenger whole hops.

TASTING NOTES

Nose	Ripe malt aroma with orange peel notes
Palate	Sweet smack of malt with light hop balance; dry finish with ripe fruit notes
Comments	Rich-tasting ale with powerful fruitiness.

LEADBOILER
OG 1063° ABV 6%
Ingredients: pale ale malt (92%), crystal malt (7%), flaked barley (1%). Challenger whole hops.

TASTING NOTES

Nose	Rich malt and hops aromas developing strong fruit notes

Palate	Powerful mouthfeel of malt and alcohol; hoppy finish with complex fruit notes
Comments	Orange-coloured strong ale with pronounced fruitiness.

ENOCH'S HAMMER
OG 1080° ABV 8%
Ingredients: pale ale malt (99%), flaked barley (1%). Challenger whole hops.

TASTING NOTES

Nose	Nose-tickling aroma of hops with ripe marmalade fruit notes
Palate	Vast attack of malt, orange and lemon peel; long finish with hoppy dryness and fruity astringency
Comments	Straw-coloured sipping beer named after Enoch Taylor whose grave can be seen at Marsden; he made an automatic shearing machine attacked by 19th-century Luddites.

XMAS ALE
OG 1080° ABV 8%
Ingredients: pale ale malt (99%), flaked barley (1%). Torrax for colour. Challenger whole hops.

TASTING NOTES

Nose	Light hops and malt aromas, fruit notes developing
Palate	Mouth-filling malt and fruit, dry finish with sultana fruit
Comments	A seasonal ale that keeps out the chill. Produced in draught and bottle-conditioned form. Linfit beers are available in the Sair Inn and in the free trade.

Malton Brewery Company Ltd

- ▭ **Crown Hotel, Wheelgate, Malton YO17 0HP.**
- ℺ **0653 697580.**
- 🏛 **Yes (small).**
- ⚐ **by arrangement.**
- *i* **Independent**

MALTON PALE ALE
OG 1033.8° ABV 3.8%
Ingredients: pale ale malt, crystal malt. Challenger whole hops. 27 units of bitterness.

TASTING NOTES
Nose	Fresh, floral hops aroma
Palate	Light, quenching malt and hops with delicate dry finish
Comments	Fine quaffing ale with good hop character, well-attenuated.

DOUBLE CHANCE BITTER
OG 1037.8° ABV 4.1%
Ingredients: pale ale malt, crystal malt. Challenger whole hops. 30 units of bitterness.

TASTING NOTES
Nose	Explosion of hops
Palate	Superb balance of malt and light fruit with intensely dry finish
Comments	Pale-coloured ale with breathtaking bitter character.

PICKWICK'S PORTER
OG 1041° ABV 4.4%
Ingredients: pale malt, crystal malt, black malt. Challenger whole hops. 28 units of bitterness.

TASTING NOTES
Nose	Heady aromas of hops and dark malt
Palate	Tart and dry balance of malt, toasted grain and pungent fruit with dry hop and chocolate finish
Comments	Jet-black stout full of dark grain and hops character.

OWD BOB
OG 1054.8˚ ABV 6%
Ingredients: pale malt, crystal malt, black malt. Challenger whole hops. 50 units of bitterness.

TASTING NOTES

Nose	Hops balanced with dark chocolate and fruit
Palate	Rich balance of malt and hops; deep finish with black malt and chocolate notes
Comments	Dark ruby-coloured winter ale.

Marston Moor Brewery

⌖ **Crown Inn, Kirk Hammerton, York YO5 8DD.**
① **0423 330341.**
🏛 **Yes (in pub).**
⚲ **Yes.**
i **Independent**

CROMWELL BITTER
OG 1037˚ ABV 3.7%
Ingredients: Maris Otter pale malt (95%), wheat malt (2.5%), crystal malt (2.5%). Challenger whole hops for bitterness, Styrian Goldings for aroma. 26 units of bitterness.

TASTING NOTES

Nose	Peppery Goldings hop resin aroma
Palate	Light, quenching balance of malt and hops, bitter-sweet finish
Comments	Refreshing session bitter with good hop character.

BREWERS PRIDE
OG 1042˚ ABV 4.1%
Ingredients: Maris Otter pale malt (95%), wheat malt (2.5%), crystal malt (2.5%). Challenger whole hops for bitterness, Styrian Goldings for aroma.

TASTING NOTES

Nose	Ripe aromas of malt and developing Goldings hops

Palate	Creamy malt in mouth, deep finish with good balance of malt and hops with some fruit notes
Comments	Amber-coloured beer with great malt appeal and fine Goldings presence.

PORTER
OG 1042˚ ABV 4.1%

Ingredients: Maris Otter pale malt (87%), roast barley (8%), wheat malt (2.5%), crystal malt (2.5%). Challenger whole hops for bitterness, Styrian Goldings for aroma.

TASTING NOTES

Nose	Roasted grain aroma with good hops character
Palate	Pronounced bitter roast notes in mouth, powerful finish with malt, hops and bitter fruit notes
Comments	Ruby-coloured, full-bodied beer with great roasted and dark malt characteristics.

BREWERS DROOP
OG 1048˚ ABV 5%

Ingredients: Maris Otter pale malt (95%), wheat malt (2.5%), crystal malt (2.5%). Challenger whole hops for bitterness, Styrian Goldings for aroma.

TASTING NOTES

Nose	Powerful smack of ripe malt with resiny Goldings notes
Palate	Rich malt in mouth; long, deep finish with good hops notes and delicate hints of fruit
Comments	Potent and potable straw-coloured beer with complex mix of malt, fruit and hops. The beers are available in the Crown Inn and in many free-trade accounts.

■■■■■■■■■■■■■■

Robinwood Brewers & Vintners

⌨ **Robinwood Brewery, Burnley Road, Todmorden OL14 8EX.**

☎ **0706 818160.**

🏛 **No.**

🏃 **No.**

i **Independent**

BEST BITTER
OG 1036˚ ABV 3.6%
Ingredients: Halcyon pale malt (94%), crystal (6%). Challenger whole hops. 32 units of bitterness.

TASTING NOTES

Nose	Rich malt aroma with good hops notes
Palate	Good balance of malt and hops in mouth, dry finish with pleasing cobnut character from crystal malt
Comments	Copper-coloured ale with warm and biscuity malt appeal.

XB
OG 1046˚ ABV 4.6%
Ingredients: Halcyon pale malt (95%), crystal malt (5%). Challenger whole hops. 34 units of bitterness.

TASTING NOTES

Nose	Delicate hop notes and light fruit
Palate	Rich malt in mouth with deep, dry finish
Comments	Amber beer, full-bodied with good malt and hops balance.

OLD FART
OG 1060˚ ABV 5.4%
Ingredients: Halcyon pale malt (74%), crystal malt (6%), roast barley (3%), pale chocolate malt (1%), malt extract (16%). Challenger whole hops. 30 units of bitterness.

TASTING NOTES

Nose	Powerful hops and rich fruit aromas
Palate	Mouth-filling mix of roast barley, raisins, sultanas and blackcurrants with massive, lingering finish full of fruit

---

Comments   Rich dark beer: 'Christmas cake!' says the brewer. Pity that a rich and complex brew is saddled with such a vulgar name.

Rooster's Brewery

▭ **Unit 20, Claro Business Park, Claro Road, Harrogate HG1 4BA.**
① **0423 561861.**
🏛 **No.**
🚶 **by arrangement.**
i **Independent**

YANKEE
OG 1042° ABV 4.3%
Ingredients: pale malt, crystal malt. Variety of hops.

TASTING NOTES
Nose   Malt and tropical fruit aromas
Palate   Soft malt in mouth, bitter finish with strong whiff of fruit
Comments   Aromatic, rounded and fruity pale yellow ale.

ROOSTER
OG 1046° ABV 4.7%
Ingredients: pale malt, crystal malt. Variety of hops.

TASTING NOTES
Nose   Treacle toffee and tropical fruit
Palate   Sweet malty marmalade in mouth. long fruity finish with good hop character

Comments	Mouth-filling copper-coloured strong ale with massive fruit and hops. Brewer Sean Franklin finds a distinct lychees fruitiness in his beers.

Rudgate Brewery Ltd

⌂ **2 Centre Park, Marston Moor Business Park, Rudgate, Tockwith, York YO5 8QF.**
① **0423 358382**
🏛 **No.**
🕺 **No.**
i **Independent**

VIKING
OG 1039˚ ABV 3.9%
Ingredients: Halcyon pale malt (90%), crystal malt (10%). 30 units of colour. Fuggles and Northdown whole hops for bitterness, Goldings for aroma. Dry hopped.

TASTING NOTES

Nose	Rich malt aroma with delicate hops developing
Palate	Full and rounded in mouth, bitter-sweet finish with light fruit, crystal cobnuts and aromatic Goldings
Comments	Rich, creamy and distinctive new Yorkshire bitter.

BATTLEAXE
OG 1044˚ ABV 4.3%
Ingredients: Halcyon pale malt (90%), crystal malt (10%). 30 units of colour. Fuggles and Northdown whole hops for bitterness, Goldings for aroma.

TASTING NOTES

Nose	Creamy malt and nuts aromas with Goldings underpinning
Palate	Mouth-filling malt and nuts in mouth, long finish with great crystal malt presence and Goldings resins
Comments	Ripe and rounded copper-coloured bitter from new brewery.

Ryburn Brewery
⌨ **Mill House, Mill House Lane, Sowerby Bridge HX6 3LN.**
☎ **0422 835413.**
🏛 **No.**
⚒ **Yes.**
i **Independent**

MILD
OG 1033° ABV 3.3%
Ingredients: Halcyon mild ale malt, roasted barley, chocolate malt, light chocolate malt, crushed wheat, flaked barley. Fuggles whole hops.

TASTING NOTES
Nose	Delectable chocolate malt and roasted grain aromas
Palate	Chocolate in mouth and finish, with roast notes and delicate hop hints
Comments	Superb and complex dark mild.

RYBURN BITTER
OG 1038° ABV 3.8%
Ingredients: Halcyon pale malt, crushed crystal malt, crushed wheat. Goldings hops for bitterness, Fuggles for aroma. Whole hops. Dry hopped.

TASTING NOTES
Nose	Complex bouquet of nutty malt and peppery hops
Palate	Rich malt in mouth, deep finish with good balance of crystal malt nuttiness and bitter hops
Comments	Finely balanced bitter-sweet tawny bitter.

RYDALE
OG 1044° ABV 4.4%
Ingredients: Halcyon pale malt, crushed crystal malt, crushed wheat. Goldings for bitterness, Fuggles for aroma. Whole hops. Dry hopped.

TASTING NOTES
Nose	Rich bouquet of nutty malt and peppery hops

Palate	Bitter-sweet malt and hops in mouth, deep hoppy finish with dark malt and fruit notes
Comments	Copper-coloured, rich tasting ale with fine balance of malt and hops.

STRONG MILD
OG 1048° ABV 4.8%
Ingredients: Halcyon mild malt, roast barley, chocolate malt, light chocolate malt, crushed wheat, flaked barley. Whole Fuggles hops.

TASTING NOTES

Nose	Massive aroma of bitter-sweet chocolate with light hops notes
Palate	Dark chewy and chocolatey malt, long dry finish full of dark malt flavours and good hops presence
Comments	Remarkable strong version of the dark mild breed.

STABBERS
OG 1050° ABV 5%
Ingredients: Halcyon pale malt, crushed crystal malt, crushed wheat. Goldings for bitterness, Fuggles for aroma. Whole hops. Dry hopped.

TASTING NOTES

Nose	Fruit cocktail of aromas with massive hops presence
Palate	Ripe fruit in mouth, big, deep finish with fruit, nuts and hops
Comments	Rounded, fruity, well-hopped strong ale.

Selby (Middlesbrough) Brewery Ltd
⌧ **131 Millgate, Selby YO8 0LL.**
① **0757 702826.**
🏛 **No.**
⚘ **No.**
i **Independent**

STRONG ALE
OG 1045° ABV 4.5%
Ingredients: Maris Otter pale ale malt (90%), crystal malt (10%). Whitbread Goldings Variety whole hops.

TASTING NOTES

Nose	Rich, inviting hops and citric fruit aromas
Palate	Sharp, tangy malt and hops in mouth with deep bitter finish
Comments	Refreshing, clean-tasting, lightly-fruity ale.

OLD TOM
OG 1065˚ ABV 6.5%
Ingredients: Maris Otter pale ale malt (90%), crystal malt (10%). Whitbread Goldings Variety whole hops.

TASTING NOTES

Nose	Pungent, tempting, pronounced floral hops and citric fruit aromas
Palate	Rounded, mouth-filling malt and fruit with deep dry finish
Comments	Distinctive, strong, copper-coloured sipping ale.

John Smith's
- ⌨ **The Brewery, Tadcaster LS24 9SA.**
- ☎ **0937 832091.**
- 🏛 **Yes.**
- 朮 **by arrangement.**
  Courage Production Ltd; subsidiary of Courage/ Foster's

JOHN SMITH'S CASK BITTER
OG 1036˚ ABV 3.8%
Ingredients: pale ale malt (78.8%), black malt (1.2%), concentrated sugar (20%). 26 units of colour. Target pellet hops. 32.5 units of bitterness.

TASTING NOTES

Nose	Light, delicate promise of hops, strong fruit developing
Palate	Malt and fruit in mouth, dry finish with some hops and pronounced orange and sultana fruit
Comments	Ruby-red beer with strong fruity input from black malt.

JOHN SMITH'S MAGNET
OG 1040° ABV 4%
Ingredients: pale ale malt (78.6%), black malt (1.4%), concentrated sugar (20%). 37 units of colour. Target pellet hops. 32.5 units of bitterness.

TASTING NOTES

Nose	Rich malt and hops with hints of orange peel
Palate	Ripe malt and hops in mouth, dry and bitter finish with hints of vanilla
Comments	Complex dark ruby ale with Yorkshire creaminess overlaying fruit and hops.

IMPERIAL RUSSIAN STOUT
(bottle conditioned)
OG 1104° ABV 10%
Ingredients: pale ale malt, amber malt, black malt and brewing sugar. Traditional English hops with 'hop rates four times that of average bitter' — indicating in the region of 24lbs per barrel.

TASTING NOTES

Nose	Fresh leather and liquorice
Palate	Stunningly dry bitter black chocolate on tongue with deep, intense finish of great hop bitterness and rich dark fruit
Comments	Brewed every two or three years, matured in oak casks and served in nip bottles, this brown-black stout was first brewed by Barclay Perkins for the Imperial Russian trade in the 19th century. Matures well in bottle: a 1969 brew tasted in 1993 was magnificent.

Samuel Smith Old Brewery (Tadcaster)

- 🖃 **The Old Brewery, High Street, Tadcaster LS24 9SB.**
- ① **0937 832225.**
- 🏛 **Yes.**
- 👷 **Yes.**
- *i* **Independent**

OLD BREWERY BITTER
OG 1037° ABV 3.8%
Ingredients: pale ale malt (91%), crystal malt (9%). Fuggles hops for bitterness, Goldings for aroma. Whole hops. 27 units of bitterness.

TASTING NOTES

Nose	Malt and delicate hops aromas
Palate	Full malt and fruit on tongue, light dry finish with vanilla notes
Comments	Full-flavoured woody bitter.

MUSEUM ALE
OG 1048° ABV 5.2%
Ingredients: pale ale malt (90%), crystal malt (10%). Fuggles hops for bitterness, Goldings for aroma.

TASTING NOTES

Nose	Rich malt and hops aromas
Palate	Complex balance of malt, light hops and developing fruit, with creamy malt finish
Comments	Complex amber beer with great malt appeal. The company has phased out brewing sugar as part of a policy of producing beers without additives.

Steam Packet Brewery

- 🖃 **Steam Packet Inn, The Bendles, Racca Green, Knottingley WF11 8AT.**
- ① **0977 674176.**
- 🏛 **Yes (in pub).**
- 👷 **No.**
- *i* **Independent**

MELLOR'S GAMEKEEPER
OG 1036˚ ABV 3.6%
Ingredients: Maris Otter pale ale malt (88%), crystal malt (12%). Challenger whole hops.

TASTING NOTES

Nose	Delicate hops and fruit aromas
Palate	Fine balance of malt and hops, smooth bitter-sweet finish
Comments	Easy-drinking amber-coloured ale.

CHATTERLEY WHEAT BEER
OG 1037˚ ABV 3.7%
Ingredients: wheat and unnamed cereal adjuncts. Challenger whole hops.

TASTING NOTES

Nose	Scented grain and hops
Palate	Bitter-sweet palate, very dry finish
Comments	Pure wheat beer 'only for connoisseurs' says the brewer; served cold with thick, creamy head.

FOXY
OG 1039˚ ABV 3.9%
Ingredients: Halcyon and Maris Otter pale ale malts, crystal malt, unnamed cereal adjuncts. Challenger and Goldings whole hops. Dry hopped.

TASTING NOTES

Nose	Rich malt aromas with strong hint of hops
Palate	Malt and hops in mouth, long finish with crystal nut and hop notes
Comments	Good drinking copper-coloured ale.

BIT O' BLACK
OG 1040˚ ABV 4%
Ingredients: Halcyon pale ale malt, crystal malt, black malt plus mixture of fruit and nuts. Challenger and Fuggles whole hops.

TASTING NOTES

Nose	Strong malt and nuts aromas
Palate	Sweet malt in mouth, nuts and fruit in finish

Comments   Most unusual 'fruit-and-nut' beer.

BARGEE
OG 1048˚ ABV 4.8%
Ingredients: Halcyon and Maris Otter pale ale malts, black malt, mixture of fruit, nuts and wheat. Challenger, Fuggles and Goldings whole hops. Dry hopped.

TASTING NOTES
Nose	Sweet malt and nuts aromas
Palate	Sweet flavours in mouth, deep finish with fruit, nuts and hops
Comments	Dark, complex and intriguing beer.

POACHER'S SWAG
OG 1050˚ ABV 5%
Ingredients: Maris Otter and Pipkin pale ale malts, crystal malt, flaked maize. Challenger whole hops. Dry hopped.

TASTING NOTES
Nose	Ripe malt aroma with strong scent of Challenger hops
Palate	Good balance of malt and hops in mouth, long bitter finish with hops and some fruit
Comments	Pale copper, complex and delicately fruity ale.

GIDDY ASS
OG 1080˚ ABV 8%
Ingredients: Halcyon and Maris Otter pale ale malts with strong percentage of crystal, plus wheat and flaked maize. Challenger and Fuggles whole hops.

MELLORS
1080
GIDDY ASS

TASTING NOTES
Nose	Sweet malt aroma
Palate	Full, ripe vinous fruit in mouth, deep bitter-sweet finish
Comments	Powerful barley wine. The brewer's name is Mellors which explains the D H Lawrence connections.

Stocks Doncaster Brewery

⌨ **The Hallcross, 33-34 Hall Gate, Doncaster DN1 3NL.**
① **0302 328213.**
🏛 **No.**
🏃 **by arrangement.**
i **Independent**

STOCKS BEST BITTER
OG 1037° ABV 3.6%
Ingredients: pale malt (98.65%), chocolate malt (1.35%).
Fuggles and Goldings whole hops.

TASTING NOTES
Nose	Light hops aroma with delicate fruit notes
Palate	Good malt and hops balance in mouth with dry finish and dark chocolate hints
Comments	Quenching, dark-coloured bitter

SELECT
OG 1044.7° ABV 4.3%
Ingredients: pale malt (98.15%), chocolate malt (1.85%).
Fuggles and Goldings whole hops.

TASTING NOTES
Nose	Earthy hops aroma with rich fruit notes developing
Palate	Smooth rounded malt in mouth with delicate bitter finish and hint of chocolate
Comments	Distinctive premium ale with good balance of malt, fruit, hops and chocolate.

OLD HORIZONTAL
OG 1054° ABV 5%
Ingredients: pale malt (97%), chocolate malt (3%). Fuggles and Goldings whole hops.

TASTING NOTES
Nose	Enticing aromas of powerful hops and chocolate
Palate	Rich balance of grain and dark chocolate with dry and nutty finish
Comments	Dark and complex strong ale.

Timothy Taylor & Co Ltd

☒ **Knowle Spring Brewery, Keighley BD21 1AW.**
① **0535 603139.**
🏛 **No.**
👥 **No.**
i **Independent**

GOLDEN MILD
OG 1033˙ ABV 3.5%
Ingredients: 100% Golden Promise
malt. 23 units of colour. Worcester
Fuggles hops for bitterness, Kent
Goldings for aroma. Whole hops.

TASTING NOTES

Nose	Light, delicate hops and malt aromas
Palate	Sweet malt in mouth, short, lightly bitter finish
Comments	Malty light mild. Best Dark Mild is the same beer with the addition of caramel.

BEST BITTER
OG 1037˙ ABV 4%
Ingredients: Golden Promise malt (95%), roasted crystal malt (5%). 29 units of colour. Worcester Fuggles and Kent Goldings for bitterness, Styrian Goldings for aroma. Whole hops.

TASTING NOTES

Nose	Floral fresh hops aroma with light fruit notes
Palate	Full and complex malt and fruit in mouth, deep, dry nutty finish
Comments	Golden bitter of exceptional quality with delectable light fruitiness.

LANDLORD
OG 1042˙ ABV 4.3%
Ingredients: Golden Promise malt (100%). 20 units of colour. Worcester Fuggles for bitterness, Kent and Styrian Goldings for aroma.

TASTING NOTES

Nose	Full hops aroma with developing orange peel and lemon notes

| *Palate* | Stunning multi-layered interweaving of malt and hops in mouth with intense hops and fruit finish |
| *Comments* | Superb beer of enormous character and complexity — a Grand Cru of the beer world. Ram Tam is the same brew with added caramel. |

PORTER
OG 1043˚ ABV 3.5%
Ingredients: Golden Promise malt, roasted crystal malt. 80 units of colour. Fuggles whole hops.

TASTING NOTES

Nose	Sweet malt and nuts aromas
Palate	Soft hops, roasted grain and nuts in mouth, dry finish with chocolate notes
Comments	Occasional creamy brew.

Joshua Tetley & Son Ltd
✉ **PO Box 142, The Brewery, Hunslet Road, Leeds LS1 1QG.**
☏ **0532 435282.**
🏛 **Yes.**
👤 **Yes.**
i **Subsidiary of Carlsberg-Tetley**

TETLEY MILD
OG 1032˚ ABV 3.2%
Ingredients: pale malt, micronised barley, liquid sugar, caramel for colour. UK hop pellets for bitterness, Northdown for aroma and dry hopping.

TASTING NOTES

Nose	Light hint of hops and malt
Palate	Chewy malt in mouth, dry, nutty finish
Comments	Easy-drinking dark mild.

TETLEY BITTER
OG 1035.5˚ ABV 3.6%
Ingredients: pale malt, micronised wheat, liquid sugar. UK hop pellets for bitterness, Northdown for aroma and dry hopping.

TASTING NOTES

Nose	Tart lemon fruit and fragrant hops aromas
Palate	Creamy malt in mouth, deep dry finish with bitter hops and lingering lemon fruit
Comments	Superb, wonderfully quenching tart bitter.

T & R Theakston Ltd

⌐ **The Brewery, Masham, Ripon HG4 4DX.**
① **0675 689544.**
🏛 **Yes.**
🕴 **Yes.**
ℹ **Subsidiary of Scottish & Newcastle Breweries**

THEAKSTON TRADITIONAL MILD
OG 1034˚ ABV 3.5%
Ingredients: pale malt, crystal malt and black malt, unmalted cereal and sugar. 70 units of colour. Fuggles and other varieties of whole and pellet hops. Dry hopped. 22 units of bitterness.

TASTING NOTES

Nose	Rich chocolate and light hops aromas
Palate	Smooth malt in mouth with pronounced roast notes, dry finish with some hop notes
Comments	Dark tawny mild with the advantage of dry hopping.

THEAKSTON BEST BITTER
OG 1038˚ ABV 3.8%
Ingredients: pale malt, crystal malt, maize-derived unmalted cereal, other sugars. 15 units of colour. Fuggles and other varieties of whole and pellet hops. Dry hopped. 24 units of bitterness.

TASTING NOTES

Nose	Pronounced hop aromas and light fruit
Palate	Delicate bitter-sweet balance in mouth; light dry finish with good hop character
Comments	Pale bitter with distinctive floral hop character. See entry under Newcastle Breweries.

THEAKSTON XB
OG 1044˚ ABV 4.5%
Ingredients: pale malt, crystal malt, maize-derived unmalted cereal and other sugars. 26 units of colour. Fuggles and other varieties of whole and pellet hops. Dry hopped. 26 units of bitterness.

TASTING NOTES
Nose	Rich floral hops and fruity, toasted grain aromas
Palate	Full malt in mouth, deep dry finish with creamy malt, hops and fruit notes
Comments	Rich and rounded fruity bitter. See entry under Newcastle Breweries.

THEAKSTON OLD PECULIER
OG 1058˚ ABV 5.6%
Ingredients: pale malt, crystal malt, unmalted cereal, sugars. 95 units of colour. Fuggles and other varieties of whole and pellet hops. Dry hopped. 29 units of bitterness.

TASTING NOTES
Nose	Massive winey bouquet of rich fruit with peppery hop notes
Palate	Toffee and roast malt in mouth, deep bitter-sweet finish with delicate hops
Comments	Dark and vinous old ale bursting with complex fruit flavours.

Trough Brewery Ltd
- ▣ **Louisa Street, Idle, Bradford BD10 8NE.**
- ① **0274 613450.**
- ▥ **No.**
- ⚐ **No.**
- *i* **Independent**

BITTER
OG 1035.5˚ ABV 4.1%
Ingredients: Halcyon and Triumph pale ale malts (50% each), sugar (8%). Fuggles, Progress and Whitbread Goldings Variety whole hops.

TASTING NOTES
Nose	Crisp hops aroma

Palate	Malt and light fruit in mouth, dry hoppy finish
Comments	Refreshing pale beer.

WILD BOAR
OG 1039.5˚ ABV 4.5%
Ingredients: Halcyon and Triumph pale malts (50% each), sugar (8%). Fuggles, Progress and Whitbread Goldings Variety whole hops.

TASTING NOTES

Nose	Ripe Goldings hops aroma with good malt notes
Palate	Fine balance of malt and hops in mouth with delicate fruit notes; dry finish with hops and fruit
Comments	Smooth and well-attenuated complex pale ale.

FESTIVAL
OG 1047˚ ABV 5%
Ingredients: Halcyon and Maris Otter pale malts (50% each), sugar (5% maximum). Goldings whole hops for aroma, Northdown for bitterness.

TASTING NOTES

Nose	Rich malt and Goldings hops aroma
Palate	Bitter-sweet malt and hops in mouth, long finish with hops and light fruit
Comments	Complex ale with massive Goldings presence.

BLIND PUGH
OG 1052˚ ABV 5%
Ingredients: Halcyon (35%) and Maris Otter (35%) pale malts, crystal malt (15%), chocolate malt (15%). Northdown and Goldings whole hops.

TASTING NOTES

Nose	Nuts, chocolate and hops aromas
Palate	Dark grain and chocolate in mouth, deep finish with chocolate and hops dominating
Comments	Rich and superb dark ale.

S H Ward & Co Ltd

☎ **Sheaf Brewery, Eccleshall Road, Sheffield S11 8HZ.**
① **0742 755155.**
🏛 **Yes.**
👤 **by arrangement.**
i **Subsidiary of Vaux Group**

MILD
OG 1032˚ ABV 3.2%
Ingredients: Halcyon, Maris Otter and Pipkin pale malts
(80%), chocolate malt, crystal malt, torrefied wheat,
invert sugar and caramel. Target and Progress whole
hops for bitterness, Fuggles for aroma. 17 units of bitterness.

TASTING NOTES

Nose	Tempting aromas of malt and chocolate
Palate	Malt and chocolate in mouth, short dry finish
Comments	Mellow dark mild.

THORNE BEST BITTER
OG 1037˚ ABV 3.9%
Ingredients: Halcyon, Maris Otter and Pipkin pale malts
(89%), crystal malt, enzymic malt, torrefied wheat, invert
sugar and caramel. Challenger whole hops for bitterness, Fuggles and Goldings for aroma. Dry hopped. 29
units of bitterness.

TASTING NOTES

Nose	Light aromas of malt and delicate hops
Palate	Toffee in mouth balanced by some hops notes, malty finish with some hops
Comments	Soft, easy-drinking bitter in need of more hops.

SHEFFIELD BEST BITTER
OG 1038˚ ABV 4%
Ingredients: Halcyon, Maris Otter and Pipkin pale malts
(89%), enzymic malt, crystal malt, torrefied wheat, invert
sugar and caramel. Challenger whole hops for bitterness, Fuggles and Goldings for aroma. 31 units of bitterness.

TASTING NOTES

Nose	Pronounced malt aroma
Palate	Full malt in mouth, rounded bitter-sweet finish
Comments	Distinctive malty ale, cleansing not cloying.

KIRBY STRONG BEER
OG 1045° ABV 5%
Ingredients: Halcyon, Maris Otter and Pipkin pale malts (89%), enzymic malt, crystal malt, torrefied wheat, invert sugar and caramel. Challenger whole hops for bitterness, Fuggles and Goldings for aroma. 31 units of bitterness.

TASTING NOTES

Nose	Malty aroma
Palate	Sweet malt in mouth and in the finish
Comments	Brown beer with ripe malt character.

Webster's Fountain Head Brewery

- ⌨ **Ovenden Wood, Halifax HX2 0TL.**
- ☎ **0422 357188.**
- 🏛 **Yes.**
- 🚶 **by arrangement.**
- *i* **Subsidiary of Courage/Foster's**

WILSONS ORIGINAL MILD
OG 1031° ABV 3%
Ingredients: pale ale malt, crystal malt, syrup (20%). 80 units of colour. Challenger, Northdown and Target hop pellets.

TASTING NOTES

Nose	Creamy burnt and roasted grain aromas
Palate	Dark malt in mouth, toffee and vanilla in dry yet sweetish finish
Comments	Easy-drinking malty mild.

GREEN LABEL BEST
OG 1033˚ ABV 3.2%
Ingredients: pale ale malt (80%), syrup (20%). 17.5 units of colour. Challenger, Northdown and Target hop pellets. 26 units of bitterness.

TASTING NOTES

Nose	Creamy malt, light fruit and hops aromas
Palate	Light balance of malt and hops in mouth, dry bitter finish with some light fruit
Comments	Light session ale with some fruit and moderate hop.

WILSONS ORIGINAL BITTER
OG 1036˚ ABV 3.6%
Ingredients: pale ale malt (70%), crystal malt (10%), syrup (20%). 21 units of colour. Challenger, Northdown and Target pellet hops. 33 units of bitterness.

TASTING NOTES

Nose	Fruity and estery aromas
Palate	Malt predominates in mouth with dry hops and vanilla finish
Comments	Creamy bitter in need of more hop attack.

WEBSTER'S YORKSHIRE BITTER
OG 1036˚ ABV 3.6%
Ingredients: pale ale malt (80%), wheat syrup (20%). 26 units of colour. Challenger, Northdown and Target pellet hops. 33 units of bitterness.

TASTING NOTES

Nose	Malt and toffee aromas
Palate	Soft vanilla and toffee flavours, dry finish with faint hop notes
Comments	A once proud regional beer turned into a bland mass-marketed brand.

Whitby's Own Brewery Ltd

⌸ **St Hilda's, The Ropery, Whitby YO22 4ET.**

☎ **0947 605914.**

i **Independent**

This small brewery brews Merry Man's Mild (OG 1037.5°, ABV 3.6%), Ammonite or Wallop (1036°, 3.9%), Woblle (1045°, 4.6%) and Force Nine (1055°, 5.6%). No other information received.

NB Whitbread Sheffield Brewery closed in the summer of 1993. Chester's Mild and Bitter were transferred to the Castle Eden Brewery in Co Durham. The future homes of the Bentley, Higsons and Trophy brands were not known as the Almanac went to press.

CENTRAL ENGLAND

Central England ranges from the pastoral delights of Shakespeare country to the great powerhouses of the industrial revolution in Birmingham and the Black Country.

At the heart of the region stands Burton upon Trent, the modern capital of brewing. It was in Burton that brewers of world renown such as Bass and Worthington developed the style of beer first called India Pale Ale and better known today as bitter — hoppy, tangy and quenching ales that replaced the darker, heavier and less refreshing porters and stouts.

Only one Burton brewery, Marston's, now uses the town's singular method of brewing, the 'union room' in which fermenting wort gushes from linked oak casks ('held in union') and circulates over a bed of yeast in troughs above. Bass, however, still uses a yeast strain developed in its sadly redundant unions and both Draught Bass and Marston's Pedigree have delicate bouquets with a hint of apple that belie their impressive strengths.

Mild still has strong roots in the region and a beer style that met the need of blue-collar workers to refresh themselves has fortunately not matched the decline of the area's industrial base. Dark nutty milds from Ansells, Batham, Bass's Highgate, and Holden, with an amber version from Banks's in Wolverhampton, are classics of their style.

Aston Manor Brewery Co Ltd

- ⌖ **Thimblemill Lane, Aston, Birmingham B7 5HS.**
- ☾ **021-328 4336.**
- 🏛 **No.**
- ⋇ **No.**
- *i* **Independent**

ASTON MANOR MILD OR CHANDLERS MILD
OG 1032° ABV 3%
Ingredients: Golden Promise pale malt, chocolate malt, brewers' invert sugar. Fuggles and Northdown whole hops. 22 units of bitterness.

TASTING NOTES

Nose	Nutty, malty aromas
Palate	Tasty flavours of nut, malt and chocolate with dry finish and some hops hints
Comments	Delectable dark mild with true West Midlands malt flavours.

ASTON MANOR BITTER OR CHANDLERS BITTER
OG 1036° ABV 3.6%
Ingredients: Golden Promise pale malt, brewers' invert sugar. Fuggles and Goldings whole hops.

TASTING NOTES

Nose	Malt, hops and delicate fruit aromas
Palate	Fine balance of sweet malt and floral hops in mouth, long, dry bitter-sweet finish with fruit notes
Comments	Complex and quenching pale bitter.

Banks's & Hanson's

- ⌖ **Wolverhampton & Dudley Breweries PLC Bath Road, Wolverhampton WV1 4NY.**
- ☾ **0902 711811.**
- 🏛 **Yes.**
- ⋇ **Yes.**
- *i* **Independent**

BANKS'S MILD ALE
OG 1036˚ ABV 3.5%
Ingredients: predominantly Maris Otter pale malt with some Halcyon and Pipkin. 40 units of colour. Worcester Fuggles and East Kent Goldings whole hops. 25 units of bitterness.

TASTING NOTES

Nose	Delicate hop aroma with fruit notes developing
Palate	Fine balance of malt and hops in mouth with dry vanilla finish and hints of cobnuts
Comments	Superb amber-coloured mild ale, the brewery's biggest selling brand.

HANSON'S MILD ALE
OG 1036˚ ABV 3.5%
Ingredients: predominantly Maris Otter pale malt with some Halcyon and Pipkin, crystal malt and caramalt. 50 units of colour. Worcester Fuggles and East Kent Goldings whole hops. 25 units of bitterness.

TASTING NOTES

Nose	Light malt and hops with caramel note
Palate	Chewy malt in mouth, dry finish with vanilla notes and some light fruit
Comments	Highly distinctive dark amber mild.

BANKS'S BITTER
OG 1038˚ ABV 3.8%
Ingredients: predominantly Maris Otter pale malt with some Halcyon and Pipkin. 23 units of colour. Worcester Fuggles and East Kent Goldings whole hops. 33 units of bitterness.

TASTING NOTES

Nose	Floral hop resins aroma with fruit notes developing
Palate	Complex balance of malt and hops in mouth; light dry finish with delicate fruit, hops and vanilla
Comments	Bitter-sweet light amber beer of great depth and character.

HANSON'S BITTER
OG 1035° ABV 3.4%
Ingredients: predominantly Maris Otter pale malt with some Halcyon and Pipkin. 25 units of colour. Worcester Fuggles and East Kent Goldings. Late copper hopped. 27 units of bitterness.

TASTING NOTES

Nose	Tempting malt, hops resin and light fruit aromas
Palate	Good balance of malt and hops in mouth, dry finish with hints of fruit
Comments	Well-crafted but lightly hopped bitter in the Midlands' tradition. W&D closed the Hanson's Brewery in Dudley in 1991 and all beers are now brewed in Wolverhampton. The company has also revealed the types of isinglass finings it uses for clearing beer: Saigon Long, Saigon Round, Penang, Brazilian Lump and Beluga 6.

Bass Brewers (Birmingham) Ltd

☞ **Mitchells & Butlers, Cape Hill Brewery, PO Box 27, Birmingham B16 0PQ.**
① **021-558 1481.**
🏛 **Yes.**
🕴 **Yes, limited access until 1994.**
i **Subsidiary of Bass PLC**

M&B MILD ALE
OG 1033.5° ABV 3.3%
Ingredients: Halcyon pale malt (94.1%), crystal malt (3.5%), black malt (2.4%); maltose syrup (17.9%) and caramel (0.3%) added in copper. 48 units of colour. Challenger and Northdown pellet hops. 24 units of bitterness.

TASTING NOTES

Nose	Roasted grain and bitter chocolate aromas
Palate	Nutty and grainy in mouth with light finish and roast and chocolate hints
Comments	Malty-sweet dark mild with pleasing chocolate notes.

M&B BREW XI
OG 1038˚ ABV 3.9%
Ingredients: 100% Pipkin pale malt. Maltose syrup (8.25%) and caramel (0.06%) added in copper. 18 units of colour. Challenger and Northdown hop pellets. 27 units of bitterness.

TASTING NOTES

Nose	Light hop resins and hint of pear drops
Palate	Sweet malt in mouth, short malt and fruit finish
Comments	Typical West Midlands malty bitter lacking hop bite.

Bass Brewers (Burton)

⌧ **137 High Street, Burton-upon-Trent DE14 1JZ.**
① **0283 511000.**
🏛 **Yes.**
⚲ **contact Bass Museum on same phone number.**
z **Subsidiary of Bass PLC**

DRAUGHT BASS
OG 1043˚ ABV 4.4%
Ingredients: 100% Halcyon cask-conditioned malt, 10% maltose syrup in copper. 19 units of colour. Challenger and Northdown hop pellets. 26 units of bitterness.

TASTING NOTES

Nose	Complex malt, toffee and sulphur aromas
Palate	Pronounced malt in mouth, delicate long finish with some hops and apple fruit
Comments	Malt-accented premium bitter. Bass has stopped dry hopping the beer, which has stressed the beer's maltiness. Sulphur aromas in Burton beers come from heavy deposits of gypsum in the soil.

Daniel Batham & Son Ltd

⌨ **Delph Brewery, Delph Road, Brierley Hill DY5 2TN.**
① **0384 77229.**
🏛 **Yes (in Vine pub).**
🏃 **by arrangement, maximum 19 people**
i **Independent**

MILD ALE
OG 1036° ABV 3.6%
Ingredients: 100% Golden Promise malt, caramel for colour. Fuggles and Northdown whole hops in copper, dry hopped with Goldings.

TASTING NOTES

Nose	Warm aromas of hop resins and malt
Palate	Rich, chewy balance of malt and nut, with light dry finish
Comments	Beautifully crafted darkish mild.

BEST BITTER
OG 1043.5° ABV 4.3%
Ingredients: 100% Golden Promise malt. Fuggles and Northdown whole hops in copper, dry hopped with Goldings.

TASTING NOTES

Nose	Floral hop flowers and rich malt aromas
Palate	Fine prickle of hops in mouth, intense dry finish with hop bitterness and light fruit
Comments	Delectable and quenching straw-coloured ale. In winter Batham produces an occasional XXX strong ale.

British Oak Brewery

⌨ **Salop Street, Eve Hill, Dudley DY1 3AX.**
① **0384 236297.**
🏛 **Yes (in British Oak pub).**
🏃 **Yes, during opening hours.**
i **Independent**

CASTLE RUIN
OG 1038˚ ABV 3.9%
Ingredients: Target pale malt, wheat malt (10%). Challenger and Fuggles whole and pellet hops for bitterness, Goldings for aroma.

TASTING NOTES

Nose	Sweet malt and peppery Goldings aromas
Palate	Well-balanced malt and hops in mouth, bitter-sweet finish with light fruit notes
Comments	Refreshing straw-coloured pale ale.

EVE'LL BITTER
OG 1042˚ ABV 4.1%
Ingredients: Target pale malt and crystal malt (89%), black malt (1%), wheat malt (10%). Challenger and Fuggles whole hops and pellets for bitterness, Goldings for aroma.

TASTING NOTES

Nose	Ripe malt and nuts aromas
Palate	Creamy nut in mouth, malty sweetness in finish with some hops and fruit notes
Comments	Tawny-coloured and malty brew.

COLONEL PICKERING'S PORTER
OG 1046˚ ABV 4.4%
Ingredients: Target pale malt and crystal malt (85%), black malt (5%), wheat malt (10%). Challenger and Fuggles whole hops and pellets for bitterness, Goldings for aroma.

TASTING NOTES

Nose	Ripe malt and chocolate aromas
Palate	Bitter chocolate in mouth balanced by creamy malt, deep dry finish with chocolate, fruit and hops notes
Comments	Dark, tangy and complex bitter-sweet porter.

DUNGEON DRAUGHT
OG 1050˚ ABV 4.8%
Ingredients: Target pale malt and crystal malt (85%), black malt (5%), wheat malt (10%). Challenger and Fuggles whole hops and pellets for bitterness, Goldings for aroma.

TASTING NOTES

Nose	Great attack of malty fruitiness and powerful hop resins
Palate	Tangy and fruity in mouth with a hint of nut, great depth of finish with malt, fruit and hops
Comments	Dark, smooth-drinking and complex strong ale.

OLD JONES
OG 1060° ABV 5.5%
Ingredients: Target pale malt and crystal malt (85%), black malt (5%), wheat malt (10%). Challenger and Fuggles whole hops and pellets for bitterness, Goldings for aroma.

TASTING NOTES

Nose	Massive malt and ripe fruit aromas with powerful tang of hops
Palate	Rich and winey in mouth, massive finish with raisins and sultana fruit, bitter chocolate and hops
Comments	Rich, dark and memorably fruity Black Country old ale. The beers are brewed for the British Oak pub and the free trade.

Brunswick Brewing Co Ltd
- ⌑ **1 Railway Terrace, Derby DE1 2RU.**
- ① **0332 290677.**
- ⏛ **Yes (in Brunswick Inn).**
- ⚗ **by arrangement.**
- *i* **Independent**

CELEBRATION MILD
OG 1033° ABV 3.3%
Ingredients: Maris Otter pale malt, crystal malt, roast barley, No 3 invert sugar. Wye Challenger whole hops.

TASTING NOTES

Nose	Nutty aromas of dark grain
Palate	Malty in mouth, dry finish with creamy roast notes
Comments	Dark, smooth-drinking mild.

BRUNSWICK RECESSION ALE
OG 1033° ABV 3.3%
Ingredients: Maris Otter pale malt and crystal malt. Northdown whole hops.

TASTING NOTES

Nose	Nutty malt aroma with hops developing
Palate	Malt dominates the mouth, dry finish with some hops
Comments	Easy-drinking amber ale.

BRUNSWICK FIRST BREW
OG 1036° ABV 3.8%
Ingredients: Maris Otter pale malt, flaked maize, torrefied wheat. Wye Challenger and Goldings whole hops.

TASTING NOTES

Nose	Rich and earthy Goldings aroma
Palate	Hops dominate mouth and dry finish
Comments	Pale and superbly hoppy ale.

FAT BOY STOUT
OG 1040° ABV 4%
Ingredients: Maris Otter pale malt, crystal malt, roast barley. Wye Challenger and Northdown whole hops.

TASTING NOTES

Nose	Sweet malt and roast aromas
Palate	Full-bodied malt in mouth, bitter-sweet finish
Comments	Dark and rich stout.

BRUNSWICK SECOND BREW
OG 1042° ABV 4.2%
Ingredients: Maris Otter pale malt, crystal malt. Wye Challenger and Goldings hops.

TASTING NOTES

Nose	Rich malt aroma with light fruit and hops
Palate	Good balance of malt and hops in mouth, sweetish finish
Comments	Rounded malty brew.

RAILWAY PORTER
OG 1045° ABV 4.5%
Ingredients: Maris Otter pale malt, roast barley, No 3 invert sugar. Goldings whole hops.

TASTING NOTES

Nose	Sweet malt and roasted grain aromas
Palate	Malt in the mouth becoming dry and bitter in finish
Comments	Mellow dark beer.

BRUNSWICK FESTIVAL ALE
OG 1046˚ ABV 4.6%
Ingredients: Maris Otter pale malt, flaked maize, torrefied wheat. Wye Challenger and Goldings hops.

TASTING NOTES

Nose	Peppery Goldings aroma
Palate	Rich malt and hops in mouth, long dry finish with powerful hops character
Comments	Ripe, full-bodied ale, stronger version of First Brew.

OLD ACCIDENTAL
OG 1050˚ ABV 4.9%
Ingredients: Maris Otter pale malt, crystal malt. Wye Challenger and Goldings whole hops.

TASTING NOTES

Nose	Goldings and rich fruit aromas
Palate	Malt, hops and fruit in mouth, rounded and deep finish with great hops character
Comments	Full-bodied, fruity ale, stronger version of Second Brew.

OWD ABUSIVE
OG 1066˚ ABV 5.9%
Ingredients: Maris Otter pale malt, crystal malt, No 3 invert sugar. Wye Challenger and Goldings whole hops.

TASTING NOTES

Nose	Massive malt and fruit aromas with hop notes developing
Palate	Sweet malt in mouth, deep finish with fruit and hops
Comments	Smooth and vinous strong ale. The beers are brewed using well water discovered when the brewery was being built. The plant is attached to the Brunswick Inn and the beers have many free trade outlets.

■■■■■■■■■■■■■■■

Burton Bridge Brewery

🖃 **24 Bridge Street, Burton-upon-Trent DE14 1SY.**
① **0283 510573.**
🏛 **Yes (in Bridge Inn).**
🕴 **Tuesday evenings.**
i **Independent**

SUMMER ALE
OG 1038° ABV 3.8%
Ingredients: 100% Pipkin pale malt. Challenger whole hops in copper, dry hopped with Styrian Goldings pellets.

TASTING NOTES
Nose	Delicate bouquet of malt and hops
Palate	Quenching malt and hops in mouth, bitter-sweet finish with fruit notes
Comments	Wonderfully refreshing pale bitter, brewed during British Summer Time: April-October.

XL
OG 1040° ABV 4%
Ingredients: Pipkin pale malt (95%), crystal malt (5%). Challenger and Target whole hops in copper (50% each), dry hopped with Target pellets.

TASTING NOTES
Nose	Rich malt aroma with strong hop notes developing
Palate	Mouth-filling blend of malt and hops with long finish full of earthy blackcurrant notes
Comments	Superb, rich clarety brew.

BRIDGE BITTER
OG 1042° ABV 4.2%
Ingredients: Pipkin pale malt (95%), crystal malt (5%). Challenger (67%) and Target (33%) whole hops in copper, dry hopped with Styrian Goldings.

TASTING NOTES
Nose	Vinous aroma with powerful hops notes
Palate	Rich fruit and malt in mouth with deep dry finish packed with sultana notes
Comments	Complex golden beer, winey and hoppy.

BURTON PORTER
OG 1045° ABV 4.%
Ingredients: Pipkin pale malt (92%), crystal malt (5%), chocolate malt (3%). Challenger and Target whole hops (50% each.)

TASTING NOTES

Nose	Light hops aroma with hints of chocolate
Palate	Warm biscuity malt in mouth with dry finish full of chocolate and hops character
Comments	Fine-tasting deep brown ale. Also available in bottle-conditioned form.

TOP DOG STOUT
OG 1050° ABV 5%
Ingredients: Pipkin pale malt (72%), chocolate malt (7%), micronised wheat (21%). 100% whole Challenger hops.

TASTING NOTES

Nose	Rich roast grain and biscuits aroma
Palate	Bitter malt and hops in mouth, deep dry finish with bitter chocolate, hops and rich fruit notes
Comments	Superb, finely-balanced stout, brewed in winter only.

BURTON FESTIVAL ALE
OG 1055° ABV 5.5%
Ingredients: Pipkin pale malt (94%), crystal malt (5%), chocolate malt (1%). Challenger and Target whole hops (50% each).

TASTING NOTES

Nose	Salty hop resins aromas
Palate	Powerful mouth-filling maltiness, shattering dry finish with vanilla notes and pronounced hops
Comments	Warming and strong old sipping ale.

OLD EXPENSIVE
OG 1065˚ ABV 6.5%
Ingredients: Pipkin malt (88%), crystal malt (5%), chocolate malt (1%), invert sugar (6%). Challenger and Target
whole hops (50% each).

TASTING NOTES

Nose	Rich port wine aroma
Palate	Massive mouth-filling malt and ripe fruit, deep finish with hops, raisins and sultanas
Comments	Vinous winter ale.

Enville Ales
⌨ **Enville Brewery, Cox Green, Stourbridge DY7 5LG.**
☎ **0384 873770/375491.**
🏛 **No.**
🍴 **Yes.**
i **Independent**

ENVILLE ALE
OG 1045˚ ABV 4.6%
Ingredients: Pipkin pale malt (88%), crystal malt (2%),
invert sugar (10%). 25 units of colour. Challenger and
Goldings hop pellets for bitterness, Saaz for aroma. Dry
hopped. 30 units of bitterness.

TASTING NOTES

Nose	Floral Saaz hops aroma
Palate	Light malt in mouth, dry hoppy finish with floral notes
Comments	Delectable balance of malt and hops with a honey note from the brewery's own brand of sugar primings

GOTHIC ALE
OG 1052˚ ABV 5.2%
Ingredients: Pipkin pale malt (77%), roast barley (10%),
dark malt (13%). Challenger and Goldings hop pellets. 35
units of bitterness.

TASTING NOTES

Nose	Rich fruit and burnt currants aroma

Palate	Smooth, rounded malt in mouth, deep finish with fruit and hops
Comments	Black beer with distinctive flavour from brewery's own 'dark honey' priming sugar.

Everards Brewery Ltd

⌐ **Castle Acres, Narborough, Leicester LE9 5BY.**
① **0533 630900.**
🏛 **Yes.**
🏃 **by arrangement.**
i **Independent**

EVERARDS MILD
OG 1036° ABV 3.3%
Ingredients: Maris Otter pale malt and crystal malt (92%), torrefied wheat, malt extract for colour. 75 units of colour. Challenger and Fuggles hop pellets for bitterness, Goldings for aroma. 15 units of bitterness.

TASTING NOTES
Nose	Malty aroma with toffee notes
Palate	Malt in mouth with some fruit notes, creamy vanilla in the finish
Comments	Dark mahogany ale with pronounced malt character

BEACON BITTER
OG 1036° ABV 3.8%
Ingredients: Maris Otter pale malt and crystal malt (91%), torrefied wheat and wheat syrup. 19 units of colour. Challenger and Fuggles hop pellets for bitterness, Goldings for aroma. Dry hopped. 25 units of bitterness.

TASTING NOTES
Nose	Delicate aromas of hops and honey
Palate	Chewy malt in mouth, light but lingering finish with with malt, hops and fruit
Comments	Light gold ale with good balance of flavours.

TIGER BEST BITTER
OG 1041˚ ABV 4.2%

Ingredients: Maris Otter pale malt and crystal malt (88%), torrefied wheat and wheat syrup. 25 units of colour. Challenger and Fuggles hop pellets for bitterness, Goldings for aroma. Dry hopped. 26 units of bitterness.

TASTING NOTES

Nose	Rich malt and hops aromas
Palate	Soft and malty in mouth, long finish with good balance of malt and hops and underlying fruitiness
Comments	Copper-coloured ale with distinctive malt and fruit notes.

OLD ORIGINAL STRONG ALE
OG 1050˚ ABV 5.2%

Ingredients: Maris Otter pale malt and crystal malt (95%), torrefied wheat and wheat syrup. 31 units of colour. Challenger and Fuggles pellet hops for bitterness, Goldings for aroma. Dry hopped. 28 units of bitterness.

TASTING NOTES

Nose	Rich malt aroma developing hops and fruit notes
Palate	Mouth-filling balance of malt and hops with deep, long dried fruit and hops finish
Comments	Luscious fruity copper-brown ale.

OLD BILL
OG 1070˚ ABV 7.3%

Ingredients: Maris Otter pale malt and crystal malt (71%), wheat syrup. 44 units of colour. Fuggles and Challenger hop pellets for bitterness, Goldings for aroma. 38 units of bitterness.

TASTING NOTES

Nose	Pronounced hops and fruit aromas
Palate	Rich malt and hops in mouth, long dry finish packed with hop bitterness and vinous fruit
Comments	Fruity strong ale available October to January.

Hanby Ales

🖃 **New Brewery, Aston Park, Soulton Road, Wem SY4 5SD.**

🕐 **0939 232432.**

🏛 **No.**

🕴 **strictly limited.**

i **Independent**

BLACK MAGIC MILD
OG 1033˚ ABV 3.3%
Ingredients: Maris Otter pale malt (88%), crystal malt (10%), black malt (2%). Fuggles whole hops.

TASTING NOTES
Nose	Pronounced malt and nut aromas
Palate	Chewy malt in mouth, bitter-sweet finish with nuts and coffee character and hint of hops
Comments	Delicious, characterful dark ale.

DRAWWELL BITTER
OG 1039˚ ABV 3.9%
Ingredients: Maris Otter pale malt (97%), crystal malt (3%). Fuggles whole hops, late hopped with Goldings.

TASTING NOTES
Nose	Rich and earthy Goldings aroma with malt notes
Palate	Full malt and hops in mouth, long finish with hops, light fruit and nutty malt
Comments	Amber ale packed with superb hops character.

SHROPSHIRE STOUT
OG 1044˚ ABV 4.5%
Ingredients: Maris Otter pale malt (73%), crystal malt (9%), black malt (12%), chocolate malt (6%). Fuggles whole hops.

TASTING NOTES
Nose	Fruity aromas with hint of chocolate
Palate	Full malt and chocolate in mouth, dry finish with hints of dark malt and hops
Comments	Ruby-black bitter-sweet beer.

NUTCRACKER BITTER
OG 1060˚ ABV 6%
Ingredients: Maris Otter pale malt (98%), crystal malt (2%). Fuggles whole hops, late hopped with Goldings.

TASTING NOTES
Nose	Massive ripe fruit and hops aromas
Palate	Malt, fruit and nuts in mouth; long, deep finish with orange and lemon fruit and good hops bitterness.
Comments	Pale fruity ale.

Hanseatic Trading Co Ltd
⌑ **West Walk Building, 110 Regent Road, Leicester LE1 7LT.**
① **0572 722215.**
🏛 **No.**
⅄ **No.**
i **Independent**

IPA
(bottle conditioned)
OG 1045˚ ABV 4.5%
Ingredients: pale ale malt, touch of malted wheat. 11 units of colour. Selection of Bramling Cross, Fuggles, Goldings and Whitbread Goldings Variety whole hops. 45-50 units of bitterness.

TASTING NOTES
Nose	Pronounced floral hops aroma
Palate	Crisp hops in mouth with long hoppy finish
Comments	Pale beer with massive hops character — a benchmark India Pale Ale.

BCA
(bottle conditioned)
OG 1045˚ ABV 4.5%
Ingredients: best pale ale malt, crystal malt, malted wheat. 38 units of colour. Aroma hops only. 35 units of bitterness.

TASTING NOTES
Nose	Complex aromas of hops, malt and barley sugar

Palate	Smooth malt and barley sugar in mouth, long hoppy finish
Comments	Amber beer of great complexity with powerful hops and barley sugar notes from crystal malt. BCA stands for Bottle Conditioned Ale.

VUSSILENSKI'S BLACK RUSSIAN (bottle conditioned)
OG 1048˚ ABV 4.8%

Ingredients: pale ale malt, black malt, crystal malt, brown malt. 140 units of colour. Fuggles and Goldings whole hops. 35 units of bitterness.

TASTING NOTES

Nose	Deep aromas of bitter chocolate, hazel nuts, hops and spices
Palate	Full malt in mouth with nuts and bitter chocolate, long dry finish with dark grain and hops
Comments	Ruby-black beer in the style of 19th-century Russian stouts, packed with complex malt, hops and fruit characteristics. The beers are brewed for Hanseatic by McMullen of Hertford.

Hardy's & Hanson's PLC

☞ **Kimberley Brewery, Kimberley, Nottingham NG16 2NS.**
① **0602 383611.**
🏛 **Yes.**
🚶 **by arrangement.**
𝑖 **Independent**

KIMBERLEY BEST MILD
OG 1035˚ ABV 3.1%

Ingredients: Pipkin mild ale malt, crystal malt, maltose, flaked maize and caramel. Challenger, Northdown and Whitbread Goldings Variety whole hops for bitterness, Goldings for aroma. 19 units of bitterness.

TASTING NOTES

Nose	Light malt aroma

Palate	Creamy malt and nut on tongue, light finish with creamy malt and faint fruit notes
Comments	Malty, smooth-drinking dark mild.

KIMBERLEY BEST BITTER
OG 1039˚ ABV 3.9%
Ingredients: Pipkin pale ale malt, maltose, flaked maize and malt extract. Challenger, Northdown and Whitbread Goldings Variety whole hops for bitterness, Goldings for aroma. 26 units of bitterness.

TASTING NOTES

Nose	Rich malt aroma with developing Goldings hop notes
Palate	Ripe malt in mouth, hops and fruit notes in finish
Comments	Distinctive malty ale; delicate hops character as a result of large addition of late hops in copper boil.

KIMBERLEY CLASSIC
OG 1047˚ ABV 4.8%
Ingredients: Pipkin pale ale malt, crystal malt, maltose. Challenger, Northdown and Whitbread Goldings Variety whole hops for bitterness, Goldings for aroma; dry hopped. 31 units of bitterness.

TASTING NOTES

Nose	Tempting aromas of malt, hops and light fruit
Palate	Quenching malt and hops in mouth, long bitter-sweet finish rich with Goldings hops
Comments	Hoppy premium ale.

Highgate Brewery
☞ **Sandymount Road, Walsall WS1 3AP.**
① **0922 23168.**
🏛 **No.**
🚶 **No.**
i **Subsidiary of Bass Brewers**

HIGHGATE MILD ALE or HIGHGATE DARK ALE
OG 1034.9˚ ABV 3.25%

Ingredients: pale malt (93%), crystal malt (1%), black malt (2.5%), maltose syrup (3.5%), caramel. 63 units of colour. Challenger and Whitbread Goldings Variety whole hops for aroma and bitterness. 22 units of bitterness.

TASTING NOTES

Nose	Malt, toffee, chocolate and light hops aromas
Palate	Smooth chewy malt in mouth, dry nutty finish
Comments	Classic dark mild full of delectable malt character. It is now sold outside its Midlands trading area as Highgate Dark Ale.

SPRINGFIELD BITTER
OG 1036˚ ABV 3.55%

Ingredients: pale ale malt (82%), maltose syrup (18%). 19 units of colour. Whitbread Goldings Variety whole hops for bitterness, Fuggles for aroma. 24 units of bitterness.

TASTING NOTES

Nose	Delicate malt and hops aromas
Palate	Malt dominates the mouth with bitter-sweet finish
Comments	Sweetish West Midlands ale, formerly brewed at the Bass Springfield Brewery in Wolverhampton.

HIGHGATE OLD ALE
OG 1055.7 ABV 5.5-6%

Ingredients: pale malt, crystal malt, black malt, maltose syrup. 75 units of colour. Challenger and Whitbread Goldings Variety whole hops for aroma and bitterness. 30 units of bitterness.

TASTING NOTES

Nose	Dark malt, chocolate, coffee and light hops aromas
Palate	Malt and chocolate in mouth, bitter-sweet finish with dark fruit and hops
Comments	Complex, rich and tasty old ale for the winter months, brewed as a parti-gyle with mild.

Holden's Brewery Ltd

✉ **George Street, Woodsetton, Dudley DY1 4LN.**
℧ **0902 880051.**
🏛 **No.**
朮 **Yes.**
i **Independent**

BLACK COUNTRY STOUT
OG 1036° ABV 3.4%
Ingredients: Maris Otter pale malt (88%), dark malts (10%), caramel (2%). 270 units of colour. Fuggles whole hops.

TASTING NOTES

Nose	Mellow hops and dark malt aromas
Palate	Smooth and creamy malt in mouth, bitter-sweet finish
Comments	Dark and mellow 'milk stout'.

BLACK COUNTRY MILD
OG 1037° ABV 3.6%
Ingredients: Maris Otter pale malt (92%), crystal and dark coloured malts (8%), brewing sugar. 50-54 units of colour. Fuggles whole hops.

TASTING NOTES

Nose	Malt with wholemeal biscuit aromas
Palate	Chewy malt and dark grain in mouth, dry hoppy finish
Comments	Tasty dark mild full of malt and hop character.

BLACK COUNTRY BITTER
OG 1039° ABV 3.9%
Ingredients: Maris Otter pale malt (90%), crystal malt (8%), brewing sugar (2%). 24-26 units of colour. Fuggles whole hops. Dry hopped.

TASTING NOTES

Nose	Crisp hops and fruity malt aromas
Palate	Malt and hops well balanced in mouth, dry hoppy finish
Comments	Golden brown bitter-sweet ale.

XB
OG 1042° ABV 4.1%
Ingredients: Maris Otter pale malt (92%), crystal malt (4%), brewing sugar (4%). 25-28 units of colour. Fuggles whole hops. Dry hopped.

TASTING NOTES

Nose	Complex aromas of ripe malt and hop resins
Palate	Malt dominates the mouth followed by deep bitter-sweet finish with malt, hops and fruit
Comments	Rich, full-tasting ale.

BLACK COUNTRY SPECIAL BITTER
OG 1050° ABV 4.8%
Ingredients: Maris Otter pale malt (90-95%), brewing sugar (5-10%). 28-32 units of colour. Fuggles whole hops. Dry hopped.

TASTING NOTES

Nose	Good balance of malt and hops with orange fruit notes
Palate	Rounded malt and fruit in mouth, long bitter-sweet finish
Comments	Rich and well-balanced strong ale.

XL
OG 1092° ABV 8.5%
Ingredients: Maris Otter pale malt (90-95%), sugar (5-10%). 40-45 units of colour. Fuggles whole hops. Dry hopped.

TASTING NOTES

Nose	Powerful vinous aromas of malt, oranges and bananas with hop notes
Palate	Malty in mouth with roast notes; long finish with hops, dark chocolate and raisins
Comments	Dark, warming and winey winter warmer.

Holt, Plant & Deakin Ltd

📧 **Dudley Road, Wolverhampton WV2 3AF.**
📞 **0902 450504.**
🏛 **Yes.**
🏃 **by arrangement.**
ℹ **Subsidiary of Carlsberg-Tetley. Mild and Bitter bearing the company's name are brewed by Tetley-Walker of Warrington; information given for only the one home-brewed ale.**

MILD
OG 1037˚ ABV 3.4%
Ingredients: see note above.

TASTING NOTES

Nose	Light malty aroma
Palate	Light hints of malt and caramel, short dry finish
Comments	Malty mild without hop balance

BITTER
OG 1037˚ ABV 3.4%
Ingredients: see note above

TASTING NOTES

Nose	Light malt and hops aromas
Palate	Malt dominates the mouth; dry finish with some hop notes
Comments	Easy-drinking bitter.

HOLTS ENTIRE
OG 1043.5˚ ABV 4.4%
Ingredients: pale malt, 'various special malts' and wheat flour. Various English whole and pellet hops.

TASTING NOTES

Nose	Malt and floral hops aromas
Palate	Well-balanced malt and hops in mouth, mellow dry finish
Comments	Smooth and creamy ale.

Home Brewery

- ⌨ **Daybrook, Nottingham NG5 6BU.**
- ① **0602 269741.**
- 🏛 **Yes.**
- 🕴 **Yes.**
- *i* **Subsidiary of Scottish & Newcastle Breweries.**

HOME MILD
OG 1036˚ ABV 3.6%
Ingredients: pale ale malt (62%), black malt (8%), crystal malt, maize, caramel for colour, priming sugar. Fuggles, Northdown, Target and Styrian hop pellets. 22 units of bitterness.

TASTING NOTES

Nose	Inviting aromas of black chocolate and light hops
Palate	Nutty, chewy malt with dry finish and roast and chocolate hints
Comments	Smooth, easy-drinking dark mild.

HOME BITTER
OG 1038˚ ABV 3.8%
Ingredients: pale ale malt (70%), maize, liquid sugar, caramel for colour. Fuggles, Northdown, Target and Styrian hop pellets; dry hopped with whole Goldings.

TASTING NOTES

Nose	Delicate hops aroma with light citric fruit notes
Palate	Good balance of malt and hop bitterness in mouth, dry finish with light fruit notes

Comments	Copper-coloured brew with refreshing light fruitiness.

Hoskins Brewery PLC

✉ **Beaumanor Brewery, Beaumanor Road, Leicester LE4 5QE.**
☎ **0533 661 122.**
🏛 **Yes.**
⚤ **Yes.**
i **Independent**

BEAUMANOR BITTER
OG 1039° ABV 3.9%
Ingredients: Maris Otter pale ale malt, crystal malt, invert sugar. Challenger whole hops.

TASTING NOTES

Nose	Peppery hops aroma, orange peel notes developing
Palate	Light nutty malt in mouth with bitter-sweet finish and some fruit notes
Comments	Pale, smooth, bitter-sweet beer.

PENN'S ALE
OG 1045° ABV 4.3%
Ingredients: Maris Otter pale malt, crystal malt, invert sugar. Challenger whole hops.

TASTING NOTES

Nose	Delicate hops aroma, developing rich fruit notes
Palate	Mouth-filling malt with deep finish and strong hints of cobnuts
Comments	Rich nutty ale.

CHURCHILL'S PRIDE
OG 1050˚ ABV 5%
Ingredients: Maris Otter pale male, crystal malt, caramel.
Challenger whole hops.

TASTING NOTES

Nose	Rich malt and fruit with some hop notes
Palate	Malt and fruit in mouth, deep bitter-sweet finish with hint of chocolate
Comments	Fruity, dark ale.

OLD NIGEL
OG 1060˚ ABV 5.7%
Ingredients: Maris Otter pale malt, crystal malt, invert
sugar. Challenger whole hops.

TASTING NOTES

Nose	Ripe malt aroma with hints of fruit and liquorice
Palate	Powerful attack of malt and fruit with deep bitter-sweet finish
Comments	Deceptively pale-coloured beer, like a German pudding wine. Named after the brewer, thought to be the youngest in the business.

Hoskins & Oldfield
⌕ **North Mills, Frog Island, Leicester LE3 5DH.**
☏ **0533 532191.**
🏛 **No.**
🕺 **by arrangement.**
i **Independent**

HOB BEST MILD
OG 1035˚
Ingredients: pale malt, crystal malt, black malt. Goldings
whole hops.

TASTING NOTES

Nose	Malt aroma with chocolate and coffee notes
Palate	Dark, bitter-sweet malt in mouth, dry finish with dark chocolate notes
Comments	Chocolatey, tasty dark mild.

HOB BITTER
OG 1041˚
Ingredients: pale malt, crystal malt. Goldings whole hops.

TASTING NOTES

Nose	Rich fruit aromas with hop notes
Palate	Bitter-sweet malt and hops in mouth, malty finish with orange and lemon fruit
Comments	Pale, malt-accented bitter. A darker version is sold as Little Matty.

TOM KELLY'S STOUT
OG 1043˚
Ingredients: pale malt, crystal malt, roasted barley, black malt. Goldings whole hops.

TASTING NOTES

Nose	Bitter chocolate and malt aromas with good hop notes
Palate	Strong dark malt in mouth, long finish with dark chocolate and hops notes
Comments	Distinctive stout with rich grain and hops character.

EXS
OG 1051˚
Ingredients: pale malt, crystal malt, Goldings whole hops.

TASTING NOTES

Nose	Powerful spicy hops aroma with ripe fruit
Palate	Rich malt and hops in mouth, deep finish with fruit and hops dominating
Comments	Full-flavoured, hoppy, fruity and spicy ale.

OLD NAVIGATION ALE
OG 1071˚
Ingredients: pale malt, crystal malt. Goldings whole hops.

TASTING NOTES

Nose	Ripe fruit aroma with good hop notes
Palate	Massive and complex bitter-sweet fruit flavours in mouth, long vinous finish with sweet fruit dominating
Comments	Rich and powerful strong old ale. The company also brews Christmas Noggin (OG 1100˚).

Sarah Hughes Brewery

⌨ **Beacon Hotel, Bilston Street, Sedgley, Dudley DY3 1JE.**
☎ **0902 883380.**
🏛 **Yes (in hotel).**
🚶 **by arrangements.**
i **Independent**

SARAH HUGHES MILD
OG 1058˚ ABV 5.5%
Ingredients: pale malt and crystal malt. Fuggles and Goldings hops.

TASTING NOTES

Nose	Rich aromas of malt and vinous fruit
Palate	Ripe malt and hops in mouth, intense dry finish with tannins and fruit
Comments	Stunning dark brown beer with a strength that recalls milds of the 19th century. Brewed by John Hughes in refurbished hotel brewery, using his grandmother's recipe. Growing free trade.

Ind Coope Burton Brewery

⌨ **107 Station Street, Burton-upon-Trent DE14 1BZ.**
☎ **0283 31111.**
🏛 **Yes.**
🚶 **Yes.**
i **Subsidiary of Carlsberg-Tetley**

ANSELLS MILD
OG 1033˚ ABV 3.2%
Ingredients: pale malt, chocolate malt, liquid sugar. UK bittering varieties of hop pellets.

TASTING NOTES

Nose	Chocolate and roast malt aromas
Palate	Rich chewy malt and nut in mouth with dry finish and dark chocolate notes
Comments	Superb dark mild with rich chocolate character.

ANSELLS BITTER
OG 1035° ABV 3.6%
Ingredients: pale malt, chocolate malt, liquid sugar. UK bittering varieties of hop pellets, Goldings for aroma and dry hopping.

TASTING NOTES

Nose	Light malt and fruit aromas
Palate	Malt in the mouth, sweet finish with hints of roast malt
Comments	Lightly-hopped, sweetish session bitter.

ABC BITTER or AYLESBURY BITTER
OG 1035° ABV 3.6%
Ingredients: pale malt, chocolate malt, liquid sugar. UK bittering varieties of hop pellets and Styrian Goldings, dry hopped with Goldings.

TASTING NOTES

Nose	Strong Goldings aromas with fruit notes
Palate	Good malty mouth-feel with dry hoppy finish
Comments	Refreshing bitter with good hops and fruit character.

BENSKINS BEST BITTER
OG 1035° ABV 3.6%
Ingredients: pale malt, chocolate malt, liquid sugar. UK bittering varieties of hop pellets and Target, dry hopped with Target.

TASTING NOTES

Nose	Malty, spicy hops and light fruit aromas
Palate	Light malt in mouth, dry bitter finish with some orange fruit notes
Comments	Tawny session bitter with good balance of malt and hops.

FRIARY MEUX BEST BITTER
OG 1035° ABV 3.6%
Ingredients: pale malt, chocolate malt, liquid sugar. UK bittering varieties of hop pellets, Styrian Goldings for aroma and dry hopping.

TASTING NOTES

Nose	Light promise of malt and hops with apple fruit notes

Palate	Malt in mouth with some fruit, dry finish
Comments	Light session bitter.

TAYLOR WALKER BEST BITTER
OG 1035˚ ABV 3.6%
Ingredients: pale malt, chocolate malt, liquid sugar. UK bittering varieties of hop pellets and Target, dry hopped with Target.

TASTING NOTES

Nose	Malty aroma with developing hop notes
Palate	Malt in mouth, bitter-sweet finish
Comments	Pleasant session bitter.

IND COOPE DRAUGHT BURTON ALE
OG 1047˚ ABV 4.8%
Ingredients: pale malt, chocolate malt, liquid sugar. UK bittering varieties of hop pellets, Styrian Goldings for aroma and dry hopping.

TASTING NOTES

Nose	Stunning aromas of malt, rich hops and marmalade fruit
Palate	Massive mouth-filling balance of malt and hops with long finish full of hops and fruit notes
Comments	Magnificent powerful ale; casks are heavily primed with sugar for secondary fermentation and the ABV can reach 5.1% or 5.2%.

Judge's Brewery

- ▣ **83 Constable Road, Hillmorton, Rugby CV21 4DA.**
- ① **0788 569831.**
- ⌂ **No.**
- 林 **Yes**
- *i* **Independent**

BARRISTER'S BITTER
OG 1037˚ ABV 3.6%
Ingredients: Halcyon pale malt (92%), crystal malt (2%), wheat malt (6%). Challenger whole hops in copper, seedless variety for dry hopping.

TASTING NOTES

Nose	Light malt and hops aromas
Palate	Delicate malt in mouth, bitter-sweet finish with good hop notes
Comments	Delicately hopped session bitter.

OLD GAVEL BENDER
OG 1050° ABV 4.9%

Ingredients: Halcyon pale malt (90%), crystal malt (3%), wheat malt (7%). Challenger whole hops in copper, seedless variety for dry hopping.

TASTING NOTES

Nose	Rich malt and fruit aromas
Palate	Full malt in mouth, big finish with fruit and hop notes
Comments	Full-bodied, slightly vinous ale.

Lichfield Brewery

- 3 Europa Way, Boley Park, Lichfield WS14 9TZ.
- 0543 419919.
- No.
- No.
- Independent

INSPIRED
OG 1040° ABV 4%

Ingredients: Maris Otter pale malt (95%), crystal malt (5%). Challenger and Goldings whole hops (50% each) for bitterness and aroma.

TASTING NOTES

Nose	Light hops and malt aromas
Palate	Smooth and fruity in mouth, short bitter finish
Comments	Refreshing light amber ale.

XPIRED
OG 1050° ABV 5%

Ingredients: Maris Otter pale malt (90%), crystal malt (10%). Challenger (60%) and Goldings (40%) whole hops for bitterness and aroma.

TASTING NOTES

Nose	Rich malt and fruit aromas
Palate	Smooth nutty malt in mouth, big finish with malt, hops and fruit
Comments	Dark and dangerously quaffable ruby ale.

Lloyds Country Beers

⌨ **John Thompson Inn, Ingleby DE7 1NW.**
☏ **0332 863426/862469.**
🏛 **Yes (in pub).**
🚶 **Yes.**
i **Independent**

CLASSIC
OG 1038˚ ABV 3.6%

Ingredients: Maris Otter pale malt (100%). Challenger whole and pellet hops for bitterness and aroma. Dry hopped.

TASTING NOTES

Nose	Rich malt aroma with light fruit hints
Palate	Malt in mouth, bitter-sweet finish with hops and fruit notes
Comments	A pale, light and quenching ale, brewed for summer drinking.

DERBY or COUNTRY BITTER
OG 1042˚ ABV 4.1%

Ingredients: Maris Otter pale malt (99%), chocolate malt (1%), barley syrup. Challenger whole and pellet hops for bitterness and aroma. Dry hopped.

TASTING NOTES

Nose	Rich promise of hops with fruit notes developing
Palate	Rounded malt in mouth with good balance of hops, deep dry finish with ripe fruit
Comments	Beautifully balanced beer full of malt and hops character.

DERBY PORTER
OG 1045˚ ABV 4.5%
Ingredients: Maris Otter pale malt (90%), chocolate malt (10%). Challenger whole and pellet hops for bitterness and aroma.

TASTING NOTES

Nose	Roasted grain aroma
Palate	Sweet malt in mouth gives way to mellow chocolate finish
Comments	Jet black, rich-tasting ale.

SKULLCRUSHER
OG 1065˚ ABV 6%
Ingredients: Maris Otter pale malt, chocolate malt and barley syrup. Challenger whole and pellet hops for bitterness and aroma. Dry hopped.

TASTING NOTES

Nose	Massive wine and ripe fruit aromas
Palate	Mouth filling deluge of malt and fruit, intense finish with hops, chocolate and sultana
Comments	Ripe and vinous fruity winter ale.

OVERDRAFT
OG 1065˚ ABV 6.1%
Ingredients: Maris Otter pale malt (100%). Challenger whole and pellet hops for aroma and bitterness.

TASTING NOTES

Nose	Powerful malt and fruit aromas with hop notes
Palate	Malty on tongue, developing long bitter and fruity finish
Comments	Deceptively pale and lightly fruity ale. Lloyd's beers have a slight sulphur hint as a result of supplies of yeast brought every week from Burton-on-Trent.

Mansfield Brewery Co PLC

⌨ **Littleworth, Mansfield NG18 1AB.**
☎ **0623 25691.**
🏛 **Yes.**
🕴 **Yes.**
i **Independent**

RIDING DARK MILD
OG 1035° ABV 3.5%
Ingredients: Halcyon pale malt (75%), crystal malt (5%), invert sugar (20%). 100 units of colour. Fuggles hop pellets. 22 units of bitterness.

TASTING NOTES

Nose	Roast malt, fruit, caramel and chocolate aromas
Palate	Creamy malt and nut in mouth, bittersweet finish with chocolate notes
Comments	Distinctively creamy dark mild.

RIDING BITTER
OG 1035° ABV 3.6%
Ingredients: Halcyon pale malt (82%), invert sugar (18%). 21 units of colour. Fuggles hop pellets for bitterness, Styrian Goldings for aroma and dry hopping. 24 units of bitterness.

TASTING NOTES

Nose	Resiny hop aroma with citric fruit notes
Palate	Malt and citric fruit in mouth, long dry finish with hops and delicate fruit notes
Comments	Pale bitter with powerful smack of hops.

OLD BAILY
OG 1045° ABV 4.8%
Ingredients: Halcyon pale malt (82%), invert sugar (18%). 28 units of colour. Fuggles hop pellets in copper and for dry hopping. 30 units of bitterness.

TASTING NOTES

Nose	Rich hops, fruit and vinous aromas
Palate	Fruity and estery in mouth, rich and hoppy finish with vanilla notes
Comments	Ripe, fruity, sherry-coloured ale.

Marston's

☎ **Marston, Thompson & Evershed PLC. PO Box 26, Shobnall Road, Burton upon Trent DE14 2BW.**
① **0283 31131.**
🏛 **Yes.**
⋔ **Yes.**
i **Independent**

MARSTON'S BITTER
OG 1037˚ ABV 3.8%
Ingredients: pale malt (92%), glucose (8%). 27 units of colour. Fuggles, Goldings and Whitbread Goldings Variety whole hops.

TASTING NOTES

Nose	Delicate Goldings aroma with light fruit notes
Palate	Bitter-sweet malt and hops in mouth, dry finish with hops and light fruit
Comments	Brilliant addition to the range, a bitter that replaced Burton Best Bitter.

PEDIGREE BITTER
OG 1043˚ ABV 4.5%
Ingredients: pale malt (83%), glucose (17%). Fuggles, Goldings and Whitbread Goldings Variety whole hops.

TASTING NOTES

Nose	Complex bouquet of malt, hops, sour fruit with sulphur notes
Palate	Multi-layered light assault of malt and hops with long, delicate finish full of hops, apple notes and slight saltiness
Comments	Luscious and delicate beer of enormous complexity, brewed in traditional 'union room' oak fermenting vessels, which also propagate yeast for the other Marston's beers. Merrie Monk is Pedigree with the addition of caramel.

OWD RODGER
OG 1080˚ ABV 7.6%
Ingredients: pale malt (73%), crystal malt (10%), glucose (17%), caramel for colour. Fuggles, Goldings and Whitbread Variety whole hops.

TASTING NOTES

Nose	Toast, malt, hops and coffee essence aromas
Palate	Enormous impact of malt and fruit, long bitter-sweet finish with sultana and raisin fruit
Comments	Rich and fruity barley wine. Marston's added an additional union room in 1992 and is now brewing a range of occasional beers under the title of 'Brewer's Choice'.

Nene Valley Brewery

🖻 **Unit 1, Midland Business Centre, Midland Road, Higham Ferrers NN9 8DN.**

① **0933 412411.**

🏛 **No.**

🕴 **Yes.**

i **Independent**

NENE VALLEY BREWERY

TROJAN BITTER
OG 1038˚ ABV 3.6%
Ingredients: pale malt (95%), crystal malt (5%), touch of raost barley. Equal amounts of Challenger, Fuggles and Goldings whole hops.

TASTING NOTES

Nose	Complex aromas of hops and light fruit
Palate	Light malt in mouth, fruit and delicate hops in finish
Comments	Hoppy, mellow bitter.

RAWHIDE
OG 1050˚ ABV 4.8%
Ingredients: pale malt (91%), crystal malt (7.5%), wheat malt (2%), touch of roast barley. Fuggles and Goldings whole hops.

TASTING NOTES

Nose	Rich malt and hops aromas
Palate	Honey and fruit jam in mouth, short dry finish
Comments	Robust, fruity and complex beer.

Parish Brewery

- ✉ **Rear of Old Brewery Inn, Somerby, nr Melton Mowbray LE14 2PZ.**
- ☎ **066477 781/866.**
- 🏛 **Yes.**
- 👥 **Yes.**
- *i* **Independent**

PARISH SPECIAL BITTER OR PSB
OG 1038˚ ABV 3.6%
Ingredients: Maris Otter pale malt (90%), crystal malt (5%), wheat malt (5%). Whole Goldings hops, late hopped in hopback. 28-32 units of bitterness.

TASTING NOTES

Nose	Massive hop resin aroma
Palate	Good balance of malt and hops in mouth with dry finish and some fruit notes
Comments	Rich, copper-coloured ale, sold for £1 a pint (spring 1993) in Brewery Inn.

POACHER'S ALE
OG 1060˚ ABV 6%
Ingredients: Maris Otter pale malt (85%), wheat malt (5%), crystal malt (8%), black malt (2%). Goldings whole hops for bitterness, Fuggles for aroma. 24 units of bitterness.

TASTING NOTES

Nose	Powerful assault of malt, hops and winey fruit
Palate	Mouth-filling sweet malt and orange peel with intense finish of malt, hops and fruit
Comments	Staggering ale in every sense: 'You don't know whether to frame it or drink it,' says owner Barrie Parish.

BAZ'S BONCE BLOWER
OG 1110˚ ABV 11%
Ingredients: Halcyon pale malt (85%), black malt (2%), crystal malt (7%), wheat malt (5%), 1% of 'a secret ingredient'. Goldings whole hops for bitterness, Bramling Cross and Fuggles for aroma. 38-42 units of bitterness.

TASTING NOTES

Nose	Whole fields of hops and malt clamber out of the glass with dark chocolate notes
Palate	Port wine character in mouth, tremendous length of finish with malt, hops, chocolate, nuts and raisins
Comments	A brown-black ale of awesome complexity; try it in a wine glass. Parish also brews Somerby Premium (OG 1042° ABV 4.2%) for the Brewery Inn only.

Rising Sun Brewery

⌨ **Rising Sun Inn, Knowle Bank Road. Shraley Brook, Audley, Stoke-on-Trent ST7 8DS.**

① **0782 720600.**

🏛 **Yes (in pub).**

🕴 **by arrangement.**

i **Independent**

SUNLIGHT
OG 1036° ABV 3.5%
Ingredients: Halcyon pale malt (96%), crystal malt (1%), flaked wheat (3%). Challenger, Fuggles and Goldings whole hops, late hopped in copper with Goldings.

TASTING NOTES

Nose	Malt, nuts and Goldings hops aromas
Palate	Quenching malt and light fruit in mouth, bitter-sweet finish with delicate fruit and hops
Comments	Golden ale with good hop 'bite'.

RISING
OG 1040° ABV 3.9%
Ingredients: Halcyon pale malt (90%), crystal malt (4%), flaked wheat (6%). Challenger, Fuggles and Goldings whole hops, late hopped in copper with Challenger.

TASTING NOTES

Nose	Hop aroma dominates with good malt undertones
Palate	Blend of malt and crystal nut in mouth, long bitter finish
Comments	Hoppy amber ale.

SETTING
OG 1045° ABV 4.4%
Ingredients: Halcyon pale malt (89%), crystal malt (5%), chocolate malt (1%), flaked wheat (5%). Challenger, Fuggles and Goldings whole hops, late hopped in copper with Goldings.

TASTING NOTES

Nose	Rich fruit and hops aromas
Palate	Malt, fruit and chocolate in mouth, deep finish with dark grain, fruit and hops
Comments	Dark brown and complex ale.

SUNSTROKE
OG 1056° ABV 5.6%
Ingredients: Halcyon pale malt (87%), crystal malt (8%), flaked wheat (5%). Challenger, Fuggles and Goldings whole hops, late copper hopped with Goldings.

TASTING NOTES

Nose	Ripe fruit and hops aromas
Palate	Massive malt and fruit in mouth, deep finish dominated by powerful hop character
Comments	Dark amber ale with great hops appeal.

TOTAL ECLIPSE
OG 1072° ABV 6.9%
Ingredients: Halcyon pale malt (83%), crystal malt (10%), flaked wheat (5%), chocolate malt (1.5%). Fuggles and Goldings whole hops, late copper hopped with Goldings.

TASTING NOTES

Nose	Dark, roasted and chocolate malts dominate aroma
Palate	Bitter malts in mouth, long finish with malt, dark fruit and hops
Comments	Dark, hoppy and bitter powerful brew.

SOLAR FLARE
OG 1100° ABV 10.9%
Ingredients: Halcyon pale malt (82%), crystal malt (11%), flaked wheat (5%), chocolate malt (1.5%). Fuggles and Goldings whole hops.

TASTING NOTES

Nose	Ripe fruit and malt aromas
Palate	Vinous fruit in mouth, deep, long finish packed with massive fruit, malt and hops
Comments	Dark and enticing barley wine. The beers are available in the pub and in the free trade.

Ruddles Brewery Ltd
- **Langham, nr Oakham, Rutland LE15 7JD.**
- **0572 756911.**
- **No.**
- **No.**
- *i* **Subsidiary of Grolsch N V, Netherlands**

RUDDLES BEST BITTER
OG 1037° ABV 3.8%
Ingredients: pale ale malt (86%), crystal malt (4%), sugar (10%). Bramling Cross, Challenger, Fuggles and Goldings whole hops.

TASTING NOTES

Nose	Malt and light fruit aromas with hop notes developing
Palate	Malt in mouth, dry finish with some fruit and hops notes
Comments	Rich amber fruity ale

RUDDLES COUNTY
Ingredients: premium ale malt (85%), crystal malt (4%), sugar (11%). Bramling Cross, Challenger, Fuggles and Goldings whole hops.

TASTING NOTES

Nose	Powerful promise of hops and winey fruit
Palate	Mouth-filling, complex balance of grain, fruit and hops with deep, rounded dry and fruity finish

Comments	Rich and tasty strong ale with powerful fruit character.

Springhead Brewery

🖃 **25 Main Street, Sutton-on-Trent, nr Newark NG23 6PF.**
① **0636 821000.**
🏛 **No.**
🕴 **No.**
i **Independent**

SPRINGHEAD BITTER
OG 1040° ABV 4%
Ingredients: Halcyon pale malt (98.5%), crystal malt (1.5%). Kent Northdown whole hops. 23 units of bitterness.

TASTING NOTES

Nose	Warm biscuity malt and bitter hops aromas
Palate	Rich malt in mouth, long finish with complex malt, fruit and hops character
Comments	Fine copper-coloured ale with a touch of sherry wineyness. The beer is brewed with a bottom-fermenting ale yeast strain originating in Canada.

Titanic Brewery

🖃 **Unit G, Harvey Works, Lingard Street, Burslem, Stoke-on-Trent ST6 1ED.**
① **0782 823447.**
🏛 **Yes (Bulls Head pub).**
🕴 **Yes.**
i **Independent**

TITANIC BEST BITTER
OG 1036° ABV 3.6%
Ingredients: Maris Otter pale malt (97%), flaked wheat (3%). Fuggles and Goldings whole hops.

TASTING NOTES

Nose	Rich hop resin aroma
Palate	Refreshing and sharp in mouth, dry hoppy finish

Comments	Pale bitter brew, a good palate cleanser; brewed in summer only.

LIFEBOAT ALE
OG 1040˚ ABV 4%
Ingredients: Maris Otter pale malt (85%), crystal malt (14%), black malt (1%). Fuggles and Goldings whole hops.

TASTING NOTES

Nose	Rich malt and Goldings hops bouquet
Palate	Sweet and nutty malt in mouth, dry malty finish with some fruit notes
Comments	Dark and nutty, full-bodied brew with fine crystal malt character.

TITANIC PREMIUM ALE
OG 1042˚ ABV 4.2%
Ingredients: Maris Otter pale malt (90%), crystal malt (5%), black malt (0.5%), flaked wheat (4.5%). Fuggles and Goldings whole hops.

TASTING NOTES

Nose	Massive hop resin aroma
Palate	Smooth balance of malt and hops in mouth, long dry finish with citric fruit notes
Comments	Pale and refreshing brew with rich hops character.

CAPTAIN SMITH'S STRONG ALE
OG 1050˚ ABV 5%
Ingredients: Maris Otter pale malt (80%), crystal malt (10%), glucose syrup (5%), flaked wheat (5%). Goldings whole hops.

TASTING NOTES

Nose	Tempting fruit and hops aroma
Palate	Massive fruit and malt in mouth balanced by deep, dry finish with powerful Goldings hop notes
Comments	Dark and potable beer named after the captain of the Titanic who came from Stoke.

WRECKAGE
OG 1080˚ ABV 8%
Ingredients: Maris Otter pale malt (80%), crystal malt (8%), black malt (2%), glucose syrup (6%), flaked wheat (4%). Fuggles whole hops.

TASTING NOTES

Nose	Complex aroma of malt, fruit and hops
Palate	Explosion of malt, fruit and hops with rich, bitter-sweet finish
Comments	Dark but subtle winter beer described by the brewer as 'liquid knockout drops'.

Wiltshire Brewery Co PLC

- **Unit 4, Block E, Stourbridge Estate, Mill Race Lane, Stourbridge DY8 1JN.**
- **0384 442040.**
- **No.**
- **Yes.**
- **Independent. Formed as a merger between Premier Ales and Wiltshire Brewery, it was bought in 1992 by United Breweries of India. It is expected that the name will change to United Breweries and the location of the brewery will move. The range of beers is liable to change.**

PITFIELD MILD OR STONEHENGE MILD
OG 1035˚ ABV 3.4%
Ingredients: Maris Otter and Pipkin pale malts, crystal malt, roast barley, caramel, dark cane sugar. Challenger, Goldings and Northdown hop pellets.

TASTING NOTES

Nose	Aromas of dark malt and roasted grain
Palate	Roast and malt in mouth, light bitter finish
Comments	Dark mild with rich malt character.

PITFIELD BITTER OR STONEHENGE BITTER
OG 1036˚ ABV 3.5-3.6%
Ingredients: Maris Otter and Pipkin pale malts, crystal malt, roast barley. Challenger, Goldings and Northdown hop pellets.

TASTING NOTES

Nose	Rich malt aroma with peppery Goldings and fruit hints
Palate	Malt in mouth with light hoppy finish
Comments	Copper-coloured ale with good hops character.

PITFIELD ESB
OG 1044° ABV 4.2%

Ingredients: Maris Otter and Pipkin pale malts, light Muscovado cane sugar. Challenger and Goldings hop pellets. Dry hopped with Goldings.

TASTING NOTES

Nose	Splendid peppery Goldings aroma
Palate	Delicate balance of malt and hops, dry finish with toffee notes and good Goldings character
Comments	Straw-coloured beer with a Pilsner characteristic of butterscotch and hops.

PITFIELD HOXTON HEAVY
OG 1048-1050° ABV 4.8%

Ingredients: Maris Otter and Pipkin pale malts, crystal malt, wheat malt and pure malt extract. Goldings and Northdown hop pellets.

TASTING NOTES

Nose	Fragrant malt, hops and orange peel aromas
Palate	Rich malt in mouth, deep bitter-sweet finish
Comments	Rounded and complex ruby-coloured ale.

OLD GRUMBLE
OG 1048° ABV 4.8%

Ingredients: Maris Otter and Pipkin pale malts, crystal malt, wheat malt, pure malt extract. Goldings and Northdown hop pellets, dry hopped with Goldings.

TASTING NOTES

Nose	Rich aromas of malt and floral hops
Palate	Full malt in mouth, with long hop and fruit finish
Comments	Copper-coloured, complex and fruity brew.

PITFIELD DARK STAR
OG 1049-1050° ABV 4.9%
Ingredients: Maris Otter and Pipkin pale malts, crystal malt, wheat malt, roast barley, pure malt extract. Goldings hop pellets.

TASTING NOTES

Nose	Blackcurrant and chocolate aromas
Palate	Rich malt, coffee and fruit in mouth with dry bitter finish
Comments	Superb tawny ale, cross between a bitter and a stout.

PITFIELD BLACK KNIGHT STOUT
OG 1050° ABV 5%
Ingredients: Maris Otter and Pipkin pale malts, roast barley, wheat malt, dark cane sugar, malt extract. Challenger and Goldings hop pellets.

TASTING NOTES

Nose	Dark aromas of raisins and chocolate
Palate	Bitter malt and hops in mouth, vinous and bitter chocolate finish
Comments	Jet-black stout with layers of fruit, chocolate and hops; brewed in winter months only.

PITFIELD LONDON PORTER
OG 1058° ABV 5.7%
Ingredients: Maris Otter and Pipkin pale malts, black malt, pure malt extract. Goldings and Northdown hop pellets.

TASTING NOTES

Nose	Biscuity, roast barley aroma
Palate	Tart balance of malt, dark chocolate and hops; deep finish with coffee notes
Comments	Dark brew of great depth and roastiness, based on 1850s Whitbread recipe.

PITFIELD MAIDEN'S RUIN
OG 1075° ABV 7.5%
Ingredients: Maris Otter and Pipkin pale malts, light muscovado cane sugar, pure malt extract. Challenger and Northdown hop pellets. Dry hopped.

TASTING NOTES

Nose	Powerful aromas of hops, alcohol and vinous fruit
Palate	Mouth-filling sweet malt and hops, deep and long finish packed with fruit
Comments	Pale coloured sipping ale with great hops and fruit character; brewed in winter months.

PITFIELD SANTA'S DOWNFALL
OG 1078° ABV 8%
Ingredients: Maris Otter and Pipkin pale malts, light muscovado cane sugar, pure malt extract, raspberry fruit. Challenger and Northdown hop pellets.

TASTING NOTES

Nose	Powerful aromas of raspberries and alcohol
Palate	Ripe balance of malt, alcohol and fruit in mouth, massive finish packed with fruit and hops
Comments	Red in colour, intriguing and complex fruit beer, brewed only in December.

Wood Brewery Ltd
✉ **Wistanstow, Craven Arms SY7 8DG.**
☎ **0588 672523.**
🏛 **Yes (in Plough Inn).**
⚲ **by arrangement.**
i **Independent**

SAM POWELL BEST BITTER
OG 1034° ABV 3%
Ingredients: pale malt (86%), crystal malt (5.5%), chocolate malt (1%), wheat flour (7.5%). Fuggles and Goldings whole hops.

TASTING NOTES

Nose	Delicate Goldings bouquet
Palate	Light malt in mouth, clean hop finish
Comments	Pale and refreshing light bitter.

SAM POWELL ORIGINAL BITTER
OG 1038° ABV 3.5%
Ingredients: pale malt (86%), crystal malt (5.5%), chocolate malt (1%), wheat flour (7.5%). Fuggles and Goldings whole hops.

TASTING NOTES

Nose	Rich tang of hops and malt
Palate	Full malt in mouth, deep bitter finish with some light fruit notes
Comments	Rounded deep-drinking bitter.

WOOD'S PARISH BITTER
OG 1040° ABV 3.7%
Ingredients: premium pale ale malt (96%), crystal malt (4%). Fuggles in copper, dry hopped with whole Goldings.

TASTING NOTES

Nose	Rich hop resin aroma
Palate	Clean and quenching malt and hops in mouth, long finish full of floral hop character
Comments	Light-coloured, superbly balanced, hoppy beer.

WOOD'S SPECIAL BITTER
OG 1043° ABV 4%
Ingredients: premium pale ale malt (91%), crystal malt (9%). Fuggles whole hops.

TASTING NOTES

Nose	Complex bouquet of malt, hops and fruit
Palate	Rich malt in mouth, dry finish with hops, fruit and nut notes
Comments	Russet-coloured ale, multi-layered and memorable.

SAM POWELL OLD SAM
OG 1048° ABV 4.3%
Ingredients: pale malt (86.5%), crystal malt (5.5%), chocolate malt (1%), wheat flour (7%). Fuggles and Goldings whole hops.

TASTING NOTES

Nose	Dry roast malt aroma

| Palate | Rich winey flavour with bitter hop edge, dry finish with chocolate notes |
| Comments | Dark copper ale with warm malt and hops character. |

WOOD'S WONDERFUL
OG 1050° ABV 4.75%
Ingredients: premium pale ale malt (92%), crystal malt (7%), chocolate malt (1%). Fuggles in copper, whole Goldings for cask hopping.

TASTING NOTES
Nose	Great attack of hop flowers and fruit jam
Palate	Generous malt and fruit in mouth, deep, dry slightly tannic finish
Comments	Wonderful indeed! Powerful ruby brew of memorable complexity.

WOOD'S CHRISTMAS CRACKER
OG 1060° ABV 6%
Ingredients: premium pale ale malt (83%), crystal malt (16%), chocolate malt (1%). Fuggles in copper, whole Goldings hops for cask hopping.

TASTING NOTES
Nose	Enormous bouquet of hops, raisins and sultanas
Palate	Rich and vinous in mouth, intense rich finish with hops, dark chocolate, coffee and fruit notes
Comments	Dark ruby winter brew, ideal with Christmas pudding. Wood's also brews an occasional Recession Bitter selling at 99p in 1993.

Wye Valley Brewery

🖃 **69 St Owen Street, Hereford HR1 2JQ.**
① **0432 274968.**
🏛 **Yes.**
🏃 **Yes.**
i **Independent**

HEREFORD BITTER
OG 1036° ABV 3.5%
Ingredients: Maris Otter pale malt (85%), crystal malt (5%), wheat malt. Target whole hops.

TASTING NOTES

Nose	Inviting hops and light citric fruit aromas
Palate	Refreshing balance of malt and hops in mouth with hops dominating the finish
Comments	Golden ale with superb quenching flavour.

HPA
OG 1040° ABV 4%
Ingredients: Maris Otter pale malt (90%), wheat malt (10%). Target whole hops.

TASTING NOTES

Nose	Rich malt and hops aromas
Palate	Creamy balance of malt and hops in mouth, long dry finish with some vanilla notes
Comments	Finely balanced pale beer rich with malt and hops.

HEREFORD SUPREME
OG 1043° ABV 4.3%
Ingredients: Maris Otter pale malt (80%), crystal malt (12%), wheat malt (8%). Target whole hops.

TASTING NOTES

Nose	Superb malt and hops aromas with fruit notes developing
Palate	Rich fruit and malt in mouth, deep finish with long hops character and hints of vanilla and sultanas
Comments	Dark golden beer with many layers of complex bitter-sweet flavours.

BREW 69
OG 1055˚ ABV 5.6%
Ingredients: Maris Otter pale malt (95%), crystal malt (5%). Target whole hops.

TASTING NOTES

Nose	Rich aromatic malt, hops and fruit bouquet
Palate	Mouth-filling fruit and malt, deep finish with hop resin and ripe fruit
Comments	Pale, powerful barley wine; a fine nightcap.

EASTERN ENGLAND

East Anglia is the major barley growing region of Britain, blessed with fine chalky soil that produces grain low in nitrogen — ideal for brewing.

Beers from Eastern England are generous and rounded in palate but any sweetness is offset by good hop rates. The end results are ales of great complexity and depth.

The region lost many of its breweries during a wave of takeovers and closures in the 1970s. Norwich, once a great brewing city, now has just one small micro. But there is growing choice as the region's independents are augmented by small micro-breweries producing beers of great quality: Mauldon and Woodfordes won CAMRA's Champion Beer of Britain award in 1991 and 1992 respectively.

Adnams & Co PLC

☐ **Sole Bay Brewery, East Green, Southwold IP18 6JW.**
① **0502 722424.**
🏛 **No.**
🕿 **Trade only.**
i **Independent**

MILD
OG 1034˚ ABV 3.2%
Ingredients: Maris Otter pale malt, crystal malt, invert, Laevuline and priming sugars, caramel for colour. 120 units of colour. Fuggles and Goldings whole hops. 20 units of bitterness.

TASTING NOTES

Nose	Light malt and hops aromas
Palate	Soft yet rich malt in mouth, gentle finish with good chewy malt and hops undertones
Comments	Fine dark and mellow mild.

BITTER (BB)
OG 1036˚ ABV 3.8%
Ingredients: Maris Otter pale ale malt, invert sugar, caramel for colour. 26 units of colour. Fuggles and Goldings whole hops, with Challenger. Dry hopped with Fuggles. 33 units of bitterness.

TASTING NOTES

Nose	Superb bouquet of tangy orange fruit and peppery hops
Palate	Rich malt in mouth balanced by good hop attack, long finish packed with citric fruit and hop resin notes
Comments	Aromatic, generously hopped and fruity beer with a hint of salt.

OLD
OG 1042˚ ABV 4.1%
Ingredients: Maris Otter pale ale malt, invert, Laevuline and priming sugars, caramel for colour. 100 units of colour. Fuggles and Goldings whole hops. 23 units of bitterness.

TASTING NOTES

Nose	Gentle malt aroma with hop notes developing
Palate	Soft malt in mouth, good chewy malt and hops finish
Comments	Mellow, dark winter beer.

EXTRA
OG 1043˚ ABV 4.5%

Ingredients: Maris Otter pale ale malt, Dixon's crystal malt, invert sugar, caramel for colour. 30 units of colour. Fuggles and Goldings whole hops, some Challenger; Fuggles added to hopback. 36 units of bitterness.

TASTING NOTES

Nose	Powerful spicy hops and fruit bouquet
Palate	Rich balance of malt and hops resin, deep dry finish with fruit notes
Comments	Tangy and complex strong bitter.

BROADSIDE
OG 1049˚ ABV 4.8%

Ingredients: Maris Otter pale ale malt, Dixon's crystal malt, invert sugar, caramel for colour. 38 units of colour. Fuggles and Goldings whole hops, some Challenger; late hopped with Fuggles. 33 units of bitterness.

TASTING NOTES

Nose	Rich promise of hops and grain
Palate	Sweet malt and fruit in mouth, light dry finish
Comments	Potable, complex and fruity strong ale.

TALLY-HO
OG 1075˚ ABV 6.2%

Ingredients: Maris Otter pale ale malt, crystal malt, invert and Laevuline sugars, caramel for colour. 120 units of colour. Fuggles and Goldings whole hops. 28 units of bitterness.

TASTING NOTES

Nose	Rich vinous and spice aromas
Palate	Malt, fruit and hops in mouth, long, rounded and complex finish with raisin and sultana notes
Comments	Classic barley wine brewed for Christmas season.

Banks & Taylor Brewery Ltd

▣ **The Brewery, Shefford SG17 5DZ.**
① **0462 815080.**
🏛 **No.**
⚚ **No.**
i **Independent**

SHEFFORD MILD
OG 1035˚ ABV 3.5%
Ingredients: pale malt (95%), crystal malt (5%), caramel. Challenger whole hops for bitterness, Fuggles and Goldings for aroma. 30 units of bitterness.

TASTING NOTES

Nose	Pleasing malt, nut and hops aromas
Palate	Creamy malt in mouth, delicate bitter-sweet finish
Comments	Smooth drinking darkish mild with good hop notes.

SHEFFORD BITTER
OG 1038˚ ABV 3.8%
Ingredients: pale malt (95%), crystal malt (5%). Challenger, Fuggles and Goldings whole hops. 40 units of bitterness.

TASTING NOTES

Nose	Strong hop resin aroma with delicate fruit notes
Palate	Light clean grain and hops in mouth with quenching bitter finish
Comments	Refreshing well-hopped and tasty session bitter.

SHEFFORD PALE ALE
OG 1041˚ ABV 4%
Ingredients: pale malt (87%), crystal malt (7%), wheat malt (6%). Fuggles and Goldings whole hops. 36 units of bitterness.

TASTING NOTES

Nose	Rich malt and hops aromas with citric fruit developing
Palate	Full rounded malt and hops in mouth, deep dry finish with strong fruit notes

Comments   Well-crafted, rounded ale.

EDWIN TAYLOR'S EXTRA STOUT
OG 1045˚ ABV 4.5%
Ingredients: pale malt (84%), roast barley (16%). Challenger and Hallertau whole hops. 48 units of bitterness.

TASTING NOTES
Nose	Pungent aromas of roasted grain, bitter chocolate and hop resins
Palate	Ripe malt with strong roast notes in mouth, deep finish with rich balance of hops, bitter malt and chocolate
Comments	Superb stout with exceptional hop character and bitter dark malt.

OLD BAT
OG 1045˚ ABV 4.5%
Ingredients: 100% Halcyon pale malt. Fuggles, Goldings and Hallertau whole hops.

TASTING NOTES
Nose	Powerful bouquet of citric fruit, malt and hops
Palate	Quenching malt and fruit in mouth, deep finish with great attack of fruit and hops
Comments	Pale and luscious barley wine.

SHEFFORD OLD STRONG (SOS)
OG 1050˚ ABV 5%
Ingredients: pale malt (95%), crystal malt (5%). Fuggles and Goldings whole hops.

TASTING NOTES
Nose	Rich aromas of hop resins and ripe, jammy fruit
Palate	Rich, mouth-filling grain with good bitter balance, intense finish with sultana and raisin notes
Comments	Powerful and fruity ale. Shefford Old Dark (SOD) is the same beer with caramel for colour.

2XS
OG 1059˚ ABV 5.8%
Ingredients: pale malt (92%), crystal malt (8%). Challenger, Fuggles and Goldings whole hops. 40 units of bitterness.

TASTING NOTES

Nose	Enormous attack of rich malt, spicy hops and citric fruit
Palate	Mouth-filling malt and hops, long bitter-sweet finish with ripe fruit
Comments	Fruity, copper-coloured strong ale.

BLACK BAT
OG 1064˚ ABV 6.4%
Ingredients: pale malt (90%), crystal malt (10%). Challenger, Fuggles and Goldings whole hops. 42 units of bitterness.

TASTING NOTES

Nose	Rich creamy malt and nut with strong hop notes
Palate	Vast fruity malt and hops in mouth, deep bitter-sweet finish with delicious balance of hops and nutty malt
Comments	Potent and complex strong, copper-coloured ale.

George Bateman & Son Ltd
⌧ **Salem Bridge Brewery, Wainfleet, Skegness PE24 4JE.**
① **0754 880317.**
🏛 **Yes.**
🏃 **by arrangement.**
i **Independent**

DARK MILD
OG 1033˚ ABV 3%
Ingredients: Pipkin pale ale malt (60%), crystal malt (12%), wheat (4%), invert sugar (19%), caramel for colour (5%). Goldings whole hops.

TASTING NOTES

Nose	Biscuit and hazelnut aromas

Palate	Chewy malt in mouth, dry finish with roast malt and caramel notes
Comments	Tasty mild full of dark malt character.

XB BITTER
OG 1036° ABV 3.8%

Ingredients: Pipkin pale ale malt (73.5%), crystal malt (6%), wheat (2.5%), invert sugar (18%). Challenger and Goldings whole hops.

TASTING NOTES

Nose	Delicate malt and hops aromas, light orange fruit notes
Palate	Light, refreshing balance of malt and hops in mouth with long dry finish full of hops character
Comments	Rounded and distinctively hoppy beer

XXXB BITTER
OG 1048° ABV 5%

Ingredients: Pipkin pale ale malt (72%), crystal malt (7.5%), wheat (2.5%), invert sugar (18%). Challenger and Goldings whole hops.

TASTING NOTES

Nose	Ripe malt and hops aromas with hint of banana fruit
Palate	Sweet malt in mouth balanced by strong hop notes, deep, rounded finish with strong hops presence and rich fruit
Comments	Superb, complex premium bitter, four times winner of its class in Champion Beer of Britain competition.

SALEM PORTER
OG 1050° ABV 5%

Ingredients: Pipkin pale ale malt (75%), crystal malt (8%), roast barley (3%), wheat (2%), invert sugar (12%). 105 units of colour. Challenger and Goldings whole hops.

TASTING NOTES

Nose	Powerful roasted grain aroma
Palate	Dry nutty malt in mouth, long hoppy finish
Comments	Dark, complex, multi-layered dark beer.

VICTORY ALE
OG 1056° ABV 6%
Ingredients: Pipkin pale ale malt (66%), crystal malt (4.5%), wheat (4.5%), invert sugar (25%). Goldings whole hops.

TASTING NOTES

Nose	Luscious aromas of hops, oranges and pear drops
Palate	Full malt in mouth, intense finish with complex balance of hop bitterness and fruit
Comments	Delightful mellow ale brewed to celebrate the brewery's victory against closure in the mid-1980s.

Crouch Vale Brewery Ltd

- ⌖ **12 Redhills Road, South Woodham Ferrers, nr Chelmsford CM3 5UP.**
- ① **0245 322744.**
- 🏛 **No.**
- ⚑ **by arrangement.**
- *i* **Independent**

BEST MILD
OG 1036° ABV 3.5%
Ingredients: pale malt (95%: grist varies between Halcyon, Pipkin, Maris Otter and Triumph), roast barley (5%). 50 units of colour. Challenger and East Kent Goldings whole hops. 30 units of bitterness.

TASTING NOTES

Nose	Powerful aroma of roast barley with malt hints
Palate	Malt and roast in mouth, creamy finish
Comments	Easy-drinking mild with lingering bitterness.

WOODHAM IPA BITTER
OG 1036° ABV 3.5%
Ingredients: pale malt (95%), crystal malt (5%). 25 units of colour. Challenger whole hops for bitterness, East Kent Goldings for aroma. Dry hopped. 32 units of bitterness.

TASTING NOTES

Nose	Floral Goldings hop aroma
Palate	Sharp balance of malt and hops in mouth, finish packed with hops character
Comments	Refreshing light bitter with superb hoppiness

BEST BITTER
OG 1038˚ ABV 4%
Ingredients: pale malt (93%), crystal malt (7%). 31 units of colour. Challenger whole hops for bitterness, East Kent Goldings for aroma. Dry hopped. 35 units of bitterness.

TASTING NOTES

Nose	Rich hops aroma with fruit developing
Palate	Rich fruit in mouth leading to long dry finish with fine balance of malt and hops
Comments	Red-brown ale with uncompromising bitterness.

MILLENIUM GOLD
OG 1042˚ ABV 4.2%
Ingredients: 100% pale malt. 22 units of colour. Challenger whole hops for bitterness, East Kent Goldings for aroma. Dry hopped. 35 units of bitterness.

TASTING NOTES

Nose	Strong floral hop aroma with malt notes
Palate	Rich balance of malt, hops and fruit in mouth, sharp hoppy finish
Comments	Golden beer with fine malt, fruit and hops character.

STRONG ANGLIAN SPECIAL (SAS)
OG 1048˚ ABV 5%
Ingredients: pale malt (94%), crystal malt (6%). 29 units of colour. Challenger whole hops for bitterness, East Kent Goldings for aroma. Dry hopped. 37 units of bitterness.

TASTING NOTES

Nose	Fine aromas of malt, hop resins and fruit
Palate	Dry malt and hops in mouth, intense bitter, fruity finish
Comments	Deceptively light-bodied brew with sharp hop edge.

ESSEX PORTER
OG 1050˚ ABV 5%
Ingredients: pale malt (90%), crystal malt (5%), roast barley (5%). 98 units of colour. Challenger whole hops for bitterness, East Kent Goldings for aroma.

TASTING NOTES

Nose	Fruit and roast barley aromas
Palate	Nuts and fruit in mouth, dry bitter finish
Comments	Dark, rich and smooth bitter-sweet ale.

SANTA'S REVENGE
OG 1058˚ ABV 5.8%
Ingredients: pale malt (75%), crystal malt (5%), sugar (20%). 23 units of colour. Challenger whole hops for bitterness, East Kent Goldings for aroma. Dry hopped. 37 units of bitterness.

TASTING NOTES

Nose	Rich malt aroma with good waft of hops
Palate	Enticing hops in mouth, rich and ripe finish full of malt, fruit and hops
Comments	Fascinatingly complex strong ale: recipe can vary from year to year.

WILLIE WARMER
OG 1060˚ ABV 6.5%
Ingredients: pale malt (70%), roast barley (5%), sugar (25%). 100 units of colour. Challenger whole hops for bitterness, East Kent Goldings for aroma. 40 units of bitterness.

TASTING NOTES

Nose	Vast aromas of roasted grain and fruit
Palate	Sweet malt in mouth balanced by hops, rich roast barley finish with hints of fruit and nuts
Comments	Powerful, fruity sipping ale.

Elgood & Sons Ltd
- **North Brink Brewery, Wisbech PE13 1LN.**
- **0945 583160.**
- **No.**
- **No.**
- **Independent**

CAMBRIDGE BITTER
OG 1035° ABV 3.8%

Ingredients: Triumph pale ale malt, wheat flour, maize, roast barley, invert sugar. 28 units of colour. Fuggles whole hops.

TASTING NOTES

Nose	Delicate hops aroma with malt and some fruit
Palate	Refreshing balance of malt and hops in mouth, dry finish with some fruit notes
Comments	Fruity, fine-tasting bitter.

GSB OR GREYHOUND STRONG BITTER
OG 1045° ABV 5.2%

Ingredients: Triumph pale ale malt, wheat flour, maize, roast barley, invert sugar. 32 units of colour. Fuggles whole hops.

TASTING NOTES

Nose	Light hops aroma with some fruit notes developing
Palate	Rich malt and fruit in mouth, long bitter-sweet finish
Comments	Well-balanced, mahogany-coloured premium ale.

WINTER WARMER
OG 1080° ABV 9%

Ingredients: mild ale malt, wheat, maize, roast barley, invert sugar. Fuggles whole hops.

TASTING NOTES

Nose	Rich malt and biscuity roast grain aromas

Palate	Powerful mouth-filling roast barley and ripe fruit with long, deep vinous finish
Comments	Robust barley wine, highly attenuated, from Cambridgeshire's sole commercial brewery.

Forbes Ales

i **Oulton Broad, Lowestoft: this company was up for sale when the Almanac went to press.**

Greene King PLC

- ▭ **Westgate Brewery, Bury St Edmunds IP33 1QT.**
- ① **0284 763222.**
- 🏛 **Yes.**
- ⚲ **by arrangement.**
- *i* **Independent**

XX DARK MILD
OG 1030° ABV 3%
Ingredients: pale ale malt, coloured malt and sugar, small proportion of caramel for colour. English pellet hops. 19 units of bitterness.

TASTING NOTES

Nose	Dark grain and chocolate with hint of hops
Palate	Malt dominates the mouth, dry finish with chocolate notes
Comments	Fine chewy dark mild.

GREENE KING IPA
OG 1035° ABV 3.6%
Ingredients: pale ale malt, coloured malt and sugar, small proportion of caramel for colour. English hop pellets and hop oil. 24 units of bitterness.

TASTING NOTES

Nose	Delicate hop notes and yeasty esters
Palate	Good balance of hops and malt in mouth, bitter finish with hint of orange fruit
Comments	Tangy and distinctive tawny ale

RAYMENTS SPECIAL BITTER
OG 1040˚ ABV 4.3%
Ingredients: pale ale malt, high percentage of roasted malts, sugar, small proportion of caramel for colour. English hop pellets and oil. 26 units of bitterness.

TASTING NOTES

Nose	Rich bouquet of hops and roasted grain
Palate	Malt and fruit in mouth, bitter-sweet finish becoming dry with some tart fruit
Comments	Amber-coloured ale with a fascinating 'Scottish' feel to aroma and palate from roasted barley.

ABBOT ALE
OG 1048˚ ABV 5%
Ingredients: pale ale malt, coloured malt and sugar, small proportion of caramel for colour. English hop pellets and hop oil; dry hopped with hop oil. 36 units of bitterness.

TASTING NOTES

Nose	Massive aromas of hop resins and ripe fruit
Palate	Rich malt and marmalade fruit in mouth with superb hop balance; intense bitter-sweet finish
Comments	Strong beer of enormous complexity, any tendency towards sweetness deterred by powerful balance of hops. Greene King also brews a Winter Ale (OG 1052˚).

Hull Brewery Co Ltd
☎ **144-148 English Street, Hull HU3 2BT.**
✆ **0482 586364/5.**
🏛 **No.**
🚶 **Yes.**
i **Independent**

HULL BREWERY MILD
OG 1033˚ ABV 3.3%
Ingredients: 100% Maris Otter pale malt with black malt for colour and sucramel. Fuggles hop pellets.

TASTING NOTES

Nose	Light hops aroma with dark malt notes
Palate	Chewy bitter-sweet malt in mouth, dry finish with hop notes
Comments	Tasty dark mild served with Yorkshire creamy head.

HULL BREWERY BITTER
OG 1036˚ ABV 3.6%
Ingredients: 100% Maris Otter pale malt with chocolate malt for colour. Goldings hop pellets.

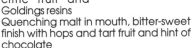

TASTING NOTES

Nose	Superb aromas of citric fruit and Goldings resins
Palate	Quenching malt in mouth, bitter-sweet finish with hops and tart fruit and hint of chocolate
Comments	Refreshing and complex copper ale.

GOVERNOR STRONG ALE
OG 1048˚ ABV 5%
Ingredients: 100% Maris Otter pale malt, chocolate malt for colour. Goldings hop pellets.

TASTING NOTES

Nose	Rich malt and hops aromas
Palate	Great malt attack in mouth, deep finish dominated by hops and tart fruit
Comments	Full-bodied amber ale with fine Goldings hops character.

McMullen & Sons Ltd
⌨ **The Hertford Brewery, 26 Old Cross, Hertford SG14 1RD.**
☎ **0992 584911.**
🏛 **Yes.**
⚒ **by arrangement.**
i **Independent**

ORIGINAL AK
OG 1033° ABV 3.8%

Ingredients: East Anglian Halcyon pale ale malt (80%), chocolate malt (1%), flaked maize (6%), maltose syrup (13%). East Kent Goldings and Whitbread Goldings Variety whole hops. 22 units of bitterness.

TASTING NOTES

Nose	Floral hop and light fruit aromas
Palate	Sweet malt, fruit and delicate hop in mouth, good dry finish with orange peel and faint chocolate notes
Comments	Superb, well-attenuated ale, once sold as light mild but now positioned as a pale ale; neither brewery nor historians are certain as to the origins of the name 'AK'.

COUNTRY BEST BITTER
OG 1041° ABV 4.6%

Ingredients: Halcyon pale ale malt (76%), crystal malt (4%), flaked maize (6%), maltose syrup (14%). East Kent Goldings and Whitbread Goldings Variety whole hops. 30 units of bitterness.

TASTING NOTES

Nose	Rich and tempting aromas of hop flowers and ripe fruit
Palate	Mouth-filling malt and fruit, deep dry finish with pronounced fruit and vanilla notes
Comments	Brilliant balance of malt and hop character; well-attenuated beer that drinks more than strength suggests.

STRONGHART
OG 1070° ABV 7%

Ingredients: Halcyon pale ale malt (74%), crystal malt (4%), flaked maize (4%), maltose syrup (18%). East Kent Goldings and Whitbread Goldings Variety whole hops. 33 units of bitterness.

TASTING NOTES

Nose	Heady aromas of hops and banana
Palate	Vinous in mouth, intense bitter-sweet finish with hops, raisins and sultanas

Comments	Liquid Christmas pudding, brewed for the festive season. McMullen is also test-marketing seasonal beers, including an IPA and a Summer Ale.

Mauldons Brewery

✉ **7 Addison Road, Chilton Industrial Estate, Sudbury CO10 6YW.**
☏ **0787 311055.**
🏛 **No.**
👫 **by arrangement.**
i **Independent**

MAULDONS BEST BITTER
OG 1037˚ ABV 3.8%
Ingredients: premium pale ale malt, crystal malt. Challenger and Goldings whole hops. 28 units of bitterness.

TASTING NOTES
Nose	Delicate hops aroma
Palate	Good balance of grain and hops with bitter-sweet finish
Comments	Excellent copper-coloured supping bitter.

PORTER
OG 1042˚ ABV 3.8%
Ingredients: premium pale ale malt, crystal malt, black malt. Challenger and Goldings whole hops. 23 units of bitterness.

TASTING NOTES
Nose	Pleasing aromas of hops and nuts
Palate	Rich nut in mouth, creamy finish with coffee and chocolate hints
Comments	Ripe and delectable black beer.

OLD XXXX
OG 1042˚ ABV 4%
Ingredients: premium pale ale malt, crystal malt. Challenger and Goldings whole hops. 25 units of bitterness.

TASTING NOTES
Nose	Sweet malt and chocolate aromas

Palate	Malt and nut in mouth, dry and bitter finish
Comments	Dark and rich ale.

SQUIRES
OG 1044˚ ABV 4.2%
Ingredients: premium pale ale malt, crystal malt. Challenger and Goldings whole hops. Dry hopped. 33 units of bitterness.

TASTING NOTES

Nose	Ripe aromas of hops and fruit
Palate	Rich rounded malt in mouth, bitter-sweet finish
Comments	Fine copper-coloured, well-balanced ale.

SUFFOLK PUNCH
OG 1050˚ ABV 4.8%
Ingredients: premium pale ale malt, crystal malt. Challenger and Goldings whole hops. 37 units of bitterness.

TASTING NOTES

Nose	Powerful bouquet of hop resins and developing fruit
Palate	Ripe malt and jammy fruit with a deep dry finish packed with Goldings character
Comments	Powerful, fruity ale with deep copper colour.

BLACK ADDER
OG 1055˚ ABV 5.3%
Ingredients: premium pale ale malt, crystal malt, black malt. Challenger and Goldings whole hops. 37 units of bitterness.

TASTING NOTES

Nose	Roast and nut aromas with strong hops developing
Palate	Fine fruity balance of hops and dark malt in mouth, intensely long, dry finish with coffee and nut notes
Comments	Memorably tasty strong stout: Champion Beer of Britain in 1991.

WHITE ADDER
OG 1055° ABV 5.3%
Ingredients: premium pale ale malt, crystal malt. Goldings whole hops. 37 units of bitterness.

TASTING NOTES

Nose	Delicate Goldings hop aroma
Palate	Bitter-sweet in mouth with hops dominating the finish
Comments	Pale, refreshing and hoppy ale.

SUFFOLK COMFORT
OG 1065° ABV 6.6%
Ingredients: premium pale ale malt, crystal malt. Challenger and Goldings whole hops. Dry hopped. 45 units of bitterness.

TASTING NOTES

Nose	Powerful peppery Goldings presence with malt notes
Palate	Rich balance of malt, crystal nuts and hops in mouth, long bitter finish with dark malt notes
Comments	Deceptively pale and potable strong ale. The brewery also brews Christmas Reserve (OG1066° 6.7%).

Nethergate Brewery Co Ltd

- ✉ **11-13 High Street, Clare, nr Sudbury CO10 8NY.**
- ☏ **0787 277244.**
- 🏛 **No.**
- ⚤ **Yes.**
- *i* **Independent**

NETHERGATE IPA
OG 1035° ABV 3.6%
Ingredients: Maris Otter pale malt (89.98%), crystal malt (5.01%), wheat flour (5.01%). 28 units of colour. Fuggles whole hops for aroma, Goldings pellets for bitterness. 27 units of bitterness.

TASTING NOTES

Nose	Light aroma of malt and hops

Palate	Malt dominates mouth, delicate dry finish with some hops notes
Comments	Straw-coloured light session bitter.

BITTER
OG 1039˚ ABV 4.1%
Ingredients: Maris Otter pale malt (88.63%), wheat flour (4.92%), crystal malt (4.92%), black malt (1.53%). 40 units of colour. Fuggles whole hops and Goldings hop pellets. 36 units of bitterness.

TASTING NOTES

Nose	Light aromas of hops, malt and some fruit notes
Palate	Rich and rounded balance of malt and hops, deep finish with fruit hints
Comments	Succulent coppery ale with a full palate suggesting greater strength.

OLD GROWLER
OG 1055˚ ABV 5.5%
Ingredients: Maris Otter pale malt (85.3%), wheat flour (3.41%), crystal malt (8.53%), black malt (2.71%). 70 units of colour. Fuggles whole hops and Goldings hop pellets. 27 units of bitterness.

TASTING NOTES

Nose	Light aromas at first, developing hops and bitter chocolate
Palate	Full and bitter-sweet in mouth, deep finish with hints of dark chocolate
Comments	Dark and smooth porter ale based on an 18th-century London recipe. Nethergate will gradually change its hops variety to Challenger.

███████████████

Nix Wincott Brewery

⌨ **Three Fyshes Inn, Bridge Street, Turvey, Bedford MK43 8ER.**

☎ **0234 881264.**

🏛 **Yes (in pub).**

🏃 **Yes.**

i **Independent**

TWO HENRYS BITTER
OG 1039˚ ABV 3.85%
Ingredients: pale malt (90%), crystal malt (10%). Fuggles and Goldings whole hops.

TASTING NOTES

Nose	Rich hops aroma with nutty hints
Palate	Rounded malt in mouth, long dry finish with hops and nuts
Comments	Amber ale with good drinkability.

THAT
OG 1048˚ ABV 4.8%
Ingredients: pale malt (90%), crystal malt (10%). Fuggles and Goldings whole hops.

TASTING NOTES

Nose	Wafts of hops, grain and ripe fruit
Palate	Malt and ripe fruit in mouth, long finish with complex hop bitterness and nutty undertones
Comments	Oak-coloured, complex ale.

OLD NIX
OG 1056.5˚ ABV 5.7%
Ingredients: pale malt (94.4%), crystal malt (5.6%). Fuggles and Goldings whole hops.

TASTING NOTES

Nose	Powerful aromas of malt and hops
Palate	Rich malt and hops in mouth, intense finish with hops, raisins and sultana

Comments   Pale but robust strong beer with great fruit appeal

WINKY'S WINTER WARMER
OG 1058˙ ABV 5.8%
Ingredients: pale malt (94.2%), crystal malt (5.8%), tiny percentage of caramel. Fuggles and Goldings whole hops.

TASTING NOTES
Nose   Ripe bouquet of malt and dates
Palate   Superb fruity flavours in mouth lead to long, dry, bitter-sweet finish with hint of burnt sugar
Comments   Rich and complex winter beer.

WINKY WOBBLER
OG 1070˙ ABV 7.25%
Ingredients: pale malt (90%), crystal malt (10%). Fuggles and Goldings whole hops.

TASTING NOTES
Nose   Massive fruit aromas of blackcurrants and raisins
Palate   Hops and bitter fruit in mouth, full and rich finish
Comments   Oak-coloured strong ale with massive fruit appeal.

Old Mill Brewery

🔲 **Mill Street, Snaith, Goole DN14 9HS.**
① **0405 861813.**
🏛 **No.**
🏃 **No.**
i **Independent**

TRADITIONAL MILD
OG 1034˙ ABV 3.4%
Ingredients: Halcyon pale malt, crystal malt, pale chocolate malt, black malt. Target hop pellets for bitterness, Styrian Goldings for aroma.

TASTING NOTES
Nose   Light aromas of hops and chocolate

Palate	Chocolate and malt in mouth, dry finish with dark chocolate hints
Comments	Dark, nutty mild.

TRADITIONAL BITTER
OG 1037˚ ABV 3.75%
Ingredients: Halcyon pale malt, crystal malt. Target and Styrian Goldings hop pellets.

TASTING NOTES

Nose	Tempting hops and delicate fruit aromas
Palate	Ripe but balanced malt and hops in mouth, clean, dry finish with delicate fruit notes
Comments	Complex amber beer with full palate and fruit appeal.

BULLION
OG 1044˚ ABV 4.5%
Ingredients: Halcyon pale malt, crystal malt, pale chocolate malt. Target and Styrian Goldings hop pellets.

TASTING NOTES

Nose	Rich bouquet of hop resins and ripe fruit
Palate	Mouth-filling malt with hop undertones, deep bitter-sweet finish with coffee and raisin notes
Comments	Superb, quaffable dark amber ale, winner of three awards at Great British Beer Festival.

████████████

Reepham Brewery
⌨ **Unit 1, Collers Way, Reepham NR10 4SW.**
① **0603 871091.**
🏛 **No.**
🕴 **Yes.**
i **Independent**

RAPIER PALE ALE
OG 1042˚ ABV 4.2%
Ingredients: pale malt (88%), crystal malt (4%), barley syrup (8%). Fuggles and Goldings whole hops.

TASTING NOTES

Nose	Ripe aromas of malt and hops
Palate	Full, rich grain in mouth, deep dry finish
Comments	Rich and rounded pale golden bitter.

VELVET STOUT
OG 1043˚ ABV 4.3%
Ingredients: pale malt (85%), crystal malt (6%), black malt (1%), cane sugar (5%), sugar caramel 3%. Fuggles and Goldings whole hops.

TASTING NOTES

Nose	Liquorice, malt and hops aromas
Palate	Sweet burnt malt in mouth, dry finish with some hops
Comments	Dark brown, smooth and velvety stout — a 'sweet stout' in the best traditions of the style.

OLD BIRCHAM ALE
OG 1044˚ ABV 4.4%
Ingredients: pale malt (87%), crystal malt (5%), black malt (1%), sugar (7%). Fuggles and Goldings whole hops.

TASTING NOTES

Nose	Rich malt and hops aromas
Palate	Sweet fruit, nuts and malt in mouth, long finish packed with fruit
Comments	Ruby-red, full-bodied and fruity ale.

Reindeer Brewery
🖃 **10 Dereham Road, Norwich NR2 4AY.**
① **0603 666821.**
🏛 **Yes (in pub).**
🕴 **Yes.**
i **Independent**

MILD
OG 1034˚ ABV 3.4%
Ingredients: Maris Otter pale malt (75%), crystal malt (22%), chocolate malt (2%), wheat malt (1%). Kent Goldings whole hops.

TASTING NOTES

Nose	Deep nutty aroma with hint of hops
Palate	Powerful crystal malt nut in mouth, soft dry finish
Comments	Delicious ruby-red soft mild — known as 'moild' to locals.

BEVY
OG 1037˚ ABV 3.7%
Ingredients: Maris Otter pale malt (87%), crystal malt (8%), wheat malt (5%). Kent Goldings whole hops, late hopped for aroma.

TASTING NOTES

Nose	Delicate malt and hops aromas
Palate	Creamy, nutty malt in mouth, bitter-sweet finish
Comments	Golden brown quaffing bitter.

GNU BREW
OG 1042˚ ABV 4.2%
Ingredients: Maris Otter pale malt (96%), crystal malt (2%), wheat malt (2%). Kent Goldings whole hops, late hopped for aroma.

TASTING NOTES

Nose	Rich and earthy Goldings aroma
Palate	Ripe malt in mouth, bitter-sweet finish with delicate Goldings notes
Comments	Gentle straw-gold bitter.

REINDEER BITTER
OG 1047˚ ABV 4.7%
Ingredients: Maris Otter pale malt (87%), crystal malt (9%), wheat malt (4%). Kent Goldings whole hops added at three stages of copper boil.

TASTING NOTES

Nose	Ripe malt and hops aromas
Palate	Powerful malt in mouth, sweet finish with bitterness developing
Comments	Full-bodied, rich-tasting bitter.

REDNOSE
OG 1057˚ ABV 5.7%
Ingredients: Maris Otter pale malt (86%), crystal malt (13%), chocolate malt (1%). Kent Goldings whole hops.

TASTING NOTES
Nose	Dark malt and fruit aromas
Palate	Rich, deep malty sweetness in mouth, deep bitter finish
Comments	Ripe, malty and vinous winter beer. With the exception of Mild, the beers in the Reindeer pub are kept under a light CO_2 pressure but are sold in cask-conditioned form to the free trade.

T D Ridley & Sons Ltd

- ▣ **Hartford End Brewery, Chelmsford CM3 1JZ.**
- ☏ **0371 820316/820609.**
- ▥ **Yes.**
- ⚥ **by arrangement.**
- *i* **Independent**

MILD
OG 1034° ABV 3.4%
Ingredients: best pale ale malt, roast malt, invert sugar. 150 units of colour. Fuggles and Goldings whole hops. Dry hopped. 24 units of bitterness.

TASTING NOTES
Nose	Delicate roast and hops aromas
Palate	Mellow nut in mouth, dry finish
Comments	Pleasant dark-ruby mild.

IPA BITTER
OG 1034° ABV 3.5%
Ingredients: best pale ale malt, crystal malt, invert sugar. 30 units of colour. Fuggles and Goldings whole hops. Dry hopped. 28 units of bitterness.

TASTING NOTES

Nose	Aromatic hops aroma with citric fruit notes
Palate	Tangy balance of malt, hops and fruit in mouth, long dry finish
Comments	Stunning, exceptional bitter—won long overdue recognition in 1992, winning its class in Champion Beer of Britain competition.

WINTER ALE
OG 1050° ABV 5%
Ingredients: best pale ale malt, roast malt, invert sugar. 175 units of colour. Fuggles and Goldings whole hops. 31 units of bitterness.

TASTING NOTES

Nose	Floral hops aroma
Palate	Succulent fruit flavours, long dry finish
Comments	Rich, dark ruby ale available in winter months.

Scotts Brewing Company
⌨ **Crown Hotel, 151 High Street, Lowestoft NR37 1HR.**
☎ **0502 569592/537237.**
🏛 **Yes (in hotel).**
🏃 **Yes.**
i **Independent**

GOLDEN BEST BITTER
OG 1036° ABV 3.4%
Ingredients: Pipkin pale malt (98%), crystal malt (2%). Fuggles and Goldings whole hops.

TASTING NOTES

Nose	Malt and hops bouquet
Palate	Quenching malt in mouth, dry finish with hops and light fruit notes
Comments	Fine drinking tawny ale. The brewery is behind the Crown Hotel and also supplies local free trade.

Tolly Cobbold

✉ **Tollemache & Cobbold Brewery Ltd, Cliff Road, Ipswich IP3 0AZ.**
☎ **0473 231723.**
🏛 **Yes.**
🚶 **by arrangement.**
i **Independent**

MILD
OG 1032˚ ABV 3.2%
Ingredients: best pale ale malt, crystal malt, chocolate malt. Challenger, Northdown and Target hops. 18 units of bitterness.

TASTING NOTES
Nose	Good malt and chocolate aromas
Palate	Dark malt in mouth, dry finish with chocolate hop notes
Comments	Distinctive dark ale.

BITTER
OG 1035˚ ABV 3.6%
Ingredients: best pale ale malt, crystal malt, amber malt. 100% Goldings hops. 26 units of bitterness.

TASTING NOTES
Nose	Pungent hop resin aroma with hint of orange peel
Palate	Complex balance of malt in mouth, intense dry finish
Comments	Tangy, tasty distinctive bitter.

ORIGINAL
OG 1038˚ ABV 3.8%
Ingredients: best pale ale malt, invert sugar, crystal malt. Challenger, Goldings, Northdown and Target hops. 28 units of bitterness.

TASTING NOTES
Nose	Rounded aromas of hops, malt and ripe fruit
Palate	Full and bitter-sweet in mouth, deep finish with hops and fruit notes
Comments	Rich and complex Anglian ale with fine fruitiness.

OLD STRONG
OG 1047˚ ABV 4.6%
Ingredients: best pale ale malt, crystal malt, chocolate malt. Challenger, Northdown and Target hops. 24 units of bitterness.

TASTING NOTES

Nose	Hops, malt and marmalade fruit
Palate	Rich balance of ripe fruit and hop bitterness; vinous finish with Cognac notes
Comments	Strong fruity ale. The brewery has launched a new beer, Tolly Shooter (ABV 5%).

Tring Brewery Co Ltd
- **81-82 Akeman Street, Tring HP23 6AF.**
- **0442 890721.**
- **No.**
- **by arrangement.**
- *Independent*

RIDGEWAY BITTER
OG 1039˚ ABV 4%
Ingredients: Maris Otter pale malt, crystal malt, chocolate malt. Challenger and Goldings hop pellets.

TASTING NOTES

Nose	Rich malt, hops and fruit aromas
Palate	Clean balance of malt and hops in mouth, hops dominate the finish with light fruit notes
Comments	Copper-coloured, well-balanced bitter.

Charles Wells Ltd
- **Eagle Brewery, Havelock Street, Bedford MK40 4LU.**
- **0234 272766.**
- **Yes.**
- **by arrangement.**
- *Independent*

EAGLE BITTER
OG 1035˚ ABV 3.6%
Ingredients: pale malt (80-85%), crystal malt. Challenger and Goldings hop pellets. 28 units of bitterness.

TASTING NOTES

Nose	Aromatic floral hop bouquet
Palate	Light and refreshing balance of malt and hops; dry finish with orange peel notes
Comments	Superbly balanced, quenching tawny ale.

BOMBARDIER
OG 1042˚ ABV 4.2%
Ingredients: pale malt (almost 100%), crystal malt. Challenger and Goldings hop pellets. 34 units of bitterness.

TASTING NOTES

Nose	Earthy hop resin aroma
Palate	Ripe malt in mouth with good hop balance, dry finish with blackcurrant fruit notes
Comments	Deep copper-coloured, finely balanced ale.

Woodforde's Norfolk Ales
🖃 **Broadland Brewery, Woodbastwick, nr Norwich NR13 6SW.**
① **0603 720353.**
🏛 **No.**
🕴 **No.**

MARDLER'S MILD
OG 1035˚ ABV 3.4%
Ingredients: Halcyon pale malt, crystal malt, chocolate malt. Fuggles and Goldings whole hops. 20 units of bitterness.

TASTING NOTES

Nose	Strong roast malt aromas
Palate	Rich and smooth roast flavour, full bittersweet finish

Comments	Dark mild with delectable roasted grain character.

BROADSMAN BITTER
OG 1035° ABV 3.4%
Ingredients: 100% Halcyon and Pipkin pale malt and crystal malt. Fuggles and Goldings whole hops. Dry hopped. 31 units of bitterness.

TASTING NOTES

Nose	Delicate bouquet of Goldings and malt
Palate	Fine balance of malt and hops, light dry finish
Comments	Mid-brown, excellent light session bitter.

WHERRY BEST BITTER
OG 1039° ABV 3.9%
Ingredients: 100% Halcyon pale malt and crystal malt. Fuggles and Goldings whole hops. 39 units of bitterness.

TASTING NOTES

Nose	Rich malt and hops aromas
Palate	Rich malt in mouth offset by good hop character, sharp tangy finish
Comments	Ripe and complex ale.

NORFOLK PORTER
OG 1042° ABV 4.2%
Ingredients: Halcyon pale malt, crystal malt, chocolate malt. Fuggles and Goldings whole hops. Dry hopped. 22 units of bitterness.

TASTING NOTES

Nose	Superb aromas of dark grain and rich hops
Palate	Bitter-sweet dark malt in mouth, long dry finish with roast coffee and bitter fruit notes
Comments	Rich, dark, deep-tasting beer.

OLD BRAM
OG 1042° ABV 4.2%
Ingredients: Halcyon pale malt, crystal malt, chocolate malt. Fuggles and Goldings whole hops. 19 units of bitterness.

TASTING NOTES

Nose	Delicate chocolate and roast malt aromas
Palate	Fruit and roast in mouth with roast grain finish
Comments	Roasty, toasty, creamy and delectable ale.

NELSON'S REVENGE
OG 1045° ABV 4.6%
Ingredients: Halcyon pale malt and crystal malt. Fuggles and Goldings whole hops. 29 units of bitterness.

TASTING NOTES

Nose	Deep hops and malt aromas
Palate	Deep malt in mouth, tangy and fruity finish
Comments	Full-flavoured, rich and complex ale.

NORFOLK NOG
OG 1049° ABV 4.9%
Ingredients: 100% Halcyon pale malt, crystal malt and chocolate malt. Fuggles and Goldings whole hops. 18 units of bitterness.

TASTING NOTES

Nose	Dark malt and chocolate aromas with hops developing
Palate	Dark malt and fruit in mouth with dry roast grain finish
Comments	Dark, slighty vinous brew, Champion Beer of Britain 1992.

BALDRIC
OG 1052° ABV 5.5%
Ingredients: Halcyon pale malt, Cara Pils malt. Goldings whole hops. Dry hopped. 27 units of bitterness.

TASTING NOTES

Nose	Delicate hops and fruit aromas
Palate	Malt, hops and fruit in mouth, full-flavoured, dry finish
Comments	Well-balanced bitter-sweet pale beer.

HEAD CRACKER
OG 1069˚ ABV 7.5%
Ingredients: 100% Halcyon pale malt and Cara Pils malt.
Goldings whole hops. 24 units of bitterness.

TASTING NOTES

Nose	Heady bouquet of powerful hop resin, malt and fruit
Palate	Rich mouth-feel of malt and hops, deep dry finish with complex tangy fruit
Comments	Superb, deceptively pale strong sipping bitter.

THAMES VALLEY

It would be wrong to consider the breweries of the Thames Valley as living in the shadow of London, with its great if now sadly diminished brewing traditions.

'Country beer' may not be a style as such but it suggests a slow, ruminative, straw-in-the-mouth approach to life which has little truck with modern city attitudes. The 'we've been doing things this way for centuries' approach to life is epitomised by Oxford where breweries — now reduced to one — developed from ancient university brew houses established long before the hop had made its controversial arrival in England.

The general taste of Thames Valley beers is something of an amalgam of the full, fruity malt of nearby East Anglia and the tarty, hoppy edge of beers south of London. The arrival of new micro-breweries not only adds choice but is reviving the art of bottle-conditioned beers.

W H Brakspear & Sons PLC

- ▤ **The Brewery, New Street, Henley-on-Thames RG9 2BU.**
- ☎ **0491 573636.**
- 🏛 **Yes.**
- ⚘ **by arrangement.**
- *i* **Independent**

MILD or XXX
OG 1030˚ ABV 2.8%
Ingredients: Maris Otter pale ale malt, crystal malt, black malt, No 2 invert sugar. 33 units of colour. Fuggles, East Kent, Hereford and Styrian Goldings whole hops. 33 units of bitterness.

TASTING NOTES

Nose	Light hops and nuts aromas
Palate	Pleasing chewy malt in mouth, dry finish with chocolate and hop notes
Comments	Tasty, good-drinking dark mild.

BITTER or PA
OG 1035˚ ABV 3.4%
Ingredients: Maris Otter pale ale malt, crystal malt, black malt, No 2 invert sugar. 23 units of colour. Fuggles and Goldings whole hops. Dry hopped. 38 units of bitterness.

TASTING NOTES

Nose	Wholemeal biscuit and orange peel aromas
Palate	Full-flavoured malt and floral hops in mouth, delicate dry finish with massive hops character
Comments	Superb, beautifully-crafted and refreshing bitter.

SPECIAL BITTER or SBA
OG 1043˚ ABV 4%
Ingredients: Maris Otter pale ale malt, crystal malt, black malt, No 2 invert sugar. Fuggles and Goldings whole hops. Dry hopped.

TASTING NOTES

Nose	Rich malt, hops and fruit aromas
Palate	Ripe, rounded malt and fruit in mouth, bitter-sweet finish with orange and banana notes
Comments	Coppery and fruity strong bitter. The winter brew Old or XXXX is the same beer with added colour.

Chiltern Brewery

⌑ **Nash Lee Road, Terrick, Aylesbury HP17 0TQ.**
☎ **0296 613647.**
🏛 **Yes.**
🎎 **by arrangement.**
i **Independent**

CHILTERN ALE
OG 1038° ABV 3.7%
Ingredients: Maris Otter pale ale malt (90%), crystal malt (10%), invert sugar. Challenger whole hops for bitterness, Fuggles and Goldings for aroma.

TASTING NOTES

Nose	Light bouquet of hop resins and hint of nut
Palate	Tart balance of malt and hops with long dry finish and fruit notes
Comments	Tangy, refreshing light bitter.

BEECHWOOD BITTER
OG 1043° ABV 4.3%
Ingredients: Maris Otter pale ale malt (90%), crystal malt (10%), invert sugar. Challenger whole hops for bitterness, Fuggles and Goldings for aroma.

TASTING NOTES

Nose	Rich aromas of malt, hops and nutty grain
Palate	Hearty malt in mouth, deep dry finish with fruit and nut notes
Comments	Rounded, well-balanced ale, cleansing and quaffable.

THREE HUNDREDS OLD ALE
(Draught and bottle conditioned)
OG 1050˚ ABV 4.9%

Ingredients: Maris Otter pale ale malt (85%), crystal malt (15%), invert sugar. Challenger whole hops for bitterness, Fuggles and Goldings for aroma.

TASTING NOTES

Nose	Dark barley aromas with fruit notes developing
Palate	Bitter-sweet malt and hops in mouth give way to deep dry finish with complex hops and bitter fruit and nut notes
Comments	Deep chestnut-coloured ale of enormous complexity; there is even a hint of chestnuts in the finish. Bottled version is conditioned in the brewery for at least four weeks before it is released. Yeast is added to the bottle to encourage the second fermentation. The beer will improve with age.

BODGERS BARLEY WINE
(bottle conditioned)
OG 1080˚ ABV 8.5%

Ingredients: Maris Otter pale ale malt (100%), invert sugar. Challenger, Fuggles and Goldings who hops.

TASTING NOTES

Nose	Spicy hops and enormous dry malt aromas
Palate	Great hop attack in mouth leading to long, bitter finish with hops and bitter malt notes
Comments	Delight to the eye with a rich, varnished-wood colour; a beer for post-prandial sipping and savouring.

███████████████████████

Hook Norton Brewery Co Ltd

- ⌨ **Brewery Lane, Hook Norton, Banbury OX15 5NY.**
- ☎ **0608 737210.**
- 🏛 **No.**
- 👥 **strictly limited.**
- *i* **Independent**

BEST MILD
OG 1032° ABV 2.9%
Ingredients: Maris Otter pale malt (94%), flaked maize (6%), caramel for colour. Challenger, Fuggles and Goldings whole hops.

TASTING NOTES

Nose	Light malt and nut aromas
Palate	Malt in mouth with good hop finish and some fruit notes
Comments	Distinctive and tasty light mild.

BEST BITTER
OG 1036° ABV 3.3%
Ingredients: Maris Otter pale malt (94%), flaked maize (6%), caramel for colour. Challenger, Fuggles and Goldings whole hops.

TASTING NOTES

Nose	Pronounced hop resins aroma with malt and fruit developing
Palate	Light, dry grain and hops in mouth with delicate finish and some citric fruit notes
Comments	Distinctive pale bitter with some fruity complexity.

OLD HOOKY
OG 1049° ABV 4.3%
Ingredients: Maris Otter pale malt (94%), flaked maize (6%), caramel for colour. Challenger, Fuggles and Goldings whole hops.

TASTING NOTES

Nose	Rich promise of malt and ripe fruit
Palate	Stunning and complex balance of grain, fruit and hop bitterness in mouth, deep bitter-sweet finish with raisin notes

Comments	A fine old ale: 'Treat it with respect' the brewer advises.

Morland & Co PLC

🖃 **PO Box 5, The Brewery, Ock Street, Abingdon OX14 5DD.**
℧ **0235 553377.**
🏛 **Yes.**
⋔ **Yes.**
i **Independent**

ORIGINAL BITTER
OG 1035˚ ABV 4%
Ingredients: pale malt, crystal malt, brewing sugar. Challenger whole hops for bitterness, Goldings for aroma. 33-37 units of bitterness.

TASTING NOTES
Nose	Fresh floral hop aroma
Palate	Dry and quenching with a light hoppy finish
Comments	Strong Goldings character makes this a refreshing session beer.

OLD MASTERS
OG 1040˚ ABV 4.6%
Ingredients: pale malt, crystal malt, brewing sugar. Challenger whole hops for bitterness, Goldings for aroma. 36-40 units of bitterness.

TASTING NOTES
Nose	Ripe malt and hops aromas
Palate	Full malt body in mouth with bitter undertones, long dry finish and fruit notes
Comments	Rounded ale with good fruit character.

OLD SPECKLED HEN
OG 1050˚ ABV 5.2%
Ingredients: pale ale malt, crystal malt, brewing sugar. Challenger whole hops for bitterness, Goldings for aroma. 30-35 units of bitterness.

TASTING NOTES
Nose	Superb floral Goldings hops aroma

| Palate | Full malt and hops in mouth, long dry finish with hops and delicate fruit notes |
| Comments | Richly coloured and fruit flavoured strong ale with generous hop support; launched to commemorate the 50th anniversary of the MG car company in Abingdon. |

Morrells Brewery Ltd

▣ **The Lion Brewery, St Thomas Street, Oxford OX1 1LA.**
☎ **0865 792013.**
🏛 **Yes.**
⚲ **by arrangement.**
i **Independent**

DARK MILD
OG 1037˚ ABV 3.7%
Ingredients: Pipkin pale ale malt (80%), crystal malt (8%), roasted barley (4%), torrefied wheat. Challenger hop pellets for bitterness, Goldings for aroma. 26 units of bitterness.

TASTING NOTES

Nose	Light aromas of malt, nut and hops
Palate	Malt in mouth, short dry finish with roasted notes
Comments	Pleasant malty dark ale.

BEST BITTER
OG 1036˚ ABV 3.7%
Ingredients: Pipkin pale ale malt (85%), crystal malt (8%), some torrefied wheat. Challenger hop pellets for bitterness, Goldings for aroma. 26 units of bitterness.

TASTING NOTES

Nose	Rich aromas of hop resins and citric fruit
Palate	Delicate balance of grain and hops with light, dry finish and faint notes of orange peel
Comments	Carefully balanced, copper-coloured beer.

STRONG COUNTRY BITTER
OG 1037˚ ABV 3.9%
Ingredients: pale malt (65%), crystal malt (7.5%), torrefied wheat (15%), invert sugar (12.5%). 90% hop extract, 10% Target pellets; dry hopped with Target.

TASTING NOTES

Nose	Pleasant hops aroma with hint of banana fruit
Palate	Malt and hops in mouth; dry, tart finish
Comments	Pale, flinty bitter, brewed for Whitbread to the group's recipe.

VARSITY
OG 1041˚ ABV 4.3%
Ingredients: Pipkin pale ale malt (85%), crystal malt (8%), some torrefied wheat. Challenger hop pellets for bitterness, Goldings for aroma. 29 units of bitterness.

TASTING NOTES

Nose	Powerful aromas of malt and hops with fruit developing
Palate	Full malt and hops in mouth, deep, bitter-sweet finish with hints of vanilla
Comments	Rich and satisfying ale.

GRADUATE
OG 1048˚ ABV 5.2%
Ingredients: Pipkin pale ale malt (83%), crystal malt (9%), some torrefied wheat. Challenger hop pellets for bitterness, Goldings for aroma. 28 units of bitterness.

TASTING NOTES

Nose	Malty, fruity, estery aromas
Palate	Rounded bitter-sweet flavours in mouth, light hoppy finish
Comments	Rich and warming premium ale.

COLLEGE ALE
OG 1072˚ ABV 6%
Ingredients: Pipkin pale malt (84%), crystal malt (8.5%), some torrefied wheat. Challenger hop pellets for bitterness, Goldings for aroma. 28 units of bitterness.

TASTING NOTES

Nose	Pronounced aromas of roasted grain and rich marmalade fruit

Palate	Heady, sweetish malt and fruit in mouth, dense, bitter-sweet finish with nuts, raisins and sultanas
Comments	Ripe, golden winter brew: 'To warm the inner man' says the brewer.

Old Luxters Farm Brewery

⌗ **Old Luxters Farmhouse, Hambleden, Henley-on-Thames RG9 6JW.**
① **0491 638330.**
🏛 **Yes.**
⚥ **by arrangement.**
i **Independent**

OLD LUXTERS BARN ALE
OG 1042.5˚ ABV 5%
Ingredients: pale malt (94%), crystal malt (5%), chocolate malt (1%). Whole Fuggles hops for bitterness, Goldings for aroma; late hopped in copper.

TASTING NOTES
Nose	Good balance of malt and hops aroma
Palate	Full malt in mouth offset by clean bitterness; bitter-sweet finish with hint of chocolate
Comments	Copper-coloured, well-crafted premium bitter.

Rebellion Beer Co

⌗ **The Marlow Brewery, Unit J, Rose Industrial Estate, Marlow Bottom Road, Marlow SL7 3ND.**
① **0628 476594.**
🏛 **No.**
⚥ **by arrangement.**
i **Independent**

REBELLION IPA
OG 1039˚ ABV 3.9%
Ingredients: Maris Otter pale malt (92%), blend of crystal and dark malts (8%). Challenger and Goldings whole and hop pellets. 28 units of bitterness.

TASTING NOTES
Nose	Floral hop and fruit aromas

Palate	Malt and nutty dark malt in mouth, dry, bitter and lightly fruity finish
Comments	Complex tawny ale with good hop and fruit character.

Wychwood Brewery

⌨ **Two Rivers, Station Lane, Witney OX8 6BH.**
① **0993 702574.**
🏛 **No.**
🏃 **No.**
i **Independent**

SHIRES BITTER
OG 1036˚ ABV 3.4%
Ingredients: premium pale malt (95.5%), crystal malt (4%), chocolate malt (0.5%). Progress whole hops in copper, dry hopped with Hallertau.

TASTING NOTES

Nose	Fresh hop resins aroma
Palate	Light balance of hops and malt in mouth with dry hoppy finish
Comments	Deep copper-coloured, good-drinking session bitter.

FIDDLERS ELBOW
OG 1040˚ ABV 4%
Ingredients: premium pale malt and wheat malt. Challenger and Styrian Goldings whole hops.

TASTING NOTES

Nose	Dry malt and Goldings aromas
Palate	Good balance of malt and hops in mouth, dry, creamy finish with hop notes
Comments	Very pale, well-balanced beer brewed between May and October.

WYCHWOOD BEST
OG 1044˚ ABV 4.8%
Ingredients: premium pale malt (96%), crystal malt (3.75%), chocolate malt (0.25%). Progress whole hops in copper, dry hopped with Styrian Goldings.

TASTING NOTES

Nose	Nostril-tickling wafts of Goldings with malt notes
Palate	Full malt in mouth with good hop balance, rich fruity finish
Comments	Rounded, light copper ale, the result of three weeks' conditioning in the brewery.

DR THIRSTY'S DRAUGHT
OG 1050° ABV 5.2%
Ingredients: premium pale malt (90%), crystal malt (5%), chocolate malt (5%). Progress whole hops in copper, dry hopped with Hallertau.

TASTING NOTES

Nose	Rich nutty malt aroma with good Hallertau hop notes
Palate	Good malt and hops balance in mouth, long finish with hops and delicate hint of bitter chocolate
Comments	Full-flavoured, distinctive strong bitter.

HOBGOBLIN
OG 1058° ABV 6.5%
Ingredients: premium pale malt (95.5%), crystal malt (4%), chocolate (0.5%). Progress whole hops in copper, dry hopped with Styrian Goldings and Hallertau.

TASTING NOTES

Nose	Malt and dark chocolate aromas with good hop notes
Palate	Full and rounded malt in mouth; deep, dry hop and fruit finish
Comments	Plum-coloured strong ale, exceptionally dry as it is brewed out to high alcohol level.

LONDON

London, once a major international brewing centre, is now reduced to two family-owned companies, Fullers and Youngs.

Since the last edition of the Almanac, Guinness, badly advised by its marketing gurus, has phased out the classic bottle-conditioned Original stout —just as interest in natural beers in bottles was reviving.

Youngs proved more in touch with the beer world by launching a dark Porter. It was the brown and dark beers of London, known as Entire or Porter, that built London's brewing fame in the 18th and 19th centuries as a major exporter to such unlikely places as the American colonies and Tsarist Russia.

Most of the still-famous names in commercial brewing history — Charrington, Courage, Truman and Whitbread for example — sprang to fame and fortune in London. Now Courage, alone of the national brewers, has a brewery in the capital and its Mortlake factory, bought from Grand Metropolitan in 1991, produces just lagers and keg beers. Others have moved to greenfield sites alongside motorways as part of the trend towards centralised mega-breweries.

Fullers and Youngs keep the beer flag flying. Their bitters have a pronounced hop character that stresses both London's proximity to the hop fields of Kent and the preference of past generations of working-class Londoners who earned money picking hops and who liked the bite and edge which the plant gave to their ale.

Fuller's

☞ **Fuller Smith & Turner PLC, Griffin Brewery, Chiswick Lane South W4 2QB.**
℧ **081-994 3691.**
🏛 **Yes.**
🚶 **by arrangement.**
i **Independent**

CHISWICK BITTER
OG 1034° ABV 3.5%
Ingredients: pale malt, crystal malt, flaked maize, caramel for colour. Challenger, Goldings, Northdown and Target whole and pellet hops. 28 units of bitterness.

TASTING NOTES

Nose	Stunning hop resin and light fruit bouquet
Palate	Cleansing and quenching balance of malt and hops, light finish with delicate fruit notes
Comments	Superbly quaffable light bitter, a hymn of praise to the joys of the hop.

LONDON PRIDE
OG 1040° ABV 4.1%
Ingredients: pale malt, crystal malt, flaked maize, caramel for colour. Challenger, Northdown and Target hop pellets. 30 units of bitterness.

TASTING NOTES

Nose	Ripe developing aromas of malt, hops and fruit
Palate	Multi-layered delight of malt and hops; deep, intense finish with hops and ripening fruit
Comments	Astonishingly complex beer for its gravity, a marvellous melange of malt, hops and fruit.

MR HARRY
OG 1048° ABV 4.7%
Ingredients: pale malt (90%), crystal malt (10%). 42 units of colour. Challenger, Northdown and Target hop pellets. 42 units of bitterness.

TASTING NOTES

Nose	Rich malt aroma with hint of hops
Palate	Full, rounded malt and nut in mouth, deep finish with malt, hops and light fruit
Comments	Ripe ale brewed for the winter months.

ESB (EXTRA SPECIAL BITTER)
OG 1053˚ ABV 5.5%

Ingredients: pale malt, crystal malt, flaked maize, cara-mel for colour. Challenger, Goldings and Target whole and pellet hops. 35 units of bitterness.

TASTING NOTES

Nose	Explosion of malt, hops and Cooper's marmalade
Palate	Enormous attack of malt and fruit with hop underpinning; profound finish with strong Goldings character and hints of orange, lemon, gooseberry and some tannin
Comments	A beer for a Bacchanalia with a cupboardful of awards from CAMRA competitions. In 1993 Fuller's test-mar-keted a dark mild called Hock.

Young & Co PLC
⌖ **Ram Brewery, High Street, Wandsworth SW18 4JD.**
① **081-8700141.**
🏛 **Yes.**
⽊ **Yes.**
i **Independent**

BITTER
OG 1036˚ ABV 3.7%

Ingredients: Maris Otter pale ale malt (91%), torrefied barley (4%), brewing sugar (5%). 14 units of colour. Fug-gles and Goldings whole hops. 32-34 units of bitterness.

TASTING NOTES

Nose	Lilting aromas of Goldings and malt with delicate citric fruits
Palate	Tart balance of malt and hops, intense finish with orange and lemon notes
Comments	Cockney ale with stunning hoppy edge.

PORTER
OG 1040° ABV 4%
Ingredients: Maris Otter pale ale malt, chocolate malt, crystal malt, brewing sugar. 100 units of colour. Fuggles and Goldings whole hops. 30 units of bitterness.

TASTING NOTES

Nose	Roasted grain and chocolate aromas
Palate	Light malt and hops in mouth, dry finish with chocolate and coffee notes
Comments	Superb dark addition to the Young's range.

SPECIAL BITTER
OG 1046° ABV 4.8%
Ingredients: Maris Otter pale ale malt (91%), torrefied barley (4%), brewing sugar (5%). 20 units of colour. Fuggles and Goldings whole hops, dry hopped with Target. 32 units of bitterness.

TASTING NOTES

Nose	Ripe malt and hops aromas with orange fruit developing
Palate	Rounded malt with good hop underpinning, deep bitter-sweet finish with citric fruit notes
Comments	Beautifully crafted premium bitter.

WINTER WARMER
OG 1055° ABV 5%
Ingredients: Maris Otter pale ale malt, crystal malt, brewing sugar. Fuggles and Goldings whole hops. 30 units of bitterness.

TASTING NOTES

Nose	Warm. biscuity aromas with vinous notes
Palate	Generous malt and hops in mouth with rich port wine finish
Comments	Ruby old ale brewed for the winter months.

SOUTH-EAST ENGLAND

Hops are grown in other regions, Worcestershire in particular, but Kent is fondly regarded as the hop garden of England.

Travellers to and from the Kentish ports have seen for centuries a landscape criss-crossed by tall, wired frames that encourage hop bines to climb towards the sun and rain. And in between the hop fields there are the strangely cowled oast houses in which hops are dried and cured following picking.

The bucolic picture is tinged with nostalgia, for the Kent hop industry has declined dramatically in size and too many of the oast houses have been turned into weekend cottages. The rise of European lager and the importing of cheap hops from as far afield as Slovenia and even China led to a sharp fall in demand for English hops in the 1980s. But there is still a powerful attachment to traditional English varieties and the revival of cask ale has brought life back to the hop fields.

It is not surprising that the ales of South-east England, brewed in the heart of the hop country, have a tang and a bite that linger tartly and refreshingly on the palate.

Arundel Brewery

- ⌖ **Ford Airfield, Arundel BN18 0BE.**
- ☏ **0903 733111.**
- 🏛 **No.**
- ⚭ **by arrangement.**
- *i* **Independent**

ARUNDEL BEST BITTER
OG 1040° ABV 4%

Ingredients: pale malt (88%), crystal malt (12%). Kent Fuggles and Goldings whole hops.

TASTING NOTES

Nose	Malt aroma with hint of hops
Palate	Fine balance of malt and hops in mouth, lingering bitter finish
Comments	Clean-tasting and refreshing bitter.

ARUNDEL STRONGHOLD
OG 1050° ABV 5%

Ingredients: pale malt (90%), crystal malt (10%). Kent Fuggles and Goldings whole hops.

TASTING NOTES

Nose	Rich hops aroma with hint of nut
Palate	Powerful malt and crystal nut in mouth, deep, complex finish with hops and bitter-sweet malt and fruit
Comments	Multi-layered, mahogany-coloured premium ale.

OLD KNUCKER
OG 1055° ABV 5.5%

Ingredients: pale malt (82%), crystal malt (12%), chocolate malt (6%). Kent Fuggles and Goldings whole hops.

TASTING NOTES

Nose	Rich fruit aroma with malt undertones
Palate	Roast malt and fruit in mouth, deep finish with hops, fruit and chocolate
Comments	Complex dark ale: the brewer recommends it should be mulled in winter.

Ballards Brewery

⌨ **Unit C, The Old Sawmill, Nyewood, Rogate, Petersfield GU31 5HA.**

☎ **0730 821 362/821 301.**

i **Independent**

🏛 **No.**

⭐ **Yes.**

MIDHURST MILD
OG 1034° ABV 3.3%
Ingredients: Pipkin pale ale malt (74%), crystal malt (8.5%), chocolate malt (6%), torrefied wheat (11.5%). Fuggles whole hops.

TASTING NOTES

Nose	Dark malt and hops aromas
Palate	Smooth, chewy malt in mouth, chocolate and hops in finish
Comments	Dark brown mild ale with good hop character; brewed in summer months.

TROTTON BITTER
OG 1036° ABV 3.5%
Ingredients: Pipkin and Triumph pale malts (90%), crystal malt (10%). Whole Fuggles for bitterness, Goldings for aroma.

TASTING NOTES

Nose	Rich balance of malt and hops
Palate	Bitter-sweet malt and hops in mouth, balanced finish with light fruit notes
Comments	Fine-tasting, copper-coloured bitter.

BEST BITTER
OG 1042° ABV 4.1%
Ingredients: Pipkin and Triumph pale malts (90%), crystal malt (10%). Fuggles whole hops for bitterness, Goldings for aroma.

TASTING NOTES
Nose	Floral hop resin aroma with fruit notes
Palate	Full malt and hops and in mouth, long finish with pronounced nut from dark malt
Comments	Refreshing copper-coloured ale.

WASSAIL
OG 1060˚ ABV 5.7%
Ingredients: Pipkin and Triumph pale malts (85%), crystal malt (15%). Fuggles whole hops for bitterness, Goldings for aroma.

TASTING NOTES
Nose	Rich malt and fruit aromas
Palate	Malt and fruit in mouth, deep hoppy finish with sultana and raisin fruit
Comments	Complex, dark, bitter-sweet beer.

BALLARD'S OLD EPISCOPAL
OG 1092˚ ABV 9%
Ingredients: Pipkin pale malt (90%), crystal malt (9.8%), chocolate malt (16%). Fuggles and Goldings whole hops.

TASTING NOTES
Nose	Ripe, dark nutty malt aroma
Palate	Sweet, fruity malt balanced by hops, deep vinous finish
Comments	Mid-brown, rich, complex and fruity strong ale.

Goacher's

▣ **P & DJ Goacher, 5 Hayle Mill Cottages, Bockingford, Maidstone ME15 6DT.**
℧ **0622 682112.**
🏛 **No.**
🖈 **Yes.**
i **Independent**

REAL MILD MAIDSTONE ALE
OG 1033˚ ABV 3.2%
Ingredients: Halcyon and Maris Otter pale malts (86.5%), crystal and chocolate malts (13.5%). Kent Progress whole hops.

TASTING NOTES

Nose	Rich coffee and chocolate aromas
Palate	Dark malt in mouth, bitter-sweet finish with coffee, chocolate and hops
Comments	Dark and richly tasty mild ale.

FINE LIGHT MAIDSTONE ALE
OG 1036˚ ABV 3.7%
Ingredients: 100% pale and crystal malts. Mid-Kent Goldings and Progress whole hops.

TASTING NOTES

Nose	Intense hops aroma with delicate citric fruit notes
Palate	Mellow balance of hops and malt in mouth, refreshing finish
Comments	Superb, pale bitter filtered over additional hops in hopback.

BEST DARK MAIDSTONE ALE
OG 1040˚ ABV 4.1%
Ingredients: 100% pale, crystal, black and chocolate malts. East Kent Goldings and Progress whole hops.

TASTING NOTES

Nose	Complex aromas of roasted malt, coffee and tart fruit
Palate	Deep chewy grain in mouth, long, dry finish with hops and dark chocolate notes
Comments	Deep copper-coloured, complex beer.

OLD MAIDSTONE ALE
OG 1066˚ ABV 6.7%
Ingredients: 100% pale, crystal, black and chocolate malts. East Kent Goldings whole hops.

TASTING NOTES

Nose	Meaty, toffee, Ribena aromas
Palate	Shockingly dry malt and tart fruit in mouth, intense finish with hops, raisins and sultanas
Comments	Powerful dark winter brew full of intriguing, complex tannic flavours, conditioned in cask in brewery for a minimum of one month.

Harvey & Son (Lewes) Ltd

⌨ **Bridge Wharf Brewery, 6 Cliffe High Street, Lewes BN7 2AH.**

☎ **0273 480209.**

🏛 **Yes (in brewery shop).**

⚒ **Yes (12 months' waiting list).**

i **Independent**

XX MILD ALE
OG 1030° ABV 3%
Ingredients: mild ale malt and crystal malt, black and caramel sugars. Bramling Cross, Fuggles and Goldings whole hops, most locally grown.

TASTING NOTES
Nose	Light nutty grain aroma
Palate	Soft, sweet malt in mouth, short finish with delicate hop notes
Comments	Easy drinking dark mild.

SUSSEX BITTER OR PA
OG 1033° ABV 3.5%
Ingredients: Pipkin and Maris Otter pale malts, crystal malt, flaked maize and sugars. Bramling Cross, Fuggles, Goldings and Progress whole hops.

TASTING NOTES
Nose	Sweet malt offset by delicate hops aroma
Palate	Good cleansing balance of malt and hops with dry finish
Comments	Light and quenching session bitter.

SUSSEX BEST BITTER (BB)
OG 1040° ABV 4%
Ingredients: Maris Otter and Pipkin pale malts, crystal malt, flaked maize and brewing sugars. Bramling Cross, Fuggles, Goldings and Progress whole hops.

TASTING NOTES
Nose	Tempting bouquet of rich malt and tangy hops
Palate	Rounded balance of malt and hops in mouth with deep, dry finish and fruit notes
Comments	Fine bitter-sweet bitter.

SUSSEX OLD (XXXX)
OG 1043˚ ABV 4.2%
Ingredients: mild ale and crystal malt, black and caramel sugars. Bramling Cross, Fuggles and Goldings whole hops.

TASTING NOTES

Nose	Soft aromas of malt, dried fruit and coffee
Palate	Mellow malt and fruit in mouth, deep finish with good hops sparkle and complex fruit notes
Comments	Dark, soft and warming winter brew.

ARMADA ALE
OG 1046˚ ABV 4.5%
Ingredients: Pipkin and Maris Otter pale malts, crystal malt, flaked maize and brewing sugar. Bramling Cross, Fuggles and Goldings whole hops.

TASTING NOTES

Nose	Tangy hops aroma with malt and some fruit notes
Palate	Rich malt and hops in mouth, big, well-balanced finish with pronounced fruitiness
Comments	Splendid premium ale with great hops character; Elizabethan (OG 1090˚), a bottled barley wine, is occasionally sold on draught.

Hogs Back Brewery

⌨ **Manor Farm, The Street, Tongham GU10 1DE.**
☎ **0252 782328.**
🏛 **Yes.**
🚶 **Yes.**
i **Independent**

TEA (TRADITIONAL ENGLISH ALE)
OG 1044˚ ABV 4.2%
Ingredients: Pipkin pale malt (92.5%), crystal malt (7.5%). Surrey Fuggles and Team Valley Goldings whole hops.

TASTING NOTES

Nose	Floral hops aroma with some fruit

Palate	Rich malt in mouth, bitter-sweet finish with fine hop notes
Comments	Full-bodied, deep golden ale full of ripe malt flavours.

OTT (OLD TONGHAM ALE)
OG 1066˚ ABV 6.5%
Ingredients: Pipkin pale malt (85%), crystal malt (9%), chocolate malt (6%). Fuggles and Goldings whole hops.

TASTING NOTES

Nose	Chocolate and blackcurrant fruit aromas
Palate	Dark nutty, roasted malt in mouth, deep bitter-sweet finish with coffee and chocolate notes
Comments	Rich ruby-black winter ale.

SANTA'S WOBBLE
OG 1077˚ ABV 7.5%
Ingredients: Pipkin pale malt (93%), crystal malt (7%). Fuggles and Goldings whole hops.

TASTING NOTES

Nose	Spicy tropical fruits and hops aromas
Palate	Vinous fruit in mouth, deep bitter-sweet finish with hops and banana fruit
Comments	Full-bodied, copper-red barley wine.

King & Barnes Ltd
- ◻ **18 Bishopric, Horsham RH12 1QP.**
- ① **0403 270 470.**
- 🏛 **Yes.**
- 👥 **Yes (mornings and evenings).**
- *i* **Independent**

SUSSEX MILD
OG 1034˚ ABV 3.5%
Ingredients: pale ale malt, crystal malt, chocolate malt, enzymic malt, flaked maize, invert sugar. Challenger, Goldings and Whitbread Goldings Variety whole hops; late hopped. 21 units of bitterness.

TASTING NOTES

Nose	Delightful light hops and nut aromas
Palate	Sweet malt in mouth, dry nutty finish
Comments	Smooth drinking ruby ale.

SUSSEX BITTER
OG 1034˚ ABV 3.5%

Ingredients: pale ale malt, crystal malt, chocolate malt, enzymic malt, flaked maize, invert sugar. Challenger, Goldings and Whitbread Goldings Variety whole hops; late hopped. 31.5 units of bitterness.

TASTING NOTES

Nose	Rich vanilla and fresh-cut grass aromas
Palate	Delicate malt and hops in mouth, fragrant hop flower finish
Comments	Superb and refreshing light bitter.

BROADWOOD
OG 1040˚ ABV 4%

Ingredients: pale malt, crystal malt, enzymic malt, maize, invert sugar and caramel. Challenger and Whitbread Goldings Variety whole hops. 37 units of bitterness.

TASTING NOTES

Nose	Tempting, balanced aromas of malt and hops
Palate	Malt and some fruit in mouth, rich and fruity finish
Comments	Refreshing, copper-coloured premium ale.

OLD ALE
OG 1046˚ ABV 4.1%

Ingredients: pale malt, crystal malt, flaked barley, chocolate malt, invert sugar. Challenger and Whitbread Goldings Variety whole hops. 27 units of bitterness.

TASTING NOTES

Nose	Rich malt aroma with fruit notes developing
Palate	Full malt and fruit in mouth, rich hops and nut finish

Comments   Rounded, warming dark winter brew.

FESTIVE
(draught and bottle-conditioned)
OG 1050˚ ABV 4.8%
Ingredients: pale malt, crystal malt, enzymic malt, maize and caramel. Challenger, Goldings and Whitbread Goldings Variety whole hops. 41.5 units of bitterness.

TASTING NOTES

Nose	Inviting Goldings hops aroma with fruit notes developing
Palate	Mouth-filling sweet grain with good hops balance, deep finish with banana and dried fruit notes
Comments	Powerful dark copper ale with complex balance of flavours.

Kemptown Brewery Co Ltd

- 🖃 **33 Upper St James's Street, Brighton BN2 1JN.**
- ① **0273 602521.**
- 🏛 **Yes (in Hand in Hand pub).**
- 🕺 **Yes.**
- *i* **Independent**

Est. 1989

KEMPTOWN BITTER
OG 1040˚ ABV 4%
Ingredients: pale malt (95%), crystal malt (5%). Challenger, Fuggles and Goldings whole hops. 38 units of bitterness.

TASTING NOTES

Nose	Floral hops aroma
Palate	Dry malt and hops in mouth, delicate fruit in finish
Comments	Pale gold beer with refreshing balance of flavours.

CELEBRATED STAGGERING ALE
OG 1050˚ ABV 5%
Ingredients: pale malt (90%), crystal malt (10%). Fuggles and Goldings whole hops. 40 units of bitterness.

TASTING NOTES

Nose	Fruity and dark nutty malt

| Palate | Ripe malt in mouth, big finish with hops, fruit and nuts |
| Comments | Rich and complex tawny ale. |

SID (STAGGERING IN THE DARK)
OG 1052˚ ABV 5.2%

Ingredients: pale malt (90%), crystal malt (8%), chocolate malt (2%). Challenger and Goldings whole hops. 40 units of bitterness.

TASTING NOTES

Nose	Floral hops, nuts and hints of chocolate
Palate	Malt dominates the mouth, big finish with dark malt and chocolate with powerful Goldings presence
Comments	Ruby-red and complex ale.

OLD GRUMPY
OG 1060˚ ABV 6.2%

Ingredients: pale malt (90%), crystal malt (9%), chocolate malt (1%). Challenger, Fuggles and Goldings whole hops.

TASTING NOTES

Nose	Rich, winey fruit and hops
Palate	Rounded malt in mouth, long, bittersweet finish with hops, fruit and chocolate
Comments	Vinous and hoppy strong ale.

Larkins Brewery Ltd

⌧ **Larkins Farm, Chiddingstone, Edenbridge TN8 7BB.**
☎ **0892 870328.**
🏛 **No.**
👥 **Yes.**
i **Independent**

TRADITIONAL
OG 1034-35˚ ABV 3.4%

Ingredients: Halcyon pale malt (90%), crystal malt (10%), small % of chocolate malt for colour. Fuggles and Whitbread Goldings Variety whole hops for bitterness, East Kent Goldings for aroma. 39 units of bitterness.

TASTING NOTES

Nose	Stunning Goldings floral hops aroma
Palate	Light, delicate malt and hops in mouth, strong hop character in finish
Comments	Delectable golden, refreshing and well-hopped beer.

BEST BITTER
OG 1044-45˚ ABV 4.7%
Ingredients: Halcyon pale malt (90%), crystal malt (10%), some chocolate malt for colour. Fuggles and East Kent Goldings whole hops. 45 units of bitterness.

TASTING NOTES

Nose	Pronounced malt, hop flowers and ripe fruit aromas
Palate	Ripe malt and tart fruit in mouth, intense finish full of hops and fruit character
Comments	Deep copper-coloured ale with enormous hop appeal.

SOVEREIGN BITTER
OG 1040˚ ABV 4%
Ingredients: Halcyon pale malt (90%), crystal malt (10%), dash of chocolate malt for colour. Fuggles and Whitbread Goldings Variety whole hops for bitterness, East Kent Goldings for aroma. 36 units of bitterness.

TASTING NOTES

Nose	Powerful bouquet of malt and hops
Palate	Full-bodied malt in mouth, deep dry finish with great hops presence and powerful fruit notes
Comments	Golden bitter with fine balance of hops and fruit.

PORTER
OG 1052-54˚ ABV 5.5%
Ingredients: Halcyon pale malt (88%), crystal malt (7%), chocolate malt (5%). Fuggles and East Kent Goldings whole hops. 59 units of bitterness.

TASTING NOTES

Nose	Strong hops aroma with dark chocolate notes
Palate	Bitter-sweet balance of malt and hops in mouth, deep fruit and chocolate finish

Comments   Dark, complex and rich-tasting beer.
East Kent Goldings used in Larkins' beers
are grown and dried on their own farm.

Pilgrim Brewery

- ☑ **West Street, Reigate RH2 9BL.**
- ☎ **073 72 22651.**
- 🏛 **No.**
- ⚲ **by arrangement.**
- *i* **Independent**

SURREY PALE ALE
OG 1038˚ ABV 3.7%
Ingredients: pale malt (85%), crystal malt (8%), torrefied
wheat (7%). East Kent Goldings whole hops in copper
and cask.

TASTING NOTES
Nose   Light, tempting hop flowers aromas with
delicate citric fruit notes
Palate   Cleansing hops and malt in mouth, light
dry finish with faint lemon notes
Comments   Well-balanced and refreshing ale.

PORTER
OG 1041˚ ABV 4%
Ingredients: pale malt (80%), crystal malt (4%), torrefied
wheat (4%), roast barley (4%). East Kent Goldings copper
hops.

TASTING NOTES
Nose   Rich aromas of hops and roasted grain
Palate   Chewy malt and dark chocolate in
mouth, dry finish with coffee notes
Comments   Fine-tasting dark beer.

PROGRESS
OG 1041˚ ABV 4%
Ingredients: pale malt (80%), crystal malt (12%), torrefied
wheat (4%), roast barley (1%). East Kent Goldings whole
hops in copper.

TASTING NOTES
Nose   Ripe malt and fruit with hop notes

Palate	Ripe malt in mouth, deep, rounded bitter-sweet finish with hops and fruit
Comments	Rich tasting ale with delectable fruit notes.

SARACEN STOUT
OG 1048° ABV 4.7%
Ingredients: pale malt and crystal malt. East Kent Goldings whole hops in copper.

TASTING NOTES

Nose	Dark nutty malt and floral hops
Palate	Dark malt dominates the mouth with deep finish packed with bitter dark malt and hops
Comments	Splendid dark stout full of tasty malt and hop character.

TALISMAN WINTER WARMER
OG 1048° ABV 4.8%
Ingredients: pale malt (82%), crystal malt (11%), torrefied wheat (3%), roast barley (2%), molasses (2%). East Kent Goldings whole hops in copper.

TASTING NOTES

Nose	Deep aromas of hops, fruit and tannin
Palate	Superb mouthfeel of malt and tart fruit, deep finish with hops, vanilla and banana notes
Comments	Richly warming, fruity winter ale.

Shepherd Neame Ltd

⌧ **17 Court Street, Faversham ME13 7AX.**
① **0795 532206.**
🏛 **Yes.**
🏃 **Yes.**
i **Independent**

MASTER BREW BITTER
OG 1036° ABV 3.8%
Ingredients: pale malt (75%), crystal malt (8%), amber malt (5%), wheat malt (4%), torrefied wheat (8%) and glucose sugar. East Kent Omega, Target and Zenith hop pellets with Goldings hop oil.

TASTING NOTES

Nose	Powerful smack of hop resins
Palate	Dry malt in mouth with long finish full of hops and light fruit
Comments	Stunning beer full of fine hop fields character.

MASTER BREW BEST BITTER
OG 1039° ABV 4%

Ingredients: pale malt (75%), crystal malt (8%), amber malt (5%), wheat malt (4%), torrefied wheat (8%) and glucose syrup. East Kent Omega, Target and Zenith hop pellets with Goldings hop oil.

TASTING NOTES

Nose	Tart wafts of hops with tangy fruit developing
Palate	Fine balance of malt and fruit in mouth, dry finish with citric fruit notes
Comments	Big, bold beer full of hop character; Stock Ale is a winter version with added colour.

SPITFIRE ALE
OG 1045° ABV 4.7%

Ingredients: pale malt (75%), crystal malt (8%), amber malt (5%), wheat malt (4%), torrefied wheat (8%) and glucose syrup. East Kent Omega, Target and Zenith hop pellets with Goldings hop oil.

TASTING NOTES

Nose	Rich malt and hops aromas with fruit notes
Palate	Good malt and hops balance in mouth, long bitter finish packed with hops character
Comments	Fine premium ale with good balance of hops and fruit.

ORIGINAL PORTER
OG 1049° ABV 5.2%

Ingredients: pale malt (65%), crystal malt (12%), chocolate malt (7%), torrefied wheat (8%), glucose (8%). 60-80 units of colour. Kent Goldings and Target hop pellets. 30 units of bitterness.

TASTING NOTES

Nose	Powerful aromas of dark malt and liquorice
Palate	Dark malt packs the mouth, deep finish with malt, hops and bitter fruit
Comments	Superb dark beer with fruit, hops and slightly astringent dark malt.

BISHOPS FINGER
OG 1052˚ ABV 5.4%

Ingredients: pale malt (75%), crystal malt (8%), amber malt (5%), wheat malt (4%), torrefied wheat (8%) and glucose syrup. East Kent Omega, Target and Zenith hop pellets with Goldings hop oil.

TASTING NOTES

Nose	Powerful bouquet of malt, nuts, fruit and hops
Palate	Rich malt and fruit on tongue, long, complex finish with great hops character with ripe dried fruit notes
Comments	Warming barley wine also available in bottle.

SOUTH-WEST ENGLAND

This is Wessex, Thomas Hardy country. So powerful is his influence that Dorchester brewers Eldridge Pope name two beers in his honour. The bottle-conditioned Thomas Hardy's Ale is not for everyday drinking but the brewers of the region supply a goodly amount of tasty supping beers.

Sadly, the trend towards stronger 'premium' beers has led to the decline of what were dismissively called 'boy's bitters', low in gravity but highly potable and packed with hop character. Palmer's Best Bitter is a rare example of the breed as is Whitbread's West Country Pale Ale from its brewery in Cheltenham that specialises in replicating ales, such as Flowers and Fremlins, whose roots lie in other parts of the country.

The genuine beers of Wessex have noticeably full and dry palates, tending towards a fruity astringency in Gale's ales and to a delectable hint of crystal malt nuttiness in Hall and Woodhouse's and Palmer's products.

In the Cotswolds, Claude Arkell's Donnington idyll reaffirms one's faith in small craft breweries, with superb ale from serene surroundings sold in fine old stone pubs. His is the inspiration for a clutch of new small 'micros' which add to the pleasures of the region.

■■■■■■■■

Archers Ales Ltd
- ⌨ **London Street, Swindon SN1 5DY.**
- ✆ **0793 496789.**
- 🏛 **Yes (sort of).**
- 👥 **Yes; trade and CAMRA groups only.**
- *i* **Independent.**

VILLAGE BITTER
OG 1035˚ ABV 3.2%
Ingredients: pale malt (95%), crystal malt (5%). Progress and Whitbread Goldings Variety whole hops, late hopped towards end of copper boil with East Kent Goldings pellets.

TASTING NOTES

Nose	Light hops aroma
Palate	Delicate balance of malt and hops, with clean finish
Comments	Refreshing session bitter.

BEST BITTER
OG 1040˚ ABV 4.1%
Ingredients: pale malt (95%), crystal malt (95%). Fuggles and Sunshine whole hops, late hopped with East Kent Goldings pellets.

TASTING NOTES

Nose	Powerful smack of hops and spices
Palate	Tart and tangy malt and hops in mouth, dry finish with some citric notes
Comments	Uncompromisingly hoppy beer.

GOLDEN BITTER
OG 1046˚ ABV 4.7%
Ingredients: 100% blended pale malts, Progress and Whitbread Goldings Variety whole hops, late hopped with East Kent Goldings pellets.

TASTING NOTES

Nose	Powerful Goldings aroma with citric fruit notes
Palate	Malt in the mouth with deep finish with strong hop character and delicate fruit
Comments	Pale strong ale with fine balance of malt, hops and fruit.

BLACKJACK PORTER
OG 1046˚ ABV 4.6%

Ingredients: pale malts (88%), black and other dark malts (10%), wheat malt (2%). Fuggles and Whitbread Goldings Variety whole hops, late hopped with East Kent Goldings pellets.

TASTING NOTES

Nose	Dark fruit and malt aromas
Palate	Burnt malt in the mouth, bitter-sweet finish with good hop character and fruit and coffee notes
Comments	Superb black beer with creamy head and good retention from use of wheat malt. Brewed October to April.

HEADBANGER or OLD COBLEIGH'S
OG 1065˚ ABV 6.5%

Ingredients: pale malt (95%), crystal malt (5%). Progress and Whitbread Goldings Variety whole hops, late hopped with East Kent Goldings pellets.

TASTING NOTES

Nose	Massive hops and marmalade fruit aromas
Palate	Rich and complex flavours merging into a long finish full of hops, banana, sultana and other fruit notes
Comments	Ripe and complex strong ale, sipped with caution and appreciation.

Arkell's Brewery Ltd

✈ **Kingsdown Brewery, Upper Stratton, Swindon SN2 6RU.**

☎ **0793 823026.**

🏛 **Yes.**

👤 **by invitation.**

i **Independent.**

ARKELL'S BREWERY

2B
OG 1032° ABV 3.2%
Ingredients: Pipkin pale malt (92%), crystal malt (6%), sugar (2%). 25 units of colour. Fuggles and Goldings whole hops, late copper hopped with Goldings. 28 units of bitterness.

TASTING NOTES

Nose	Light and aromatic hops
Palate	Slightly tart with dry hop finish
Comments	Fine quaffable session bitter.

MASH TUN MILD
OG 1036° ABV 3.5%
Ingredients: Pipkin pale ale malt (66%), crystal and chocolate malts (30%), sugar (4%). 100 units of colour. Fuggles whole hops. 24 units of bitterness.

TASTING NOTES

Nose	Smooth and tempting aromas of malt, chocolate and hops
Palate	Full flavours of dark malt in mouth, dry but creamy finish with fine nuts and chocolate character
Comments	Fine dark mild with delicious dark malt character.

3B
OG 1040° ABV 4%
Ingredients: Pipkin pale ale malt (88%), crystal malt (10%), sugar (2%). 35 units of colour. Fuggles and Goldings whole hops, late copper hopped with Goldings. 30 units of bitterness.

TASTING NOTES

Nose	Powerful hop flowers aroma with malt undertones
Palate	Delicate, beautifully balanced malt and hops with lingering dry finish and hints of nuts
Comments	Memorable and complex amber ale.

KINGSDOWN ALE
OG 1052° ABV 5.2%
Ingredients: Pipkin pale ale malt (86%), crystal malt (12%), sugar (2%). 43 units of colour. Fuggles and Goldings whole hops, late copper hopped with Goldings. 32 units of bitterness.

TASTING NOTES

Nose	Rich aromas of hops and fruit
Palate	Ripe malt in mouth, deep bitter-sweet finish with fruit notes
Comments	Fruity, distinctive tawny strong ale.

NOEL
OG 1055° ABV 5.5%
Ingredients: Pipkin pale ale malt (92%), crystal malt (6%), sugar (2%). 30 units of colour. Fuggles and Goldings whole hops, late copper hopped with Goldings. 36 units of bitterness.

TASTING NOTES

Nose	Ripe malt, hops and fruit aromas
Palate	Full malt and hops in mouth, clean, dry finish with massive hop character and delicate fruit
Comments	Pale golden beer packed with malt and hops.

Bunce's Brewery

☞ **The Old Mill, Netheravon, Salisbury SP4 9QB.**
① **0980 70631.**
🏛 **No.**
🚶 **by arrangement.**
i **Independent.**

BENCHMARK
OG 1035° ABV 3.5%
Ingredients: Maris Otter pale malt (84%), crystal malt (7.5%), torrefied wheat (8.5%). Goldings and Omega whole hops.

TASTING NOTES

Nose	Tart, aromatic hops and light fruit

Palate	Good malt feel in mouth, fresh quenching finish
Comments	Light refreshing bitter with delicate fruit.

VICE
OG 1035° ABV 3.2%
Ingredients: Maris Otter pale malt, malted wheat, percentages not revealed. Goldings whole hops.

TASTING NOTES

Nose	Tart lemon aroma
Palate	Fresh and delicate fruit and hops in mouth, clean lightly fruity finish
Comments	Splendidly refreshing wheat beer. The name is a pun on the German 'Weiss' (wheat). Brewed in summer only.

BEST BITTER
OG 1042° ABV 4.1%
Ingredients: Maris Otter pale malt (84%), crystal malt (7.5%), torrefied wheat (8.5%). Goldings and Omega whole hops.

TASTING NOTES

Nose	Delicate hop flower aroma
Palate	Fruity and slightly acidic in mouth, leading to dry, hoppy finish
Comments	Golden, splendidly refreshing and aromatic ale.

PIGSWILL
OG 1040° ABV 4.0%
Ingredients: Maris Otter pale malt, crystal malt, torrefied wheat. Goldings whole hops.

TASTING NOTES

Nose	Inviting hops aroma
Palate	Good balance of malt and hops in mouth, dry and bitter with a hint of fruit
Comments	Beautifully balanced session bitter, first brewed for the Two Pigs pubs at Corsham, now commercially available.

OLD SMOKEY
OG 1050˚ ABV 5.0%
Ingredients: Maris Otter pale malt (88%), black malt (3.5%), torrefied wheat (8.5%). Goldings and Omega whole hops.

TASTING NOTES

Nose	Spicy aroma with a hint of wood smoke
Palate	Dry, chewy dark malt in mouth, long, rounded bitter-sweet finish with hops and bitter coffee
Comments	Rich, slightly sulphury and wonderfully complex dark ale.

Cheriton Brewhouse
- ▭ **Cheriton, Alresford SO24 0QQ.**
- ℺ **0962 771166.**
- 🏛 **Yes.**
- ⚐ **Yes.**
- *i* **Independent**

POTS ALE
OG 1037˚ ABV 3.8%
Ingredients: Halcyon pale malt (225kgs per 10 barrels), crystal malt (8kgs). Challenger whole hops.

TASTING NOTES

Nose	Floral hops aroma with hint of nutty malt
Palate	Fine balance of malt and hops in mouth, dry hoppy finish with hint of fruit
Comments	Pale gold and well-hopped beer, available in the Flowerpots Inn next to the brewery and the local free trade. A second beer, Brandymount Bitter (ABV 4.8%) is planned.

Cook Brewery Co
- ▭ **44 Burley Road, Bockhampton, nr Christchurch BH23 7AJ.**
- ℺ **0425 73721.**
- 🏛 **No.**
- ⚐ **No.**
- *i* **Independent.**

YARDARM SPECIAL BITTER
OG 1052° ABV 5.2%
Ingredients: best pale malt (90%), crystal malt (10%), plus 2 pints of ground black malt per 5 barrels. Fuggles whole hops for aroma, Target for bitterness.

TASTING NOTES

Nose	Rich aromas of nutty malt and spicy hops
Palate	Rounded malt in mouth, deep finish with cobnuts, hints of chocolate and coffee and hops
Comments	Aromatic ruby ale with complex flavours.

Donnington Brewery
📧 **Stow-on-the Wold, nr Cheltenham GL54 1EP.**
☎ **0451 30603.**
🏛 **No.**
⚔ **No.**
i **Independent**

XXX
OG 1036° ABV 3.5%
Ingredients: Maris Otter pale malt (90%), invert sugar (10%). Fuggles hop pellets.

TASTING NOTES

Nose	Light and delicate hop aroma
Palate	Sweet grain in mouth with hints of fruit, chocolate and liquorice in the finish
Comments	Delectable dark beer, available in only a few outlets.

BB
OG 1036° ABV 3.5%
Ingredients: Maris Otter pale malt (90%), invert sugar (10%). Fuggles hop pellets.

TASTING NOTES

Nose	Rich promise of malt with light hop aroma
Palate	Nutty malt in mouth, long dry finish

Comments   Malty, copper-coloured bitter.

SBA
OG 1044˚ ABV 4%
Ingredients: Maris Otter pale malt (90%), invert sugar (10%). Fuggles hop pellets.

TASTING NOTES
Nose	Warm malt aroma with fruit notes developing
Palate	Rich and rounded malt and hops in mouth, dry finish with hints of fruit
Comments	Succulent ale, ideal companion for a genuine ploughman's lunch.

Eldridge Pope & Co PLC
⌐ **Dorchester Brewery, Weymouth Avenue, Dorchester DT1 1QT.**
① **0305 251251.**
🏛 **Yes.**
🚶 **Yes.**
i **Independent**

DORCHESTER BITTER
OG 1032˚ ABV 3.3%
Ingredients: Pipkin pale malt, crystal malt, brewing sugar. Challenger and Northdown whole hops, dry hopped with Goldings. 21 units of bitterness.

TASTING NOTES
Nose	Delicate hop resin aroma
Palate	Light malt and hops in mouth, lingering hop finish
Comments	Quaffable amber ale.

BEST BITTER
OG 1036˚ ABV 3.8%
Ingredients: Pipkin pale malt, crystal malt and brewing sugar. Challenger and Northdown whole hops, dry hopped with Goldings. 25 units of bitterness.

TASTING NOTES
Nose	Light malt and floral hops aromas with fruit notes developing

| Palate | Crisp balance of malt and hops in mouth, long, tart finish with hints of fruit |
| Comments | Refreshing amber ale. |

THOMAS HARDY COUNTRY BITTER
(cask and bottle conditioned)
OG 1041˚ ABV 4.2%

Ingredients: Pipkin pale malt, crystal malt and brewing sugar. Challenger and Northdown whole hops, dry hopped with Goldings. 27 units of bitterness.

TASTING NOTES

Nose	Fine balance of hop resins and malt with delicate fruit notes
Palate	Full flavours of malt and hops, long finish with good hop character and a mellow fruitiness
Comments	Quenching, fruity ale.

BLACKDOWN PORTER
OG 1040˚ ABV 4%

Ingredients: Pipkin pale malt, roasted malt. 150 units of colour. Challenger and Northdown whole hops, Goldings for aroma. 30 units of bitterness.

TASTING NOTES

Nose	Roasted, toasted grain aromas and delicate hops
Palate	Hints of chocolate, liquorice and fruit, bitter-sweet finish with hops and dark malt
Comments	Splendid new porter, full of dark delights, based on genuine old porter recipes.

ROYAL OAK
OG 1048˚ ABV 5%

Ingredients: Pipkin pale malt, crystal malt and brewing sugar. Challenger and Northdown whole hops, dry hopped with Goldings. 30 units of bitterness.

TASTING NOTES

Nose	Rich floral hops and banana fruit aromas
Palate	Mouth-filling malt and fruit with delicate, bitter-sweet finish with pronounced pear drops character
Comments	Deep amber ale of great complexity.

THOMAS HARDY'S ALE
(bottle conditioned)
OG 1125˚ ABV 12%

Ingredients: 100% Pipkin pale malt. Challenger, Goldings and Northdown whole hops, dry hopped with Styrian Goldings for aroma. 75 units of bitterness.

TASTING NOTES

Nose	'Brisk as a volcano'
Palate	'Full in body; piquant, yet without a twang; free from streakiness'
Comments	'Luminous as an autumn sunset...the most beautiful colour that the eye of an artist in beer could desire': tasting notes by Mr T. Hardy of Casterbridge. Each bottle is individually numbered and will improve with age.

Freeminer Brewery Ltd

⌨ **The Laurels, Sling, Coleford, Forest of Dean GL16 7XX.**
℺ **0594 810408.**
🏛 **No.**
朸 **by arrangement.**
i **Independent.**

FREEMINER BITTER
OG 1038˚ ABV 4%

Ingredients: Maris Otter pale malt, crystal malt, wheat malt. Worcester Fuggles and Goldings whole hops. 30 units of bitterness.

TASTING NOTES

Nose	Floral hop and elderflower aromas
Palate	Bitter in mouth, floral finish with delicate fruit and nut
Comments	Chestnut brown beer with enormous hop appeal. New small brewery planning a stout and a premium bitter.

George Gale & Co Ltd

⬡ **The Brewery, Horndean, Portsmouth PO8 0DA.**
℧ **0705 571212.**
🏛 **Yes.**
🦿 **Yes.**
i **Independent**

XXXD MILD
OG 1030° ABV 3%
Ingredients: Maris Otter pale malt (82%), sugar (18%), black malt and caramel. Challenger, Fuggles and Goldings whole and hop pellets. 20 units of bitterness.

TASTING NOTES
Nose	Light hop aroma with bitter chocolate notes
Palate	Sweet malt in mouth, gentle finish with vanilla notes
Comments	Good tasting and well-balanced dark mild.

BBB or BUSTER BREW BITTER
OG 1035° ABV 3.6%
Ingredients: Maris Otter pale malt (80%), sugar (18%), torrefied wheat (2%). Challenger, Fuggles and Goldings whole and pellet hops. 25 units of bitterness.

TASTING NOTES
Nose	Rich floral hop and lemon fruit aromas
Palate	Deep and complex malt and hops in mouth with long, tart finish and slight astringency
Comments	Uncompromising tangy pale bitter.

BEST BITTER
OG 1040° ABV 3.8%
Ingredients: Maris Otter pale malt (80%), crystal malt (5%), torrefied wheat (2%), sugar (13%). Challenger, Fuggles and Goldings hop pellets. Dry hopped.

TASTING NOTES
Nose	Floral hops aroma
Palate	Malt in mouth, hops and fruit in finish
Comments	Fruity ale with good hop character.

POMPEY ROYAL
OG 1044° ABV 4.5%

Ingredients: pale malt (67.5%), crystal malt (7.5%), torrefied wheat (12.5%), sugar (12.5%). Hop extract with some Styrian pellets; dry hopped with Styrians.

TASTING NOTES

Nose	Rich hop aroma with light fruit notes
Palate	Full malt in mouth, long finish with hops and vanilla notes
Comments	Mahogany-coloured ale brewed for Whitbread.

XXXXX
OG 1044° ABV 4.2%

Ingredients: Maris Otter pale malt (88%), sugar (10%), torrefied wheat (2%), black malt and caramel. Challenger, Fuggles and Goldings whole and pellet hops. 26 units of bitterness.

TASTING NOTES

Nose	Smoky aroma with hops and hint of fruit
Palate	Sweet malt in mouth, deep and rounded hops and fruit finish
Comments	Dark and warming winter ale, blend of BBB and Prize Old Ale.

HSB
OG 1050° ABV 5%

Ingredients: Maris Otter pale malt (80%), sugar (15%), torrefied wheat (5%), black malt. Challenger, Fuggles and Goldings whole and pellet hops. 31.5 units of bitterness.

TASTING NOTES

Nose	Ripe fruit and hops aromas
Palate	Full malt with hop edge in mouth, deep finish with citric fruit and faint chocolate notes
Comments	Complex, slightly sour strong beer.

PRIZE OLD ALE
(bottle conditioned)
OG 1094° ABV 9%

Ingredients: Maris Otter pale malt (98%), black malt, wheat. Fuggles and Goldings whole and pellet hops. 47.5 units of bitterness.

TASTING NOTES

Nose	Stunning, complex aromas of hops and ripe fruit, including apple notes
Palate	Great mouth-filling malt and fruit, intensely dry, fruity finish with hints of raisins
Comments	Superb deep red barley wine in corked bottles.

Gibbs Mew PLC

⌨ **Anchor Brewery, Milford Street, Salisbury SP1 2AR.**
℗ **0722 411911.**
🏛 **No.**
🕯 **by arrangement.**
i **Independent.**

WILTSHIRE TRADITIONAL BITTER
OG 1036˚ ABV 3.5%
Ingredients: pale malt, crystal malt, chocolate malt, 3% torrefied wheat. 34 units of colour. Challenger, Fuggles and Goldings hop pellets.

TASTING NOTES

Nose	Fresh hops and malt aromas
Palate	Good malt and hops balance in mouth, delicate hop finish
Comments	Light supping bitter.

TIMOTHY CHUDLEY'S LOCAL LINE
OG 1036˚ ABV 3.5%
Ingredients: pale malt, crystal malt, chocolate malt, 3% torrefied wheat. 34 units of colour. Challenger, Fuggles and Goldings hop pellets.

TASTING NOTES

Nose	Fine floral hops aroma with malt notes
Palate	Malt and hops dominate the mouth with light bitter-sweet finish with delicate hops and fruit
Comments	Dry hopped version of Wiltshire Bitter.

PREMIUM BITTER
OG 1042˚ ABV 4%
Ingredients: pale malt, crystal malt, chocolate malt, 3% torrefied wheat. 37 units of colour. Challenger, Fuggles and Goldings hop pellets.

TASTING NOTES

Nose	Rich malt aroma with some fruit notes
Palate	Sweet malt in mouth, malty finish with some fruit
Comments	Mellow ale lacking good hop bite.

SALISBURY BEST BITTER
OG 1042° ABV 4%

Ingredients: pale malt, crystal malt, chocolate malt, 3% torrefied wheat. 37 units of colour. Challenger, Fuggles and Goldings hop pellets. Dry hopped.

TASTING NOTES

Nose	Malt aroma with pineapple fruit and delicate hops
Palate	Sweet malt in mouth, light malty finish with late dryness, some hops and dried fruit
Comments	Fruity copper-coloured bitter, dry hopped version of Premium.

DEACON
OG 1050° ABV 5%

Ingredients: Golden Promise and Pipkin pale malts, 3% torrefied wheat. 15 units of colour. Challenger, Fuggles and Goldings hop pellets.

TASTING NOTES

Nose	Rich peppery floral hops bouquet
Palate	Hops dominate the mouth leading to a bitter-sweet finish with hops, malt and delicate fruit
Comments	New straw-coloured beer with good hops character.

THE BISHOP'S TIPPLE
OG 1066° ABV 6.5%

Ingredients: pale malt, crystal malt, hint of chocolate, 3% torrefied wheat. 42 units of colour. Challenger, Fuggles and Goldings hop pellets.

TASTING NOTES

Nose	Complex malty, earthy aromas with hint of toffee

| Palate | Mouth-filling malt and fruit leading to deep vinous finish with chocolate notes |
| Comments | A barley wine to make you lose your mitre; winner of its class in 1992 Champion Beer of Britain competition. |

Goldfinch Brewery

⌑ **Tom Brown's Pub, 47 High Street, Dorchester DT1 1HU.**
① **0305 264020.**
🏛 **Yes (in pub).**
🏃 **trade and CAMRA only by arrangement.**
i **Independent**

TOM BROWN'S BEST BITTER
OG 1039˚ ABV 4%
Ingredients: pale malt (95%), crystal malt (5%). Goldings whole hops.

TASTING NOTES

Nose	Light fruit and hops aroma
Palate	Malt, fruit and hops in mouth, complex bitter-sweet finish
Comments	Pale brown, well-balanced session beer.

FLASHMAN'S CLOUT STRONG ALE
OG 1043˚ ABV 4.5%
Ingredients: pale malt (95%), crystal malt (5%). Goldings whole hops.

TASTING NOTES

Nose	Malt and honey aromas
Palate	Bitter-sweet malt and fruit in mouth, long bitter finish
Comments	Fascinating blend of flavours in a copper-coloured ale.

MIDNIGHT BLINDER PREMIUM ALE
OG 1050˚ ABV 5%
Ingredients: pale malt (91%), crystal malt (8%), chocolate (1%). Goldings whole hops.

TASTING NOTES

| Nose | Ripe fruit aromas |

Palate	Malt and ripe fruit in mouth, powerful bitter finish
Comments	Ruby-coloured ale, complex and fruity. The beers are brewed in the heart of Dorchester for Tom Brown's pub and the free trade.

Hall & Woodhouse Ltd

⌨ **The Brewery, Blandford Forum DT11 9LS.**
☎ **0258 452141.**
🏛 **Yes.**
🚶 **Yes.**
i **Independent**

COOPER'S WPA
OG 1036° ABV 3.5%
Ingredients: pale malt and crystal malt. Challenger and Fuggles whole hops.

TASTING NOTES

Nose	Floral hop aroma
Palate	Hops dominate the palate with dry finish
Comments	Quenching golden beer that drinks more than its gravity.

BADGER BEST BITTER
OG 1041° ABV 4%
Ingredients: Alexis ale malt (97%), crystal malt (3%), sugar (15%) in copper. 30 units of colour. Challenger and Northdown pellet hops. 26 units of bitterness.

TASTING NOTES

Nose	Pronounced malt and hops aromas with fruit notes
Palate	Ripe and rounded balance of malt and hops in mouth, dry hoppy finish with pleasing hint of cobnuts
Comments	Superb copper-coloured ale with good crystal malt character.

TANGLEFOOT
OG 1048° ABV 5%
Ingredients: 100% Alexis ale malt, sugar (15%) in copper. 18 units of colour. Challenger and Northdown hop pellets. Dry hopped with Styrian Goldings. 26 units of bitterness.

TASTING NOTES

Nose	Pronounced Goldings aroma with malt and citric fruit
Palate	Mouth-filling malt and hops, lingering finish with hops and fruit notes and slight hints of nuts
Comments	Pale beer of great depth and complexity. The brewery has introduced a Station Porter (OG 1059° ABV 6.1%).

Hampshire Brewery
- 5 Anton Trading Estate, Andover SP10 2NJ.
- 0264 336699.
- No.
- by arrangement.
- *i* Independent

KINGS ALFRED'S HAMPSHIRE BITTER
OG 1037° ABV 3.8%
Ingredients: pale malt, crystal malt, pale chocolate malt. Northdown whole hops.

TASTING NOTES

Nose	Ripe floral hops aroma with light fruit notes
Palate	Crisp hops on the tongue, long bitter finish with some light citric fruit
Comments	Golden brown, splendidly refreshing bitter ale.

RICHARD THE LIONHEART GOLDEN
OG 1044° ABV 4.4%
Ingredients: pale malt, crystal malt, maize, torrefied wheat. Northdown whole hops.

TASTING NOTES

Nose	Sweet malt, floral hops, hint of vanilla
Palate	Clean malt and hops in mouth, bitter-sweet finish with hint of pear drops
Comments	Quenching, straw-coloured premium ale with complex hops and fruit character.

HAMPSHIRE PORTER
OG 1046˚ ABV 4.5%
Ingredients: pale malt, crystal malt, chocolate malt plus Spanish liquorice, molasses and liquorice root. Northdown whole hops.

TASTING NOTES

Nose	Sweet malt with liquorice notes
Palate	Complex malt, roast and coffee flavours with delicate liquorice-accented finish
Comments	Fascinating and complex dark beer using 18th century-style ingredients.

ARTHUR PENDRAGON STRONG ALE
OG 1047˚ ABV 4.8%
Ingredients: pale malt, crystal malt, chocolate and pale chocolate malts. Northdown whole hops.

TASTING NOTES

Nose	Rich fruit and malt aromas
Palate	Full rich fruit in mouth, delicate hoppy finish
Comments	Tempting, smooth and deceptive ale.

WILLIAM THE CONQUEROR 1066
OG 1066˚ ABV 6.4%
Ingredients: pale malt, crystal malt, chocolate malt. Northdown whole hops.

TASTING NOTES

Nose	Ripe malt and hops aromas
Palate	Deep malt and hops in mouth, big finish with malt, fruit and hops
Comments	Ruby-red ale with deep and complex flavours. Bitter, Pendragon and Conqueror are all-malt brews.

Hop Back Brewery
- ⊡ **Wyndham Arms, 227 Estcourt Road, Salisbury SP1 3AS.**
- ① **0722 328594.**
- 🏛 **No.**
- ⋇ **Yes.**
- *i* Independent

MILD
OG 1032° ABV 3.2%
Ingredients: Pipkin pale malt (90%), crystal malt (5%), chocolate malt (2.5%), roasted barley (2.5%). Challenger and East Kent Goldings hop pellets.

TASTING NOTES

Nose	Dark malt and hops aromas
Palate	Rich toasted grain in mouth, smooth finish with hints of vanilla and hops
Comments	Fine dark mild with exceptional hop character.

GFB
OG 1035° ABV 3.5%
Ingredients: Pipkin pale malt (95%), crystal malt (5%). Challenger and East Kent Goldings hop pellets.

TASTING NOTES

Nose	Rich Goldings resiny hop bouquet
Palate	Hops dominate the mouth and dry, bitter finish
Comments	Superbly hoppy pale bitter.

SPECIAL
OG 1042° ABV 4.2%
Ingredients: Pipkin pale malt (90%), crystal malt (9%), chocolate malt (1%). Challenger and East Kent Goldings hop pellets.

TASTING NOTES

Nose	Malt and cobnuts aromas with hop notes
Palate	Bitter-sweet malt and hops in mouth, hops and crystal malt character in finish
Comments	Copper-coloured, creamy and nutty ale.

WILT ALTERNATIVE
OG 1042˚ ABV 4.2%
Ingredients: Pipkin pale malt (97%), crystal malt (3%). Challenger and East Kent Goldings hop pellets; late addition to copper with Goldings.

TASTING NOTES

Nose	Powerful peppery Goldings aroma
Palate	Hops in mouth, dry and bitter finish with light fruit notes
Comments	Refreshing pale bitter with fine hop character.

ENTIRE STOUT
OG 1042˚ ABV 4.2%
Ingredients: Pipkin pale malt (88%), crystal malt (4%), chocolate malt (4%), roasted barley (4%). Challenger and East Kent Goldings hop pellets; late copper addition of Goldings.

TASTING NOTES

Nose	Malt, hops and chocolate aromas
Palate	Dark, bitter grain and hops in mouth, deep finish with coffee, hint of liquorice and hops
Comments	Dry, bitter and hoppy Irish-style stout.

SUMMER LIGHTNING
OG 1050˚ ABV 5%
Ingredients: Pipkin pale malt (98%), crystal malt (2%). Challenger and East Kent Goldings hop pellets.

TASTING NOTES

Nose	Massive aroma of Goldings hops and citric fruit
Palate	Intensely hoppy with lemon fruit in mouth, bitter-sweet finish with hops and light fruit
Comments	Distinctive pale bitter, winner of its class in Champion Beer of Britain competition.

WHEAT BEER
OG 1051˚ ABV 5.2%
Ingredients: Pipkin pale malt (50%), wheat malt (50%). Challenger and East Kent Goldings hop pellets; late copper addition with Goldings.

TASTING NOTES

Nose	Powerful aroma of coriander
Palate	Herbal and hoppy in mouth, smooth, cleansing finish
Comments	Pale, quenching beer with fascinating herbal character.

Island Brewery

- 16 Manners View, Dodnor Industrial Estate, Newport, Isle of Wight PO30 5FA.
- 0983 520123.
- No.
- Yes.
- *i* Independent

NIPPER BITTER
OG 1038° ABV 3.8%
Ingredients: Pipkin pale malt (96%), crystal (3%), chocolate malt (1%). Challenger, Goldings and Target whole hops.

TASTING NOTES

Nose	Good floral Goldings aroma
Palate	Hops dominate the mouth with bitter-sweet finish
Comments	Easy-drinking golden brew. Nipper is Wight term for friend.

NEWPORT BEST BITTER
OG 1045° ABV 4.6%
Ingredients: Pipkin pale malt (96%), crystal (3%), chocolate malt (1%). Challenger, Goldings and Target whole hops.

TASTING NOTES

Nose	Malt and hops aromas with hint of chocolate
Palate	Malt, hops and delicate fruit in mouth, fruit, cobnuts and hops in finish
Comments	Dark ale with intriguing balance of flavours. The brewery also produces a winter beer, Old Yatesy (ABV 6%), named after head brewer David Yates.

Mole's Brewery

- ☎ **5 Merlin Way, Bowerhill, Melksham SN12 6TJ.**
- ① **0225 704734.**
- 🏛 **No.**
- 🕴 **Yes.**
- *i* **Independent**

MOLE'S CASK BITTER
OG 1040° ABV 3.9%
Ingredients: Maris Otter pale malt (90%), crystal malt (10%). Progress and Whitbread Goldings Variety whole hops.

TASTING NOTES
Nose	Malt and light fruit aromas with subtle hint of hop
Palate	Delicate malt in mouth with lingering hop finish
Comments	Cleansing balance of malt and hops; splendidly refreshing beer.

MOLE'S BREW 97
OG 1050° ABV 5%
Ingredients: Maris Otter pale malt (88%), crystal malt (12%). Fuggles and Whitbread Goldings Variety whole hops.

TASTING NOTES
Nose	Ripe malt aroma with delicate hop hints
Palate	Full malt in mouth balanced by fine hops and fruit character in finish
Comments	Red-brown beer of some complexity and good maltiness.

J C & R H Palmer Ltd

- ☎ **The Old Brewery, West Bay Road, Bridport DT6 4JA.**
- ① **0308 22396.**
- 🏛 **Yes.**
- 🕴 **Yes.**
- *i* **Independent**

BRIDPORT BITTER
OG 1031° ABV 3.2%

Ingredients: Pipkin pale malt (90%), crystal malt (5%), No 3 invert sugar (5%). 26 units of colour. Goldings and Styrian Goldings whole hops. 26 units of bitterness.

TASTING NOTES

Nose	Delicate aromas of malt and hops
Palate	Cleansing balance of malt and hops in mouth with dry, slightly nutty finish
Comments	Rare example of a Dorset 'boy's bitter' with a quenching, floral palate.

PALMER'S BEST BITTER OR IPA
OG 1039° ABV 4.2%

Ingredients: Pipkin pale malt (90%), crystal malt (5%), No 3 invert sugar (5%). 27 units of colour. Goldings and Styrian Goldings whole hops. 28 units of bitterness.

TASTING NOTES

Nose	Superb aromas of malt and Goldings hops
Palate	Full malt in mouth with intense dry, attenuated finish and fine balance of hops, fruit and nut
Comments	Fine Dorset ale with good hop character.

TALLY HO!
OG 1047° ABV 4.7%

Ingredients: Pipkin pale malt (87%), crystal malt (7%), No 3 invert sugar (6%). 80 units of colour. Goldings and Styrian Goldings whole hops. 40 units of bitterness.

TASTING NOTES

Nose	Rich roast malt and hops aromas
Palate	Sweet malt in mouth, long finish with complex balance of fruit, hops and nut
Comments	Dark, strong, fruity ale from a brewery that, apart from a little sugar, concentrates on all-malt, additive-free beer.

Poole Brewery

⌖ **Brewhouse Brewery, 68 High Street, Poole BH15 1DA.**
① **0202 682345.**
🏛 **Yes (small).**
🏃 **by arrangement, maximum 10 people.**
i **Independent**

DOLPHIN BITTER
OG 1038˚ ABV 3.9%
Ingredients: pale malt (87.5%), crystal malt (12.5%), cane sugar, caramel for colour. Fuggles whole hops for bitterness, Goldings late addition in copper. 35 units of bitterness.

TASTING NOTES
Nose	Peppery Goldings hops aroma
Palate	Fine balance of malt and hops in mouth, lingering finish with hops and nuts flavours
Comments	Deep amber, refreshing ale.

BOSUN BEST BITTER
OG 1045˚ ABV 4.5%
Ingredients: pale malt (92.5%), crystal malt (7.5%), cane sugar, caramel for colour. 100% Kent Goldings whole hops; dry hopped with 8oz (225g) per barrel. 40 units of bitterness.

TASTING NOTES
Nose	Booming Goldings hops aroma
Palate	Mellow malt in mouth with hop balance, dry and intensely hoppy finish
Comments	Rich amber ale with enormous hop character.

Ringwood Brewery

⌖ **138 Christchurch Road, Ringwood BH24 3AP.**
① **0425 471177.**
🏛 **Yes (brewery shop).**
🏃 **Yes (winter only).**
i **Independent**

BEST BITTER
OG 1039° ABV 3.8%
Ingredients: Maris Otter pale malt (89%), balance made up of coloured malts and torrefied wheat. Challenger, Goldings and Progress hop pellets. 28.5 units of bitterness.

TASTING NOTES

Nose	Tempting hop resin aroma with light fruit notes
Palate	Good malt feel in mouth, dry, tangy, fruity finish
Comments	Easy-drinking, slightly tart pale bitter.

FORTYNINER
OG 1048° ABV 4.9%
Ingredients: Maris Otter pale malt (90%), balance made up of coloured malts and torrefied wheat. Challenger, Goldings and Progress hop pellets. 34.5 units of bitterness.

TASTING NOTES

Nose	Light, fresh hop bouquet
Palate	Rounded malt in mouth with strong hop balance; deep bitter-sweet finish with delicate fruit notes
Comments	Beautifully balanced and refreshing premium ale.

XXXX PORTER
OG 1048° ABV 4.8%
Ingredients: Maris Otter pale malt (81%) with coloured malts, torrefied wheat and caramel. Challenger, Goldings and Progress hop pellets. 35 units of bitterness.

TASTING NOTES

Nose	Hops and roasted grain aromas
Palate	Dry in mouth with burnt malt notes; dry nutty finish
Comments	Smooth dark beer with delectable chewy malt character.

OLD THUMPER
OG 1058° ABV 6%
Ingredients: Maris Otter pale malt (90%), balance made up of coloured malts and torrefied wheat. Challenger, Goldings and Progress hop pellets. 39 units of bitterness.

TASTING NOTES

Nose	Peppery and spicy aromas with hint of apples and nettles
Palate	Superb balance of malt and hops in mouth; bitter-sweet finish with good hop tingle and citric fruit
Comments	Rich, warm and rounded yet marvellously delicate and fruity strong ale. Champion Beer of Britain in 1988.

Uley Brewery Ltd

⌨ **The Old Brewery, Uley, Dursley GL11 5TB.**
℧ **0453 860120.**
🏛 **No.**
🕺 **by arrangement.**
i **Independent**

ULEY BITTER
OG 1040˚ ABV 3.8%
Ingredients: pale Devonshire malt, crystal malt. Worcester Fuggles and Goldings whole hops.

TASTING NOTES

Nose	Ripe malt and hop aromas, fruit notes developing
Palate	Rich malt in mouth, deep, dry finish with citric fruit notes
Comments	Tart, hoppy, tasty bitter.

OLD SPOT PRIZE ALE
OG 1050˚ ABV 5%
Ingredients: pale Devonshire malt (85%), crystal malt (15%). Worcester Fuggles and Goldings whole hops.

OLD SPOT ALE

TASTING NOTES

Nose	Delicious hop resin aroma with ripe fruit developing
Palate	Rich, rounded malt in mouth, long bitter-sweet finish with tart fruit
Comments	Superbly balanced premium ale, accounts for 50 per cent of brewery's production.

PIG'S EAR IPA
OG 1050˚ ABV 5%
Ingredients: lager malt (100%). Worcester Fuggles and Goldings whole hops.

TASTING NOTES

Nose	Rich butterscotch and lemon aromas
Palate	Brilliant balance of light malt and hops bitterness in mouth; deep finish with hop flowers and citric fruit
Comments	A hybrid brew using lager malt and English hops; pale and deceptively strong, brewed to wean young drinkers off Euro-lager.

PIGOR MORTIS
OG 1058˚ ABV 5.5%
Ingredients: pale malt (80%), crystal malt (20%). Worcester Fuggles and Goldings whole hops.

TASTING NOTES

Nose	Delicate hops, malt and fruit bouquet
Palate	Good balance of malt and hops in mouth; deep fruit and hops finish
Comments	Rich, tawny ale. Bitter and Old Spot are brewed regularly, Pig's Ear once a month and Pigor Mortis at Xmas.

Ushers of Trowbridge PLC
- ✉ **Directors House, 68 Fore Street, Trowbridge BA14 8JF.**
- ☎ **0225 753661.**
- 🏛 **Yes.**
- 🏃 **Yes.**
- *i* **Independent**

USHER'S BEST BITTER
OG 1037˚ ABV 3.8%
Ingredients: Halcyon and Pipkin pale malts (96%), crystal malt (4%). No brewing sugars. 26 units of colour. Target pellet hops for bitterness, Styrian Goldings for aroma added late in boil. 27 units of bitterness.

TASTING NOTES

Nose	Spicy hops aroma

Palate	Toffee and malt in mouth, fruit in finish with good hop presence
Comments	Amber-coloured session bitter.

USHER'S FOUNDERS ALE
OG 1045˚ ABV 4.5%
Ingredients: Halcyon and Pipkin pale malts (93%), crystal malt (7%). No brewing sugars. 30 units of colour. Target hop pellets for bitterness, Styrian Goldings for aroma added late in copper boil. 34 units of bitterness.

TASTING NOTES

Nose	Rich floral hops aroma with fruity, estery notes
Palate	Citrus hop in mouth, fruity finish
Comments	Dark amber ale full of hop and fruit character.

1824 PARTICULAR
OG 1060˚ ABV 6.2%
Ingredients: Halcyon and Pipkin pale malts (92%), crystal malt (8%). No brewing sugars. 60 units of colour. Target hop pellets for bitterness, Styrian Goldings for aroma added late in copper boil. 33 units of bitterness.

TASTING NOTES

Nose	Rich fruity, estery aroma
Palate	Ripe malt, fruit and cobnuts in mouth, long hoppy finish with fruit notes
Comments	Powerful and complex winter ale.

Wadworth & Co Ltd
- ☎ **Northgate Brewery, Devizes SN10 1JW.**
- ① **0380 723361.**
- ⟐ **Yes.**
- ⭑ **by arrangement.**
- *i* **Independent**

HENRY WADWORTH IPA
OG 1034˚ ABV 3.8%
Ingredients: Pipkin pale malt (89%), crystal malt (3%), sugar (8%), caramel for colour adjustment. Fuggles whole hops in the copper, Goldings for aroma in hopback. 22 units of bitterness.

TASTING NOTES

Nose	Floral hops aroma with light fruit
Palate	Malt dominates the mouth with dry, hoppy finish
Comments	Well-attenuated bitter with pleasant biscuity character.

6X
OG 1040° ABV 4.3%
Ingredients: Pipkin pale malt (90%), crystal malt (3%), sugar (7%). Fuggles whole hops in copper, Goldings for aroma in hopback. 22 units of bitterness.

TASTING NOTES

Nose	Earthy hops, fruit and nutty malt aromas
Palate	Complex bitter-sweet flavours in mouth, long dry finish with vanilla notes
Comments	Copper-coloured ale of enormous depth and complexity.

FARMER'S GLORY
OG 1046° ABV 4.5%
Ingredients: Pipkin pale malt (90%), crystal malt (3%), sugar (7%). Roasted malt extract for colour and flavour. Fuggles whole hops in copper, Goldings for aroma in hopback plus pellets for dry hopping. 22 units of bitterness.

TASTING NOTES

Nose	Peppery aroma of Goldings and toasted grain
Palate	Full malt and hops in mouth, deep, dry, bitter finish
Comments	Ripe and tasty deep red strong ale.

OLD TIMER
OG 1055° ABV 5.8%
Ingredients: Pipkin pale malt (90%), crystal malt (3%), sugar (7%). Fuggles whole hops in copper, Goldings for aroma in hop back. 22 units of bitterness.

TASTING NOTES

Nose	Ripe fruit and hops aromas
Palate	Full malt and fruit in mouth, long finish full of hop bitterness with banana and sultana fruit

Comments	Aromatic winter beer: 'Ideal by a log fire,' says the head brewer. In 1992 Wadworth brewed Malt & Hops (ABV 4.5%), a harvest ale using the new season's Pipkin malt and Goldings hops; it plans to produce the beer every autumn.

Whitbread (Cheltenham)

⌨ **The Flowers Brewery, Monson Avenue, Cheltenham GL50 4EL.**

① **0242 261166.**

🏛 **Yes.**

🕺 **Yes.**

i **Part of the Whitbread Beer Company**

WEST COUNTRY PALE ALE
OG 1030.5˚ ABV 3%
Ingredients: pale ale malt (96%), crystal malt (4%), caramel (0.3%). 23 units of colour. Hop extract (85%), Whitbread Goldings Variety pellets (10%), late hopped with Styrian Goldings (5%). Target hop oil for aroma. Dry hopped with Goldings. 25 units of bitterness.

TASTING NOTES
Nose	Delicate hop aroma with malt and biscuit notes
Palate	Light and refreshing malt and hops in mouth, good hoppy finish
Comments	Quenching session bitter, good if rare example of a 'boy's bitter'.

FREMLINS BITTER
OG 1035.5˚ ABV 3.5%
Ingredients: pale ale malt (82%), crystal malt (5%), sugar (13%), caramel (0.2%). 24 units of colour. Hop extract (94%), Target pellets (5%). Dry hopped with Styrians. 24 units of bitterness.

TASTING NOTES
Nose	Spicy hops aroma
Palate	Light malt in the mouth with short and nutty finish
Comments	'Typical Kentish beer,' says the company. The geography is off-beam.

WHITBREAD BEST BITTER
OG 1036˚ ABV 3.6%

Ingredients: pale ale malt (96%), crystal malt (4%), caramel (0.3%). 29 units of colour. Hop extract (85%), Whitbread Goldings Variety (10%), late hopped with Styrian pellets (5%). Target hop oil for aroma. 26 units of bitterness.

TASTING NOTES

Nose	Light malt and nut aromas with hint of hops
Palate	Malt in mouth, medium length with malt, nuts and light fruit in finish
Comments	Amber bitter with plenty of malt character.

FLOWERS IPA
OG 1036˚ ABV 3.6%

Ingredients: standard white malt (80%), crystal malt (7.5%), sugar (12.5%). 24 units of colour. Hop extract (90%), Styrian pellets (10%), Target hop oil, late copper hopped with Styrians. 24 units of bitterness.

TASTING NOTES

Nose	Light hops aroma with hint of apple
Palate	Good balance of malt and hops in mouth, light bitter-sweet finish
Comments	Easy drinking light bitter.

FLOWERS ORIGINAL BITTER
OG 1044˚ ABV 4.5%

Ingredients: pale ale malt (80%), crystal malt (7.5%), sugar (12.5%). 27 units of colour. Hop extract (90%), Styrian pellets (10%), Target hop oil for aroma, Styrian dry hops in cask. 30 units of bitterness.

TASTING NOTES

Nose	Rich bouquet of hops and wholemeal biscuit
Palate	Full malt in mouth, dry finish with some hop character and raisin and sultana notes
Comments	Strong fruity bitter with some acidity. Who says consumer pressure does not work? Whitbread has phased out the use of large amounts of torrefied wheat — 15% in West Country Pale Ale — in its beers.

LATE ENTRY

Foxley Brewing Co Ltd
🖃 **Unit 3, Home Farm Workshops, Mildenhall**
nr Marlborough SN8 2LR
℧ **0672 515000**
Brewing Foxley Best Bitter (OG 1040˚ ABV 4%).

WEST COUNTRY

The West Country has no single, distinctive beer style. The ales of Avon and Somerset have a ripe malty fruitiness while further west there is a sharper, even astringent edge to the beers. Several companies produce deceptively strong and pale beers.

The decline in the number of large commercial brewers has been countered by the spectacular growth of micros. The lonely furrow dug by Blackawton in the late 1970s has now sprouted an astonishing number of other small producers.

The success of such companies as Cotleigh and Exmoor has moved them from the micro division into the league of small regionals, aided by a larger than usual free trade.

Ash Vine Brewery Ltd

⌑ **White Hart, Trudoxhill, Frome BA11 5DP.**
① **0373 836344.**
🏛 **Yes.**
🕴 **by arrangement.**
i **Independent**

TRUDOXHILL BITTER
OG 1034.5˚ ABV 3.3%
Ingredients: Triumph pale malt, crystal malt, wheat malt. Fuggles and Goldings hop pellets.

TASTING NOTES

Nose	Spicy Goldings hops
Palate	Malt and hops in mouth, medium dry finish with good Goldings character
Comments	Well-balanced beer that drinks more than its strength.

ASH VINE BITTER
OG 1039.8˚ ABV 3.8%
Ingredients: Triumph pale malt, crystal malt, malted wheat. Goldings and Whitbread Goldings Variety hop pellets.

TASTING NOTES

Nose	Fresh floral hops aroma with citric notes
Palate	Fine balance of malt and hops in mouth, intensely dry, hoppy finish
Comments	Pale bitter beer with pleasing light fruitiness.

CHALLENGER
OG 1042.8˚ ABV 4.1%
Ingredients: Triumph pale malt, crystal malt, malted wheat. Challenger, Fuggles and Goldings hop pellets.

TASTING NOTES

Nose	Delicate aromas of malt and hops
Palate	Malt and some fruit in mouth, dry finish with hops and nuts
Comments	Ruby ale with good hops and crystal malt character.

BLACK BESS PORTER
OG 1044.5˚ ABV 4.2%

Ingredients: Triumph pale malt, crystal malt, black malt, chocolate malt, wheat malt. Fuggles, Goldings, Whitbread Goldings Variety hop pellets.

TASTING NOTES

Nose	Dark grain, coffee and hops aromas
Palate	Hops and dark, bitter malt in mouth, bitter-sweet finish packed with dark, roasted malt
Comments	Dark brown beer with complex malt flavours

TANKER
OG 1049.8˚ ABV 4.7%

Ingredients: Triumph pale malt, crystal malt, black malt, malted wheat. Fuggles, Goldings, Whitbread Goldings Variety hop pellets.

TASTING NOTES

Nose	Ripe malt and coffee aromas offset by Goldings hops
Palate	Sweet malt in mouth leading to long, dry finish with fruit and hint of coffee
Comments	Ruby-coloured ale with great dark malt and Goldings character.

HOP AND GLORY
OG 1058.9˚ ABV 5.5%

Ingredients: Triumph pale malt, crystal malt, black malt, malted wheat. Challenger, Fuggles and Goldings hop pellets.

TASTING NOTES

Nose	Rich bouquet of peppery, spicy hops
Palate	Fruit and dark malt flavours in mouth, fruit and hops in long finish
Comments	Distinctive dark ruby ale with pronounced dark fruit.

███████████

Beer Engine

☎ **Newton St Cyres, Exeter EX5 5AX.**
① **0392 851282.**
🏛 **Yes (in pub).**
⚲ **by arrangement.**
i **Independent**

RAIL ALE
OG 1037˚ ABV 3.7%
Ingredients: pale malt (96%), crystal malt (4%). Challenger and Goldings whole hops.

TASTING NOTES
Nose	Delicate floral hops aroma
Palate	Refreshing malt and hops in mouth, light dry finish
Comments	Pleasant pale golden supping bitter.

PISTON BITTER
OG 1044˚ ABV 4.6%
Ingredients: pale malt (96.6%), crystal malt (2%), chocolate malt (1.4%). Challenger and Goldings whole hops.

TASTING NOTES
Nose	Pronounced malt and hops aromas
Palate	Good mouth-feel of malt, hops and slight chocolate, bitter-sweet finish
Comments	Tasty amber-coloured ale.

SLEEPER HEAVY
OG 1055˚ ABV 5.5%
Ingredients: pale malt (96.6%), crystal malt (2.4%), chocolate malt (1%). Challenger and Goldings whole hops.

TASTING NOTES
Nose	Rich hop resin and coffee aromas
Palate	Full malt and hops in mouth with bitter-sweet finish with hint of chocolate
Comments	Strong dark amber ale. The beers are brewed in a pub alongside the Exeter-Barnstaple railway and sold to the free trade.

Berrow Brewery

- ⌐ **Coast Road, Berrow, Burnham-on-Sea TA8 2QU.**
- ① **0278 751345.**
- 🏛 **Yes.**
- 🕅 **by arrangement.**
- *i* **Independent**

BBBB OR 4BS
OG 1038˚ ABV 3.8%
Ingredients: pale malt and crystal malt. Fuggles and Goldings whole hops.

TASTING NOTES

Nose	Fine floral hops aroma with some fruit notes
Palate	Good malt and hops balance in mouth, quenching finish with hops and fruit notes
Comments	Potable amber ale that drinks more than its gravity.

TOPSY TURVY
OG 1055˚ ABV 5.9%
Ingredients: 100% pale malt. Fuggles and Goldings whole hops. Dry hopped.

TASTING NOTES

Nose	Powerful aromas of malt and hops with some citric fruit notes
Palate	Fine balance of malt and hops, intense finish of hop bitterness and lemon and vanilla notes
Comments	Pale and complex strong ale.

Blackawton Brewery

- ⌐ **Washbourne, Totnes TQ9 7UF.**
- ① **080423 339.**
- 🏛 **No.**
- 🕅 **No.**
- *i* **Independent**

BLACKAWTON BITTER
OG 1037.5˚ ABV 3.8%
Ingredients: 100% pale and crystal malts. East Kent Goldings whole hops. 26 units of bitterness.

TASTING NOTES

Nose	Fresh, floral hop resin aroma
Palate	Good balance of malt and hops in mouth with quenching dry finish
Comments	Refreshing copper-coloured bitter.

DEVON GOLD
OG 1040.5° ABV 4.1%
Ingredients: 100% pale malt. East Kent Goldings whole hops. 21 units of bitterness.

TASTING NOTES

Nose	Light malt aroma with good hop notes
Palate	Sweet malt with vanilla hints; bitter-sweet finish with good balance of hops and delicate fruit
Comments	A pale gold beer brewed in the summer for lager-drinking visitors.

44 SPECIAL
OG 1044.5° ABV 4.5%
Ingredients: 100% pale and crystal malts. East Kent Goldings whole hops. 25 units of bitterness.

TASTING NOTES

Nose	Ripe hops and fruit aromas with fruit notes developing
Palate	Rounded malt in mouth, long dry finish with good balance of hops and fruit
Comments	Mellow, smooth copper-coloured ale.

HEADSTRONG
OG 1051.5° ABV 5.2%
Ingredients: 100% pale and crystal malts. East Kent Goldings whole hops. 25 units of bitterness.

TASTING NOTES

Nose	Ripe malt and fruit jam aromas
Palate	Sweet malt in mouth, lingering hoppy finish with fruit notes
Comments	Dark, bitter-sweet beer like a strong mild.

Branscombe Vale Brewery

- ☞ **Great Seaside Farm, Branscombe, Seaton EX12 3DP.**
- ✆ **0297 80511.**
- ⛁ **No.**
- ⚲ **by arrangement.**
- *i* **Independent**

BRANOC
OG 1040° ABV 3.8%
Ingredients: pale malt (90%), chocolate malt (0.7%), wheat flour (5%), micro maize (4%). Challenger and Goldings whole hops.

TASTING NOTES

Nose	Rich malt aroma
Palate	Full malt in mouth with long finish with hops and citric fruit
Comments	Pale and refreshing, well-balanced beer.

OLDE STOKER
OG 1055° ABV 5.4%
Ingredients: pale malt (92%), chocolate malt (3%), wheat flour (5%). Challenger and Goldings whole hops.

TASTING NOTES

Nose	Heady bouquet of malt and hops
Palate	Mellow malt in mouth, long finish with hops and hints of chocolate
Comments	Dark, rich beer with fine chocolate malt notes.

Bridgwater Brewing Company

- ☞ **Unit 1, Lovedere Farm, Goathurst, Bridgwater TA5 2DD.**
- ✆ **0278 663996.**
- ⛁ **No.**
- ⚲ **Yes.**
- *i* **Independent**

AMBER ALE
OG 1040° ABV 3.8%
Ingredients: pale malt (94%), crystal malt (6%). Kent Goldings and Styrian Goldings whole hops.

TASTING NOTES

Nose	Light malt aroma with good hop notes
Palate	Strong Goldings hops in mouth, fruit and malt in finish
Comments	Amber-coloured ale with fine balance between malts and hops.

COPPERNOB
OG 1045˚ ABV 4.4%
Ingredients: pale malt (90%), crystal malt (10%). Fuggles and Styrian Goldings whole hops.

TASTING NOTES

Nose	Rich malt aroma
Palate	Pronounced biscuity malt in mouth, full, rounded finish with hop notes and nutty crystal malt
Comments	Ruby-coloured bitter with powerful malt presence.

SUNBEAM
OG 1052˚ ABV 5.4%
Ingredients: 100% pale malt. East Kent Goldings and Styrian Goldings whole hops.

TASTING NOTES

Nose	Light malt with hints of butterscotch
Palate	Rich malt in mouth, sweet finish becoming dry with light hop notes
Comments	Straw-coloured bitter aimed at lager drinkers. The brewery also produces Carnival Special Brew (OG 1035˚ ABV 3.5%) for the annual Bridgwater Carnival.

Butcombe Brewery Ltd
- ⌑ **Butcombe, Bristol BS18 6XQ.**
- ① **0275 472240.**
- 🏛 **No.**
- 🕯 **Trade only.**
- *i* **Independent**

BUTCOMBE BITTER
OG 1039˚ ABV 4.1%
Ingredients: 100% pale and crystal malts. Northdown and Yeoman hops, German Northern Brewer. 35 units of bitterness.

TASTING NOTES

Nose	Delicate and tempting floral hops aroma
Palate	Refreshing malt and hops in mouth; dry, lingering finish with some light fruit notes
Comments	Subtle, beautifully-crafted bitter.

Cotleigh Brewery
- ⌑ **Ford Road, Wiveliscombe TA4 2RE.**
- ① **0984 24086.**
- 🏛 **No.**
- 🕯 **No.**
- *i* **Independent**

HARRIER SPA
OG 1036˚ ABV 3.6%
Ingredients: pale malt, crystal malt, chocolate malt. English whole hops.

TASTING NOTES

Nose	Delicate mellow aromas of hops with honey notes
Palate	Refreshing malt and hops in mouth, with lingering bitter-sweet finish
Comments	Fine golden bitter with pronounced floral hops character.

TAWNY BITTER
OG 1040˚ ABV 3.8%
Ingredients: pale malt, crystal malt, chocolate malt. English whole hops.

TASTING NOTES

Nose	Rich malt aroma with hop notes
Palate	Smooth and rich malt and hops in mouth, rounded finish with hop bitterness and fruit and chocolate notes
Comments	Ripe, beautifully balanced coppery ale.

OLD BUZZARD
OG 1048° ABV 4.8%
Ingredients: pale malt, crystal malt, chocolate malt. English whole hops.

TASTING NOTES

Nose	Roast chestnut and coffee aromas
Palate	Rich chewy malt in mouth, deep finish with hops and hints of bitter chocolate
Comments	Dark ruby coloured strong beer.

MONMOUTH REBELLION
OG 1050° ABV 5%
Ingredients: pale malt, chocolate malt. East Kent Goldings whole hops.

TASTING NOTES

Nose	Rich resiny Goldings aromas with chocolate notes
Palate	Full malt and hops in mouth, long dry finish with hops and dark chocolate character
Comments	Complex and rounded strong pale ale.

━━━━━━━━━

Courage Ltd
⌨ **Bath Street Brewery, Counterslip, Bristol BS1 6EX.**
① **0272 297222.**
🏛 **No.**
🕏 **No.**
i **Subsidiary of Foster's/Courage group**

BITTER ALE
OG 1031° ABV 3.2%
Ingredients: Halcyon and Pipkin white malts, crystal malt, black coloured malt, brewing sugar. 23 units of colour. Hallertau, Styrian and Target hop pellets, dry hopped with hop oil. 24 units of bitterness.

TASTING NOTES

Nose	Delicate dry hop aroma with malt and fruit notes
Palate	Light malt in mouth, refreshing light hop finish
Comments	Quenching 'boy's bitter' with pleasing hop notes.

COURAGE CASK BEST BITTER
OG 1039° ABV 4%

Ingredients: Halcyon and Pipkin white malts, crystal malt, black coloured malt, brewing sugar. 25 units of colour. Hallertau, Styrian and Target hop pellets, dry hopped with hop oil. 30 units of bitterness.

TASTING NOTES

Nose	Pronounced malt and fruit aromas with light hop notes
Palate	Malt and toffee notes in mouth, dry finish with orange fruit and some hop notes
Comments	Ruby-coloured malty and fruity ale.

DIRECTORS CASK BITTER
OG 1046° ABV 4.8%

Ingredients: Halcyon and Pipkin white malts, crystal malt, black coloured malt, brewing sugar. 28 units of colour. Hallertau, Styrian and Target hop pellets, dry hopped with hop oil. 35 units of bitterness.

TASTING NOTES

Nose	Rich malt and orange fruit aroma with dry hop notes
Palate	Full orange fruit and malt in mouth, deep bitter-sweet finish with fruit and hop notes
Comments	Rounded, full-drinking and complex strong ale. The three Bristol beers are produced by high gravity brewing, with one basic brew watered down as required.

Exe Valley Brewery

- ▭ **Land Farm. Silverton, nr Exeter EX5 4HF.**
- ☎ **0392 860406.**
- ⛪ **No.**
- ⚐ **by arrangement.**
- *i* **Independent**

EXE VALLEY BITTER
OG 1039˚ ABV 4%
Ingredients: pale malt (95%), crystal malt (5%). Fuggles and Goldings whole hops.

TASTING NOTES

Nose	Powerful hops aroma with roasted notes
Palate	Rich mouth-feel of malt and crystal malt nut, long bitter finish with pleasing nut chaacter.
Comments	Pale amber beer based on old West Country recipe. A dry hopped version is sold as Dob's Best Bitter (ABV 4.1%).

DEVON GLORY
OG 1047˚ ABV 4.8%
Ingredients: pale malt (95%), crystal malt (5%). Fuggles and Goldings whole hops.

TASTING NOTES

Nose	Rich aromas of malt, nuts and hops
Palate	Great depth in mouth of sweet malt and crystal; long rounded finish with hops, fruit and nut notes
Comments	Rich amber strong ale; dry hopped version is sold as Exeter Old Bitter (ABV 4.9%).

Exmoor Ales Ltd

- ▭ **Golden Hill Brewery, Wiveliscombe TA4 2NY.**
- ☎ **0984 23798.**
- ⛪ **No.**
- ⚐ **Yes.**
- *i* **Independent**

EXMOOR ALE
OG 1039˚ ABV 3.8%

Ingredients: pale malt, crystal malt. 30 units of colour. Challenger, Fuggles and Goldings whole hops. 40 units of bitterness.

TASTING NOTES

Nose	Rich malt aroma with fine hop notes
Palate	Ripe malt in mouth, refreshing finish with light hops and fruit notes
Comments	Fine, award-winning session bitter.

EXMOOR GOLD
OG 1045˚ ABV 4.5%

Ingredients: 100% pale malt. 10 units of colour. Challenger, Fuggles and Goldings whole hops. 40 units of bitterness.

TASTING NOTES

Nose	Stunning hop resin aroma with delicate butterscotch notes
Palate	Dry, quenching balance of malt and hops, long finish with bitter-sweet notes and light fruit
Comments	Superb golden ale, almost a hybrid with a lager butterscotch aroma and palate and the finish of a strong ale. Winner of more than 25 awards.

EXMOOR STAG
OG 1050˚ ABV 5.2%

Ingredients: 100% pale malt and crystal malt. 35 units of colour. Challenger, Fuggles and Goldings whole hops. 35 units of bitterness.

TASTING NOTES

Nose	Rich hop flowers aroma with malt overtones
Palate	Full malt and fruit in mouth, long bitter-sweet finish with hop bitterness and some fruit
Comments	Ripe and complex copper-coloured strong ale.

EXMOOR BEAST
OG 1066˚ ABV 6.6%
Ingredients: pale malt, crystal malt, chocolate malt. 120 units of colour. Challenger, Fuggles and Goldings whole hops. 40 units of bitterness.

TASTING NOTES

Nose	Complex chocolate malt and hop flowers aromas
Palate	Burnt malt in mouth, smooth and bitter finish
Comments	Dark, strong porter, brewed from October to Easter.

Furgusons Plympton Brewery
- ▣ **Valley Road, Plympton, Plymouth PL7 3LQ.**
- ✆ **0752 330171.**
- 🏛 **No.**
- ⋔ **Yes.**
- *i* **Subsidiary of Carlsberg-Tetley.**

DARTMOOR BEST BITTER
OG 1038˚ ABV 3.7%
Ingredients: Pipkin pale malt (86%), crystal malt (14%). Fuggles and Progress whole hops for bitterness, Goldings for aroma. 30 units of bitterness.

TASTING NOTES

Nose	Light hops, cobnuts and malt aromas
Palate	Malt in the mouth, dry finish with hints of toffee
Comments	Pleasant amber-coloured ale.

DARTMOOR STRONG
OG 1044˚ ABV 4.5%
Ingredients: Pipkin pale malt (93%), crystal malt (7%). Fuggles and Progress whole hops for bitterness, Goldings for aroma. 32 units of bitterness.

TASTING NOTES

Nose	Rich Goldings aroma, fruit notes developing
Palate	Full malt in mouth, dry bitter-sweet finish with slight citric notes

Comments	Golden brew with good balance of flavours.

COCKLEROASTER
OG 1060˚ ABV 5.8%
Ingredients: 100% Pipkin pale malt. 15-18 units of colour. Fuggles and Goldings whole hops. 30 units of bitterness.

TASTING NOTES

Nose	Hops, malt and yeast esters
Palate	Ripe malt and fruit in mouth, big finish with hops and fruit
Comments	Pale but powerful and fruity strong ale.

Hardington Brewery

⌨ **Albany Buildings, Dean Lane, Bedminster, Bristol BS3 1BT.**
℠ **0272 636194.**
🏛 **No.**
⚲ **No.**
i **Independent**

TRADITIONAL BITTER
OG 1037˚ ABV 3.7%
Ingredients: not revealed.

TASTING NOTES

Nose	Floral hops and citric fruit aromas
Palate	Malt, hops and light fruit in mouth, long, dry bitter finish
Comments	Amber beer with clean and refreshing flavours.

BEST BITTER
OG 1042˚ ABV 4.2%
Ingredients: not revealed.

TASTING NOTES

Nose	Pronounced floral hops aroma
Palate	Malt dominates the mouth with some citric fruit, bitter-sweet finish

Comments	Amber beer with good malt and hops balance.

MOONSHINE
OG 1048° ABV 5%
Ingredients: not revealed.

TASTING NOTES

Nose	Grain and lemon fruit aromas
Palate	Sweet malt in mouth with citric fruit, dry finish with hints of fruit and spices
Comments	Intriguing and complex beer with suggestion of wheat in recipe.

JUBILEE
OG 1050° ABV 5%
Ingredients: not revealed.

TASTING NOTES

Nose	Hops and spices aromas
Palate	Rich dark malt in mouth, dark sultana fruit in finish
Comments	Fruity brown beer.

OLD LUCIFER
OG 1054° ABV 6%
Ingredients: not revealed.

TASTING NOTES

Nose	Rich malt and hops aromas
Palate	Ripe dark malt in mouth with fruit notes, finish becomes dry with good malt and hops balance
Comments	Full-bodied, fruity, well-attenuated brown beer.

OLD ALE
OG 1065° ABV 6.5%
Ingredients: not revealed.

TASTING NOTES

Nose	Roasted malt aroma with fruit and hops developing
Palate	Dark malt, dried fruit and hops in mouth, powerful fruity finish with strong hints of cherries

Comments   Copper-coloured ale of enormous vinous
                     complexity.

Mill

- ⌑ **Unit 18c, Bradley Lane, Newton Abbot TQ12 1LZ.**
- ① **0626 63322.**
- 🏛 **No.**
- ☆ **No.**
- *i* **Independent**

JANNERS ALE
OG 1038˚ ABV 3.8%
Ingredients: pale malt, crystal malt, pale chocolate malt.
Challenger and Fuggles whole hops.

TASTING NOTES
Nose   Rich floral hops aroma
Palate   Full malt and chocolate notes in mouth,
                  deep bitter finish with powerful hop char-
                  acter
Comments   Uncompromisingly dry and bitter beer.

JANNERS OLD ORIGINAL
OG 1045˚ ABV 4.4%
Ingredients: pale malt and crystal malt. Challenger whole
hops.

TASTING NOTES
Nose   Pronounced hops aroma with ripe fruit
                  developing
Palate   Mouth-filling malt and hops; deep finish
                  with hops and fruit notes
Comments   Deceptively pale strong beer. Gravity
                  increased to 1050˚ at Xmas and sold as
                  Janners Christmas Ale. The company
                  also brews an occasional Old Dark (ABV
                  3.9%) which includes black malt in the
                  recipe.

Oakhill

- **Old Brewery, High Street, Oakhill, Bath BA3 5AS.**
- **0749 840134.**
- **No.**
- **No.**
- **Independent**

OAKHILL BITTER
OG 1039˚ ABV 3.8%
Ingredients: Triumph pale malt (93.5%), crystal malt (6.5%). Bramling Cross, Challenger, Fuggles and Goldings whole and pellet hops.

TASTING NOTES

Nose	Rich hops and malt aromas
Palate	Malt and crystal malt nuttiness in mouth, dry quenching finish with good hops and dark malt balance
Comments	Refreshing pale beer with good grain and hops balance.

BLACK MAGIC STOUT
OG 1044˚ ABV 4%
Ingredients: Triumph pale malt (80%), chocolate malt (10%), roasted barley (10%). Bramling Cross, Challenger, Fuggles and Goldings whole and pellet hops.

TASTING NOTES

Nose	Powerful aromas of bitter coffee and hops
Palate	Dark malt and toasted grain in mouth, sweet finish becoming bitter with hops and coffee notes
Comments	Superb stout packed with complex malt and hops character.

YEOMAN STRONG 1767 ALE
OG 1049˚ ABV 4.8%
Ingredients: Triumph pale malt (91.5%), crystal malt (8.5%). Bramling Cross, Challenger, Fuggles and Goldings whole and pellet hops.

TASTING NOTES

Nose	Ripe malt aroma with good hop notes
Palate	Full malt in mouth with deep bitter-sweet finish and vinous notes
Comments	Rounded and rich copper-coloured fruity strong ale.

Otter Brewery
✉ **Mathayes, Luppitt, Honiton EX14 0SA.**
① **0404 891285.**
🏛 **Yes.**
🏃 **Yes.**
i **Independent**

OTTER BITTER
OG 1036˚ ABV 3.6%
Ingredients: Halcyon and Maris Otter pale malts (92%), crystal malt (8%). Kent Challenger whole hops.

TASTING NOTES

Nose	Tempting hops and malt aromas
Palate	Refreshing balance of malt and hops, full finish with good hops character
Comments	Finely balanced session bitter with great malt and hops appeal.

OTTER ALE
OG 1044˚ ABV 4.4%
Ingredients: Halcyon and Maris Otter pale malts (92%), crystal malt (8%). Kent Challenger whole hops.

TASTING NOTES

Nose	Rich malt aromas with fruit and hop notes
Palate	Full malt and some fruit in mouth, deep nutty finish with good hop bitterness
Comments	Rounded copper-coloured ale with fine crystal malt character.

OTTER HEAD
OG 1055˚ ABV 5.6%
Ingredients: Halcyon and Maris Otter pale malts (47% each), crystal malt (6%). Kent Challenger whole hops.

TASTING NOTES

Nose	Rich malt aroma with hops and fruit notes
Palate	Ripe malt in mouth with dark fruit, full and long finish with hops and vinous fruit
Comments	Amber ale with complex hops and fruit character.

Redruth Brewery

⌨ **Foundry Row, Redruth TR10 8LA.**
① **0209 212244.**
🏛 **No.**
👷 **by arrangement.**
i **Independent**

CORNISH ORIGINAL
OG 1037˙ ABV 3.4%

Ingredients: pale malt and crystal malt (85%), invert sugar. Fuggles, Goldings and Progress pellet hops; dry hopped. 24 units of bitterness.

TASTING NOTES

Nose	Malt and hops aroma with some fruit developing
Palate	Malt dominates mouth with hop notes, dry finish with fruit notes and slight astringency
Comments	Rounded malt-accented ale. The former Cornish Steam Brewery is now reduced to one cask ale brewed under licence for Whitbread. The former owners, Devenish, sold the brewery to senior management when it quit brewing. Redruth concentrates on packaged beers for supermarkets.

Ross Brewing Company

⌨ **The Bristol Brewhouse, 117-119 Stokes Croft, Bristol BS1 3RW.**
① **0272 420306.**
🏛 **No.**
👷 **by arrangement.**
i **Independent**

CLIFTON DARK ALE
OG 1045° ABV 4%
Ingredients: organic pale malt
(90%), black malt (5%), crystal malt
(5%). Goldings whole hops.

TASTING NOTES
Nose	Strong malt aroma
Palate	Rounded toffee and malt flavours with bitter-sweet finish
Comments	Dark, malt-accented beer.

ROSS'S BEST BITTER (BOTTLED AS HARTCLIFFE BITTER)
OG 1045° ABV 4%
Ingredients: organic pale malt (95%), crystal malt (5%).
Goldings whole hops.

TASTING NOTES
Nose	Floral Goldings hops aroma with malt notes
Palate	Hops dominate the mouth, with long bitter finish with some fruit notes
Comments	Mid-brown beer with fine Goldings hop character.

SAXON STRONG ALE
OG 1055° ABV 5.5%
Ingredients: organic pale malt (100%) with apple juice
and honey. Goldings whole hops.

TASTING NOTES
Nose	Strong malt aroma
Palate	Malt in the mouth, apple and honey notes in finish
Comments	Pale beer with intriguing character of malt, hops and fruit.

ROSS'S MEDIEVAL PORTER
OG 1055° ABV 5.5%
Ingredients: organic pale malt (90%), black malt (10%)
plus ginger, liquorice and coriander. Goldings whole
hops.

TASTING NOTES
Nose	Powerful aromas of malt and ginger
Palate	Rich malt in mouth, spicy finish with complex flavours of malt, hops and herbs

Comments	Dark porter using ingredients once in widespread use in the hey-day of the beer style. Ross's beers are available in bottle-conditioned form.

Royal Clarence

Royal Clarence Hotel, The Esplanade, Burnham-on-Sea TA8 1BQ.
0278 783138.
Yes (hotel bar).
Yes.
Independent

CLARENCE PRIDE
OG 1036° ABV 3.7%
Ingredients: pale malt (89%), crystal malt (10%), black malt (1%). Fuggles and Goldings whole hops.

TASTING NOTES

Nose	Malt and Goldings hops aromas with dark, roasted malt notes
Palate	Good malt and hops balance in mouth, bitter-sweet finish with malt, hops and coffee notes
Comments	Full-flavoured beer with dark malt character.

CLARENCE REGENT
OG 1050° ABV 5.2%
Ingredients: pale malt (87%), crystal malt (10%), black malt (3%). Fuggles and Goldings whole hops.

TASTING NOTES

Nose	Full, ripe malt, hops, nuts and fruit
Palate	Rounded malt and fruit in mouth, deep finish with hops, fruit and nuts
Comments	Rich and flavoursome beer full of dark malt pleasures.

St Austell Brewery Co Ltd

☒ **63 Trevarthian Road, St Austell PL25 4BY.**
℧ **0726 74444.**
🏛 **Yes.**
🜊 **Yes.**
i **Independent**

BOSUN'S BITTER
OG 1034° ABV 3.5%
Ingredients: pale ale malt, crystal malt, torrefied wheat.
25 units of colour. Fuggles and Goldings whole hops.

TASTING NOTES

Nose	Delicate hops aroma
Palate	Light balance of malt and hops with short finish
Comments	Easy-drinking light bitter.

XXXX MILD
OG 1037° ABV 3.6%
Ingredients: pale ale malt, crystal malt, caramel for colour, torrefied wheat. 95 units of colour. Fuggles and Goldings whole hops.

TASTING NOTES

Nose	Pronounced malt and roast malt aromas
Palate	Sweet malt in mouth, dry and nutty finish
Comments	Rare dark mild, almost stout-like in character.

TINNERS BITTER
OG 1038° ABV 3.8%
Ingredients: pale ale malt, crystal malt, torrefied wheat. 28 units of colour. Fuggles and Goldings whole and pellet hops. Dry hopped.

TASTING NOTES

Nose	Light hops and buttercups aromas
Palate	Malt, hops and light fruit in mouth, lingering hop finish
Comments	Mellow, easy-drinking bitter.

HSD OR HICKS SPECIAL
OG 1050˚ ABV 5%

Ingredients: pale ale malt, crystal malt, torrefied wheat. 33 units of colour. Fuggles and Goldings whole and pellet hops. Dry hopped.

TASTING NOTES

Nose	Rich aromas of hop resins and pear drops fruit
Palate	Warm biscuity flavour in mouth, long bitter-sweet finish with ripe fruit notes
Comments	Ripe, complex strong ale known locally as 'High Speed Diesel'.

Smiles Brewing Company Ltd
☎ **Colston Yard, Colston Street, Bristol BS1 5BD.**
① **0272 297350.**
🏛 **Yes.**
👤 **by arrangement.**
i **Independent**

BREWERY BITTER
OG 1037˚ ABV 3.7%

Ingredients: pale and amber malts. East Kent Goldings whole hops.

TASTING NOTES

Nose	Fresh hops, malt and light fruit
Palate	Dry malt in mouth, long finish with hops, fruit and nuts
Comments	Golden quaffing bitter.

BEST BITTER
OG 1041˚ ABV 4.1%

Ingredients: pale and crystal malts. East Kent Goldings whole hops.

TASTING NOTES

Nose	Rich malt bouquet with delicate Goldings hops
Palate	Ripe malt in mouth, long delicately dry finish with fruit notes, hops and nuts
Comments	Red-brown complex bitter.

BRISTOL STOUT
OG 1046° ABV 4.7%
Ingredients: pale malt, wheat malt, roasted barley. East Kent Goldings whole hops.

TASTING NOTES

Nose	Roasted grain and hops aromas
Palate	Creamy malt in mouth, long bitter-sweet finish with roast malt and hop notes
Comments	Dark and dry beer with fine dark grain and hop character. Available January to April.

Summerskills Brewery

Unit 15, Pomphlett Farm Industrial Estate, Broxton Drive, Billacombe, Plymouth PL9 7BG.
① **0752 481283.**
🏛 **No.**
㕙 **by arrangement.**
i **Independent**

SUMMERSKILLS BEST BITTER
OG 1042° ABV 4.3%
Ingredients: Tucker's pale malt (92%), crystal malt (8%). Styrian and Worcester Goldings whole hops.

TASTING NOTES

Nose	Rich malt, nuts and hops with hint of honey
Palate	Full malt in mouth, long finish with good hop bitterness
Comments	Pale bitter with fine crystal malt and hops character.

WHISTLE BELLY VENGEANCE
OG 1046° ABV 4.7%
Ingredients: Tucker's pale malt (91%), crystal malt (8%), black malt (1%). Styrian and Worcester Goldings whole hops.

TASTING NOTES

Nose	Rich dark malt and hops aromas
Palate	Malt dominates mouth with hops, dark malt and liquorice notes

Comments   Dark ruby beer full of complex dark malt character.

NINJA BEER
OG 1049˚ ABV 5%
Ingredients: Tucker's pale malt (95%), crystal malt (5%). Styrian and Worcester Goldings whole hops.

TASTING NOTES

Nose   Light malt and hops aromas
Palate   Soft malt in mouth, hops and hint of toffee in finish
Comments   Dark gold beer with good balance of malt and hops.

Tally Ho

🖃 **Tally Ho Country Inn and Brewery, 14 Market Street, Hatherleigh EX20 3TN.**
🕐 **0837 810306.**
🏛 **Yes (hotel).**
🕴 **Yes.**
i **Independent**

POTBOILER'S BREW
OG 1036˚ ABV 3.5%
Ingredients: pale malt, crystal malt, chocolate malt. Goldings whole hops.

TASTING NOTES

Nose   Rich malt aroma with Goldings notes
Palate   Hints of chocolate and nuts in mouth, dry finish with good hops character
Comments   Straw-coloured beer with good malt and hop notes.

NUTTERS
OG 1048˚ ABV 4.6%
Ingredients: pale malt, crystal malt, chocolate malt, black malt. Goldings whole hops.

TASTING NOTES

Nose   Massive malt aroma with dark grain and hops

Palate	Chocolate and bitter coffee in mouth, deep malty finish with hops and dark malt
Comments	Malty beer with complex dark grain and hops character.

TARKA TIPPLE
(cask and bottle conditioned)
OG 1048° ABV 4.6%
Ingredients: pale malt, crystal malt, chocolate malt. Goldings and Styrian whole hops.

TASTING NOTES

Nose	Mellow malt and powerful hops aromas
Palate	Rich malt and spritzy hops in mouth, long dry finish with hops and hint of chocolate
Comments	Red-brown ale with fine hops character.

THURGIA
(bottle conditioned)
OG 1056° ABV 5.7%
Ingredients: pale malt, crystal malt, black malt. Goldings and Styrian whole hops.

TASTING NOTES

Nose	Fruity aromas with good hops balance
Palate	Dark malt and dry fruit in mouth, long bitter finish with hops and sultana fruit
Comments	Dark brown, complex beer. The 3.5 barrels capacity brewhouse is run by hotelier Gianni Scoz, an Italian with a penchant for English cask ale. Thurgia is Ancient Greek for 'Natural Magic'.

Thompsons

📧 **London Inn, 11 West Street, Ashburton TQ13 7BD.**
① **0364 52478.**
🏛 **Yes.**
🏃 **Yes.**
i **Independent**

BEST BITTER
OG 1040° ABV 4.2%
Ingredients: Tucker's pale malt (94%), crystal malt (6%). Whitbread Goldings Variety whole hops.

TASTING NOTES

Nose	Rich malt aromas with some fruit developing
Palate	Full malt and fruit in mouth, deep, dry bitter finish
Comments	Malty, fruity bitter.

IPA
OG 1045° ABV 4.6%
Ingredients: Tucker's pale malt (99%), black malt (1%). Whitbread Goldings Variety whole hops.

TASTING NOTES

Nose	Powerful bouquet of sweet malt and ripe fruit
Palate	Bitter-sweet malt in mouth leading to dry finish with bitter hops and tart fruit notes
Comments	Complex and distinctive copper ale.

FIGUREHEAD
OG 1050° ABV 5.3%
Ingredients: Tucker's pale malt (96%), crystal malt (3%), black malt (1%). Whitbread Goldings Variety whole hops.

TASTING NOTES

Nose	Rich vinous malt and fruit aromas
Palate	Full malt in mouth, fruit and hops in long bitter finish with dark fruit notes
Comments	Ripe and distinctive winter ale. The brewery is also planning Celebration Porter (ABV 4.2%) and Botwrights Man-o-War (ABV 5%).

Wickwar Brewing Company

⌨ **The Old Cider Mill, Station Road, Wickwar GL12 8NB.**
☎ **0454 294168.**
🏛 **No.**
🚶 **Yes (25 maximum).**
i **Independent**

BRAND OAK BITTER
OG 1039° ABV 4%
Ingredients: pale malt, crystal malt, chocolate malt. Challenger and Fuggles whole hops; late hopped in copper.

TASTING NOTES
Nose   Malt, fruit and hops aromas
Palate   Rich malt and powerful hops in mouth,
              long bitter-sweet finish with hints of nuts
              and fruit
Comments   Superb amber ale full of malt and hops
              character.

OLDE MERRYFORD ALE
OG 1049˚ ABV 5.1%
Ingredients: pale malt, chocolate
malt. Challenger and Fuggles
whole hops; late hopped in copper.

TASTING NOTES
Nose   Pronounced fruit
              and hops aromas
Palate   Bitter-sweet malt and hops in mouth,
              long finish with ripe fruit and hop bitter-
              ness; becoming dry
Comments   Tawny ale with fine balance of complex
              aromas and flavours. The brewery also
              produces an occasional Station Porter
              (ABV 6.1%) based on a Victorian recipe.

WALES

There is an affinity between the beers of south Wales and the English West Midlands. Both still produce substantial quantities of dark mild while the bitters often have a malty sweetness.

The connection is obvious: both regions were once powerhouses of industry and in Wales workers leaving pit or foundry needed copious quantities of light, quaffable and sweetish beers to replace lost energy.

Wales has suffered grievously from brewery closures and there is no beer style as such to discuss in the north of the country because of the lack of producers save for a few plucky micros. As ever, the best advice in Wales is to use your Brains!

S A Brain & Company Ltd

▣ **The Old Brewery, St Mary Street, PO Box 53, Cardiff CF1 1SP.**

① **0222 399022.**

🏛 **No.**

⚔ **strictly limited.**

i **Independent**

RED DRAGON DARK
OG 1035˚ ABV 3.5%
Ingredients: pale malt, chocolate malt, invert and glucose sugars. Fuggles and Goldings whole hops.

TASTING NOTES

Nose	Delicate hops and chocolate aromas
Palate	Malt and slight nut in mouth, light dry finish
Comments	Rich ruby mild, fine tasting and eminently quaffable.

BITTER or LIGHT
OG 1035˚ ABV 3.7%
Ingredients: pale malt, crystal malt, invert and glucose sugars. Fuggles and Goldings whole hops.

TASTING NOTES

Nose	Fragrant malt and hops bouquet
Palate	Sweet malt in mouth, dry but quenching well-hopped finish
Comments	Refreshing amber-coloured light bitter.

SA BEST BITTER
OG 1042˚ ABV 4.2%
Ingredients: pale malt, crystal malt, invert and glucose sugars. Fuggles and Goldings whole hops.

TASTING NOTES

Nose	Rich malt and hops aromas with developing fruit
Palate	Full malt in mouth, deep bitter-sweet finish with hops and fruit notes
Comments	Superb deep amber beer known to devotees as 'Skull Attack'.

Bullmastiff Brewery

⌕ **11 Bessemer Road, Grangetown, Cardiff.**
① **0222 665292.**
🏛 **No.**
🏃 **No.**
i **Independent**

BREWERY BITTER
OG 1036° ABV 3.5%
Ingredients: Maris Otter pale malt (85%), crystal malt (15%) plus sugar (5%) in copper. Worcester Goldings hop pellets.

TASTING NOTES

Nose	Tempting hop resin aroma with dark fruit notes
Palate	Pronounced cobnuts in mouth, deep dry finish with Goldings and dark sultana fruit
Comments	Tasty beer with rich crystal malt character.

BEST BITTER
OG 1040° ABV 4%
Ingredients: Maris Otter pale malt (85%), crystal malt (15%), plus sugar (5%) in copper. Worcester Goldings hop pellets.

TASTING NOTES

Nose	Delicate aromas of malt, hops and dark fruit
Palate	Bitter-sweet malt and hops in mouth, light dry finish with tart fruit and nuts
Comments	Tawny ale with rich dark fruit character from generous use of crystal malt.

EBONY DARK
OG 1040° ABV 4%
Ingredients: Pipkin pale malt (85%), crystal malt (6%), chocolate (9%) plus dark sugar (5%) in copper. Fuggles hop pellets.

TASTING NOTES

Nose	Rich aromas of hops and dark chocolate

Palate	Deep mouth-filling dark grain, dry finish packed with hops, chocolate and vanilla notes
Comments	Complex ale with dark malt character.

SON OF A BITCH
OG 1062° ABV 6.5%
Ingredients: Maris Otter pale malt (90%), crystal malt (10%) with sugar (5%) in copper. Worcester Goldings hop pellets.

TASTING NOTES

Nose	Ripe malt and Goldings hop bouquet
Palate	Winey mix of malt and fruit with deep, rounded bitter-sweet finish.
Comments	Strong and fruity ale.

Crown Buckley
⌨ **The Brewery, Gilbert Road, Llanelli SA15 3PP.**
① **0554 777004.**
🏛 **Yes.**
🍺 **trade and CAMRA groups only.**
ℹ **Subsidiary of Harp Lager Co/Guinness. A possible management buy-out was rumoured as the Almanac went to press.**

BUCKLEYS DARK MILD
OG 1034° ABV 3.4%
Ingredients: Maris Otter pale malt, black malt, torrefied wheat, invert sugar. Challenger, Fuggles and Goldings hop pellets.

TASTING NOTES

Nose	Pronounced dark malt aroma
Palate	Chewy dark malt in mouth, dry finish with light hops and chocolate notes
Comments	Tasty dark mild.

BUCKLEYS BEST BITTER
OG 1036° ABV 3.7%
Ingredients: Maris Otter pale malt, torrefied wheat, invert sugar. Challenger, Fuggles and Goldings hop pellets.

TASTING NOTES

Nose	Resiny Goldings aroma with good balance of malt
Palate	Rounded malt in mouth, full finish with hops and nuts character
Comments	Well-balanced malt and hops makes this a good-drinking session bitter.

SBB
OG 1036˚ ABV 3.7%
Ingredients: Maris Otter pale malt, torrefied wheat, invert sugar. Challenger, Fuggles and Goldings hop pellets.

TASTING NOTES

Nose	Fruity, estery aromas
Palate	Mellow malt in mouth, rich finish with hops and rich fruit notes
Comments	Tangy and distinctive ale.

REVEREND JAMES ORIGINAL BITTER
OG 1045˚ ABV 4.5%
Ingredients: Maris Otter pale malt, torrefied wheat, invert sugar. Challenger, Fuggles and Goldings hop pellets.

TASTING NOTES

Nose	Spicy hop aroma with good malt notes
Palate	Aromatic hops and full malt in mouth, long bitter-sweet finish with hop bitterness and some fruit
Comments	Fine hops and fruit character in a beer described by the head brewer as having an 'old fashioned flavour—not commonly available these days'.

Felinfoel Brewery Co Ltd

⌨ **Farmers' Row, Felinfoel, Llanelli SA14 8LB.**
☎ **0554 773357.**
🏛 **No.**
👥 **trade only.**
i **Independent**

TRADITIONAL DARK
OG 1032° ABV 3.4%
Ingredients: Pipkin pale malt (75%), crystal malt (3%), torrefied wheat (12%), No 1 invert sugar. 75 units of colour. Bramling Cross, Challenger and Whitbread Goldings Variety whole hops. 28 units of bitterness.

TASTING NOTES

Nose	Gentle caramel and toffee aromas
Palate	Smooth malt in mouth, full finish with good nutty notes
Comments	Deep reddish-brown ale with pleasing dark malt character

BITTER ALE
OG 1032° ABV 3.4%
Ingredients: Pipkin pale malt (75%), crystal malt (3%), torrefied wheat (12%), No 1 invert sugar (10%). 20 units of colour. Bramling Cross, Challenger and Whitbread Goldings Vareity whole hops. 28 units of bitterness.

TASTING NOTES

Nose	Delicate hops aroma
Palate	Rich malt and hops in mouth, bitter-sweet finish with quenching light hops and fruit
Comments	Honey-coloured beer, well-rounded for its strength.

DOUBLE DRAGON
OG 1048° ABV 5%
Ingredients: Pipkin pale malt (75%), crystal malt (3%), torrefied wheat (12%), No 1 invert sugar (10%). 30 units of colour. Bramling Cross, Challenger and Whitbread Goldings Variety whole hops. 25 units of bitterness.

TASTING NOTES

Nose	Distinctive ripe fruit with delicate hop notes
Palate	Full malt and vinous fruit in mouth; deep, complex finish with hops, fruit and faint toffee notes
Comments	Beautifully crafted fruity golden ale.

Plassey Brewery

- Eyton, Wrexham LL13 0SP.
- 0978 780922.
- **Yes.**
- **Yes.**
- *i* **Independent**

BITTER
OG 1040˚ ABV 4%
Ingredients: pale malt (95%), crystal malt (5%). Fuggles and German Hallertau and Tettnang whole and pellet hops; Tettnang for aroma. 32 units of bitterness.

TASTING NOTES

Nose	Light hops aroma
Palate	Rounded malt in mouth with hop notes, long dry finish with good hops character
Comments	Pale and refreshing hoppy beer.

CWRW TUDNO
OG 1047˚ ABV 5%
Ingredients: pale malt (97%), crystal malt (2%), chocolate malt (1%). Hallertau, Northern Brewer and Tettnang whole and pellet hops; Tettnang for aroma. 35 units of bitterness.

TASTING NOTES

Nose	Rich, spicy hops aroma with malt notes
Palate	Full malt in mouth, long, bitter finish with powerful hop character plus fruit and hint of chocolate
Comments	Rich golden beer with superb hop aroma and flavour. Plassey also brews Dragon's Breath (OG 1060˚), a winter warmer.

Snowdonia Brewing Company

⌑ **Snowdonia Brewery, The Bryn Arms, Gellilydan, nr Blaenau Ffestiniog LL41 4EH.**
① **0766 85379.**
🏛 **Yes (in pub).**
🏃 **Yes.**
i **Independent**

MEL Y MOELWYN
OG 1037˚ ABV 3.7%
Ingredients: Maris Otter pale malt, crystal malt, touch of black malt. Fuggles and Goldings whole hops.

TASTING NOTES
Nose	Delicate fruit and honey aroma with touch of hops
Palate	Hops in the mouth, fruity and dry bitter finish
Comments	Bitter-sweet, well-balanced bitter. The name means 'Honey of the Moelwyn Mountains'.

CHOIR PORTER
OG 1045˚ ABV 4.5%
Ingredients: Maris Otter pale malt, crystal malt, black malt. Fuggles whole hops.

TASTING NOTES
Nose	Malt aroma with hint of chocolate
Palate	Light hops and dark malt in mouth, smooth and bitter-sweet finish with good malt character
Comments	Rich, dark and tuneful porter

SNOWDON
OG 1050˚ ABV 5%
Ingredients: Maris Otter pale malt, crystal malt. Goldings whole hops added twice during boil.

TASTING NOTES
Nose	Malt, hops and fruit bouquet
Palate	Rich malt and hops in mouth, long dry finish with hops and fruit notes

Comments	Red-brown ale with complex fruity palate. The beers are brewed in the Snowdonia National Park using local spring water.

Welsh Brewers Ltd

- 🖃 **Crawshay Street, Cardiff CF1 1TR.**
- ① **0222 233071.**
- 🏛 **Yes.**
- 🕴 **by arrangement.**
- *i* **Subsidiary of Bass**

WORTHINGTON DARK
OG 1032.5˚ ABV 3.3%
Ingredients: pale malt (83%), copper sugars, sucrose as priming sugar. 70 units of colour. Challenger and Northdown hop pellets. 20 units of bitterness.

TASTING NOTES

Nose	Rich malt aroma
Palate	Sweet malt in mouth, short bitter-sweet finish
Comments	Malty, creamy mild.

HANCOCK'S HB
OG 1036.5˚ ABV 3.8%
Ingredients: Halcyon and Pipkin pale malt (84%), high maltose syrup. 22 units of colour. Challenger and Northdown hop pellets. 22 units of bitterness.

TASTING NOTES

Nose	Light malt and hops aroma
Palate	Sweet malt in mouth, light dry finish
Comments	Pleasant, undemanding beer.

WORTHINGTON BEST BITTER
OG 1036.5˚ ABV 3.8%
Ingredients: pale malt (84%), copper sugars, sucrose as priming sugar. 22 units of colour. Challenger and Northdown hop pellets. 22 units of bitterness.

TASTING NOTES

Nose	Malt and fruit aromas with light hop notes
Palate	Malt dominates the mouth; short bitter-sweet finish

Comments   Pale, underhopped beer now sold nationally.

LATE ENTRY

Bragdy Dyffryn Clwyd Brewery
Old Butter Market, Denbigh, Clwyd
Due to begin brewing in 1993 with two bitters OG 1038° and 1042°.

NORTH-WEST ENGLAND

North-west England, a region encompassing great cities and tranquil countryside, has breweries in profusion, though here as in the rest of Britain takeover attrition has whittled down the numbers.

Boddingtons sold its brewery to Whitbread in order to concentrate on pub retailing, a course followed by Greenall Whitley, whose beers are produced by the Tetley-Walker plant in Warrington.

Meanwhile Scottish & Newcastle closed its Matthew Brown brewery in Blackburn and Robinsons of Stockport surprised no-one by axeing its Hartley subsidiary in Ulverston.

In spite of these dispiriting activities and the absurdity of 'Boddingtons Bitter' brewed by Whitbread on sale in Boddingtons pubs under separate ownership, there is still a good choice in the North-west. Beers range from the lagerish pale gold of Whitbread's Boddingtons Bitter to darker brews, including several surviving milds. There are some malty ales but the tendency is towards dry, fruity and even tart bitters.

Manchester is a remarkable city for choice, with a number of independent brewers surviving the clutches of the giants and producing beers of great quality which are remarkable value for money.

Boddingtons

✉ **Whitbread Beer Company, Boddingtons Brewery, PO Box 23, Strangeways, Manchester M60 3WB.**
✆ **061-828 2000.**
🏛 **Yes.**
🕴 **Yes.**
i **Subsidiary of Whitbread PLC**

BODDINGTONS MILD
OG 1032˚ ABV 3%
Ingredients: pale ale malt (83%), crystal malt (10%), chocolate malt (3%), cane sugar (4%), trace of caramel. 80 units of colour. Fuggles and Goldings whole hops. 24 units of bitterness.

TASTING NOTES

Nose	Light fruit and dark malt aromas
Palate	Chewy malt in mouth, light finish with dark chocolate notes
Comments	Well-balanced tawny ale with good malt character.

OLDHAM MILD
OG 1032˚ ABV 3%
Ingredients: pale ale malt (83%), crystal malt (10%), chocolate malt (3%), cane sugar (4%), trace of caramel. 80 units of colour. Fuggles and Goldings whole hops. 24 units of bitterness.

TASTING NOTES

Nose	Light roasted malt aroma
Palate	Malt and chocolate in mouth, light hops and nuts finish
Comments	Dark mild hard to distinguish from its Boddingtons stablemate.

BODDINGTONS BITTER
OG 1035˚ ABV 3.8%
Ingredients: pale ale malt (95%), patent malt (2%), cane sugar (3%), primed with cane sugar. 14 units of colour. Fuggles, Goldings, Whitbread Goldings Variety whole hops.

TASTING NOTES

Nose	Complex floral hops, lemon and spices aromas
Palate	Flinty dryness in mouth, long, hard finish with hop bitterness and tart fruit
Comments	Remarkable well-attenuated light gold bitter with complex hops and citric fruit character.

OLDHAM BEST BITTER
OG 1038˚ ABV 3.8%
Ingredients: pale ale malt (86%), crystal malt (6%) cane sugar (8%), primed with cane sugar. 23 units of colour. Fuggles and Goldings whole hops, late addition of Goldings in copper. 32 units of bitterness.

TASTING NOTES

Nose	Heady bouquet of malt and hops with fruit notes developing
Palate	Big, rounded malt and fruit in mouth, deep bitter-sweet finish with vinous fruit and cobnuts
Comments	Superb copper-coloured ale that deserves to break out from the shadow of Boddingtons Bitter.

Burtonwood Brewery PLC
- **Burtonwood Village, nr Warrington WA5 4PJ.**
- **0925225131.**
- **Yes.**
- **by arrangement.**
- **Independent**

BURTONWOOD MILD
OG 1032˚ ABV 3%
Ingredients: Maris Otter and Pipkin pale malts (50% each), crystal malt (8%), black malt (8%), torrefied wheat (7%), liquid sugar. 135 units of colour. Brewers Gold, Chal-

lenger, Fuggles, Northern Brewer and Whitbread Goldings Variety English and German hop pellets. Dry hopped. 22 units of bitterness.

TASTING NOTES

Nose	Rich aroma of toasted grain with hop notes developing
Palate	Rich nutty malt in mouth, good hop finish with hint of chocolate
Comments	Characterful dark mild.

BURTONWOOD BITTER
OG 1036˚ ABV 3.7%

Ingredients: Maris Otter and Pipkin pale malts (50% each), crystal malt (7%), torrefied wheat (7%), liquid sugar (9%). 24 units of colour. Brewers Gold, Challenger, Fuggles, Northern Brewer, Whitbread Goldings Variety hop pellets. Dry hopped. 22 units of bitterness.

TASTING NOTES

Nose	Fine aromatic bouquet of hop resins and nutty malt
Palate	Mellow malt in mouth with fruit notes, long finish full of hops and light fruit character
Comments	Delectable, superbly balanced fruity bitter.

JAMES FORSHAW'S BITTER
OG 1038.9˚ ABV 4%

Ingredients: Maris Otter and Pipkin pale malts (50% each), crystal malt (11%), torrefied wheat (8%), liquid sugar. 36 units of colour. Brewers Gold, Challenger, Fuggles, Northern Brewer, Whitbread Goldings Variety hop pellets. Dry hopped. 35 units of bitterness.

TASTING NOTES

Nose	Ripe malt and hops aromas
Palate	Bitter-sweet malt and hops in mouth, leading to long, dry finish with good hops and light fruit notes
Comments	Fruity and hoppy tawny ale.

Robert Cain & Co Ltd

⌑ **Stanhope Street, Liverpool L8 5XJ.**
① **051-709 8734.**
🏛 **Yes.**
🚶 **Yes.**
ℹ **Independent owned by Faxe Jyske of Denmark**

CAINS DARK MILD
OG 1033˚ ABV 3.2%
Ingredients: blend of spring and winter barley malts, small percentage of roasted malt, chocolate malt and torrefied wheat. 130-150 units of colour. Target hop pellets with some American, Australian and New Zealand varieties.

TASTING NOTES

Nose	Hops, nuts, malt and roasted grain aromas
Palate	Full malt in mouth; bitter-sweet finish with hints of chocolate and nuts
Comments	Black mild with subtle and delectable dark malt character.

CAINS BITTER
OG 1038˚ ABV not stated
Ingredients: Maris Otter pale malt, percentage of sugar and chocolate malt, roasted malt. English varieties of hops; late hopped with Goldings, dry hopped in cask with Goldings.

TASTING NOTES

Nose	Rich Goldings hop resin aroma with malt notes
Palate	Bitter-sweet in mouth with roast notes, long finish with quenching hop bitterness and light fruit notes
Comments	Superb, beautifully-balanced aromatic bitter

CAINS FORMIDABLE ALE
OG 1048˚ ABV 5.1%
Ingredients: Maris Otter pale malt, small percentage of sugar and torrefied wheat. 14-16 units of colour. English Target hops with some American, Australian and New Zealand varieties, with Northdown aroma hops.

TASTING NOTES

Nose	Delicate flowery, aromatic hops aroma
Palate	Hops dominate the mouth, bitter-sweet finish with some fruit notes
Comments	Pale, distinctive beer with complex fruit character.

Coach House Brewing Co Ltd

⌨ **Wharf Street, Howley, Warrington WA1 2DQ.**
① **0925 232800.**
🏛 **No.**
🕴 **Yes.**
i **Independent**

COACHMAN'S BEST BITTER
OG 1037˚ ABV 3.7%

Ingredients: Maris Otter pale malt (86%), crystal malt (14%). 30 units of colour. Fuggles and Goldings whole hops. Dry hopped. 28 units of bitterness.

TASTING NOTES

Nose	Rich hops and fruit aromas
Palate	Malt and crystal nut dominate the mouth, bitter, fruity finish with good hop notes
Comments	Pale brown distinctive beer with hops and crystal malt character.

GUNPOWDER STRONG MILD
OG 1039˚ ABV 3.8%

Ingredients: Maris Otter pale malt (94%), crystal malt (3%), chocolate (3%). 200 units of colour. Fuggles and Goldings whole hops. 28 units of bitterness.

TASTING NOTES

Nose	Strong dark roasted malt aroma
Palate	Full roasted malt in mouth, bitter-sweet finish becoming dry with hops and chocolate notes
Comments	Remarkable mild with great hops and dark malt character.

INNKEEPERS SPECIAL RESERVE
OG 1045˚ ABV 4.5%

Ingredients: Maris Otter pale malt (84%), crystal malt (16%). 42 units of colour. Fuggles and Goldings whole hops. Dry hopped. 32 units of bitterness.

TASTING NOTES

Nose	Stunning Goldings hops peppery aroma
Palate	Malt and fruit in mouth, great depth in finish with hops and dark fruit
Comments	Dark ruby-coloured ale with fascinating blend of hops and dark malt.

SQUIRES GOLD
OG 1042˚ ABV 4.2%

Ingredients: Maris Otter pale malt (87.5%), amber malt (12.5%). 21 units of colour. German Hallertau and Hersbrucker, New Zealand Pacific Gem hop pellets. Dry hopped. 38 units of bitterness.

TASTING NOTES

Nose	Roasted coffee aroma
Palate	Dark malt with liquorice notes in mouth, hop bitterness and dark glacé fruit in finish
Comments	Remarkable golden beer with great complexity of flavours.

BLUNDERBUS
OG 1055˚ ABV 5.5%

Ingredients: Maris Otter pale malt (90.25%), chocolate malt (6.50%), black malt (3.25%). 240 units of colour. Fuggles and Goldings whole hops. 40 units of bitterness.

TASTING NOTES

Nose	Massive Goldings hops aroma with dark malt notes
Palate	Dark malt and chocolate in mouth, fruit, liquorice, spices in big finish
Comments	Smoky, roasted malt, well-hopped beer: 'as black as night' says the brewer.

ANNIVERSARY ALE
OG 1060˚ ABV 6%
Ingredients: Maris Otter pale malt (91%), crystal malt (9%). 38 units of colour. Fuggles and Goldings whole hops. Dry hopped. 35 units of bitterness.

TASTING NOTES

Nose	Rich bouquet of malt, hops and fruit
Palate	Full malt in mouth with some fruit, bitter finish with hops and fruit
Comments	Nut-brown beer with massive hops and vinous fruit character. Coach House, set up by former Greenall Whitley senior managers, also brews two seasonal beers, Ostlers Summer Pale Ale (ABV 3.9%), and Taverners Autumn Ale (5%) plus Three Kings Christmas Ale (ABV 6.5%).

■■■■■■■■
Dent Brewery

- ▭ **Hollins, Cowgill, Dent LA10 5TQ.**
- ☽ **05875 326.**
- 🏛 **Yes.**
- ⚲ **Yes (not more than six people).**
- *i* **Independent**

DENT BITTER
OG 1036˚ ABV 3.8%
Ingredients: Halcyon pale malt (95%), crystal malt (4.5%), roast barley (4.5%). Northdown whole hops.

TASTING NOTES

Nose	Rich hops aroma with light fruit notes
Palate	Bitter-sweet in mouth, light, hoppy and quenching finish
Comments	Good balance of hoppy bitterness and sweetness from yeast strain supplied by Youngers (S&N).

RAMSBOTTOM
OG 1044˚ ABV 4.7%
Ingredients: Halcyon pale malt (90%), crystal malt (9%), roast barley (1%). Northdown whole hops.

TASTING NOTES

Nose	Ripe malt aroma with good hops balance
Palate	Full malt in mouth, deep finish with good hops character and delicious fruit notes
Comments	Rich and rounded ale with complex crystal malt and hops character.

T'OWD TUP
OG 1055˚ ABV 6%
Ingredients: Halcyon pale malt (86%), crystal malt (9.5%), roast barley (4.5%). Northdown whole hops.

TASTING NOTES

Nose	Soft roasted malt fragrance
Palate	Hops and dark malt dominate mouth, lingering hoppy and slightly astringent finish
Comments	Dark, roast-accented stout.

Hesket Newmarket Brewery
⌖ **Old Crown Barn, Hesket Newmarket CA7 8JG.**
① **06974 78288.**
🏛 **No.**
🍴 **Yes.**
i **Independent**

BLENCATHRA BITTER
OG 1035˚ ABV 3.25%
Ingredients: pale malt (84%), crystal malt (13%), chocolate malt (3%). Fuggles, Goldings and Hallertau hops.

TASTING NOTES

Nose	Light malt and spicy Goldings aromas
Palate	Malt and cobnuts in mouth, bitter-sweet finish with hops, fruit and nuts
Comments	Smooth-drinking light bitter with rich crystal malt character.

SKIDDAW SPECIAL
OG 1035˚ ABV 3.25%
Ingredients: pale malt (92%), crystal malt (8%). Fuggles, Goldings and Hallertau hops.

TASTING NOTES

Nose	Malt and hops aroma with some delicate citric notes
Palate	Rounded malt in mouth, long bitter finish with good hops character and quenching fruitiness
Comments	Pale, refreshing, well-hopped bitter.

GREAT COCKUP PORTER
OG 1035˚ ABV 2.6%

Ingredients: pale malt (37%), glucose (37%), crystal malt (15%), chocolate malt (12%). Fuggles, Goldings and Hallertau hops.

TASTING NOTES

Nose	Dark fruit and chocolate aroma
Palate	Chocolate dominates the mouth, bittersweet finish with hops, light fruit and chocolate
Comments	Intriguing beer with the strength of a mild and complex flavours of dark malt and hops.

DORIS'S 90th BIRTHDAY ALE
OG 1045˚ ABV 4.25%

Ingredients: pale malt (92%), crystal malt (8%). Fuggles, Goldings and Hallertau hops.

TASTING NOTES

Nose	Great Goldings hop resin aroma with malt and fruit notes
Palate	Full malt and hops in mouth, deep bittersweet finish with hops and fruit
Comments	Rich and complex premium bitter.

OLD CARROCK STRONG ALE
OG 1060˚ ABV 5.75%

Ingredients: pale malt (83%), crystal malt (17%). Fuggles, Goldings and Hallertau hops.

TASTING NOTES

Nose	Rich and ripe malt, hops and marmalade fruit
Palate	Massive malt and fruit flavours leading to deep and long finish with great hops and fruit appeal

Comments   Full-flavoured, copper-coloured strong
            ale. The brewery supplies its beer to the
            Old Crown Inn and a growing free trade.

Joseph Holt PLC

☞ **Derby Brewery, Empire Street, Cheetham,
  Manchester M3 1JD.**
① **061-834 3285.**
🏛 **No.**
🖈 **No.**
i **Independent**

MILD
OG 1033° ABV 3.2%
Ingredients: Halcyon, Pipkin and Triumph pale malts,
crystal malt, black malt, flaked maize, dark invert sugar.
Goldings and Northdown whole hops. 30 units of bitter-
ness.

TASTING NOTES
Nose   Dry malt, hops and chocolate notes
Palate   Light balance of malt and hops, com-
            plex bitter-sweet finish with hops and
            black chocolate notes
Comments   Splendid dark mild with fine hop charac-
            ter.

BITTER
OG 1039° ABV 4%
Ingredients: Halcyon, Pipkin and Triumph pale malts,
black malt, flaked maize, light invert sugar. Goldings and
Northdown whole hops. 40 units of bitterness.

TASTING NOTES
Nose   Superb hops bouquet with tart fruit notes
Palate   Quenching balance of malt and hops,
            deep, bitter, hoppy finish with some cit-
            ric fruit
Comments   Classic bitter beer with enormous hop
            character.

Hydes' Anvil Brewery Ltd

- ✉ **46 Moss Lane West, Manchester M15 5PH.**
- ① **061-226 1317.**
- 🏛 **Yes.**
- 👭 **by arrangement.**
- *i* **Independent**

ANVIL MILD
OG 1032° ABV 3.5%
Ingredients: 100% Maris Otter pale malt, crystal malt and caramel for colour, invert priming sugar. Fuggles whole hops. Dry hopped. 21 units of bitterness.

TASTING NOTES

Nose	Gentle malt and hops aromas
Palate	Malt dominates the mouth with short, delicate finish with light fruit notes
Comments	Pleasant, refreshing ruby-coloured mild.

ANVIL LIGHT
OG 1034° ABV 3.7%
Ingredients: 100% Maris Otter pale malt, crystal malt and caramel for colour, invert priming sugar. Fuggles whole hops. Dry hopped. 23 units of bitterness.

TASTING NOTES

Nose	Delicate promise of hops
Palate	Light, quenching balance of malt and hops, refreshing bitter-sweet finish
Comments	Light, well-attenuated, amber-coloured mild.

ANVIL BITTER
OG 1036° ABV 3.8%
Ingredients: 100% Maris Otter pale malt, crystal malt and caramel for colour, invert priming sugar. 50% Fuggles and 50% Styrian Goldings whole hops. 28 units of bitterness.

TASTING NOTES

Nose	Rich hop resin aroma with light fruit notes
Palate	Full malt and hops in mouth, dry, tart finish with quenching hops and fruit
Comments	Superb bitter that drinks more than its strength.

Jennings Bros PLC

⌕ **Castle Brewery, Cockermouth CA13 9NE.**
☎ **0900 823214.**
🏛 **Yes.**
⚲ **by arrangement.**
i **Independent**

DARK MILD
OG 1031˚ ABV 3.1%
Ingredients: pale malt, torrefied wheat, invert sugar,
black malt. Challenger, Fuggles and Goldings whole
hops.

TASTING NOTES
Nose	Nuts and malt aromas with delicate hop notes
Palate	Rich grainy flavours with mellow, bitter-sweet finish
Comments	Dark malty mild with some hop notes.

JENNINGS BITTER
OG 1035˚ ABV 3.4%
Ingredients: pale malt, torrefied wheat, invert sugar,
small percentage black malt. Challenger, Fuggles and
Goldings whole hops.

TASTING NOTES
Nose	Complex aroma of tangy hop resins and rich malt
Palate	Pronounced flavours of rich malt and hop bitterness with long, tart finish
Comments	Brilliant copper-coloured bitter with a distinctive tangy palate and finish.

JENNINGS CUMBERLAND ALE
OG 1040˚ ABV 3.8%
Ingredients: pale malt, torrefied wheat, invert sugar.
Challenger, Fuggles and Goldings whole hops.

TASTING NOTES
Nose	Aromatic malt and hops aromas with fruit notes
Palate	Malt and hops dominate mouth; long, dry finish with good hops character and citric fruit notes

Comments   Quenching, pale bitter with fine bal-
            ance of malt, hops and tart fruit.

JENNINGS SNECK-LIFTER
OG 1055° ABV 5.1%
Ingredients: pale malt, torrefied wheat, invert sugar,
small percentage of black malt. Challenger, Fuggles
and Goldings whole hops.

TASTING NOTES
Nose   Rich malt and fruit with good hops notes
Palate   Ripe fruit and malt in mouth, deep finish
            with fruit and hops dominating
Comments   Full-flavoured and rounded strong ale.
            Jennings is marketing Oatmeal Stout
            (ABV 3.8%) brewed by Broughton of Scot-
            land; it will brew the beer itself from mid-
            1993.

J W Lees & Company (Brewing) Ltd
⌨ **Greengate Brewery, Middleton Junction,
Manchester M24 2AX.**
① **061-643 2487.**
🏛 **No.**
🕴 **Yes.**
i **Independent**

GB MILD
OG 1032° ABV 3.5%
Ingredients: Maris Otter pale malt, invert sugar (10%).
Fuggles and East Kent Goldings whole and pellet hops.
23 units of bitterness.

TASTING NOTES
Nose   Sweet malt aroma
Palate   Tasty malt in mouth, dry and nutty finish
Comments   Earthy medium dark mild with good malt
            character.

BITTER
OG 1037° ABV 4%
Ingredients: Maris Otter pale malt, caramel for colour
adjustment. Fuggles and East Kent Goldings whole and
pellet hops. 27 units of bitterness.

TASTING NOTES

Nose	Rich malt, orange fruit and Goldings hops
Palate	Malt dominates the mouth with dry and bitter finish with fine citric fruit and hops
Comments	Robust and fruity bitter — a superb and under-rated beer.

MOONRAKER
OG 1073˚ ABV 7.5%
Ingredients: Maris Otter pale malt, caramel for colour adjustment. Fuggles and East Kent Goldings whole and pellet hops. 30 units of bitterness.

TASTING NOTES

Nose	Ripe vinous attack of malt and fruit
Palate	Big malt and hop prickle in mouth, intense bitter-sweet finish with rich fruit notes
Comments	Deep, warming winter barley wine.

HARVEST ALE
OG 1120˚ ABV 11.5%
Ingredients: 100% Maris Otter pale malt. East Kent Goldings whole hops. 34 units of bitterness.

TASTING NOTES

Nose	Rich, fruity, vinous aroma with hop overtones
Palate	Enormous bitter-sweet fruit in mouth, malt, hops and fruit in deep finish
Comments	Famous bottled beer now produced in draught form once a year 'to celebrate the first first malt and hops of the harvest', says the brewer. Ripe, sherry-type fruit and great hop appeal.

Thomas McGuinness Brewing Company

- Cask & Feather, 1 Oldham Road, Rochdale OL16 1VA.
- 0706 711476.
- Yes.
- Yes.
- *i* Independent

McGUINNESS BEST BITTER
OG 1038˚ ABV 4.1%
Ingredients: Pipkin pale malt (94%), torrefied wheat (4%), crystal malt (2%). Fuggles whole hops.

TASTING NOTES

Nose	Delicate malt and hops aromas
Palate	Bitter-sweet in mouth with hops dominating the finish
Comments	Smooth, well-balanced bitter

JUNCTION BITTER
OG 1042˚ ABV 4.5%
Ingredients: Pipkin pale malt (94%), roasted malt (2%), torrefied wheat (4%). Challenger and Fuggles whole hops.

TASTING NOTES

Nose	Delicate roast malt and Fuggles aromas
Palate	Delicate hops and creamy malt in mouth, bitter-sweet finish
Comments	Fine bitter with creamy note from roasted malt and good hop character.

TOMMY DODD PORTER
OG 1050˚ ABV 5.6%
Ingredients: Pipkin pale malt (92%), torrefied wheat (3%), roast barley (5%). Challenger and Fuggles whole hops.

TASTING NOTES

Nose	Delicate roasted grain and chocolate aromas
Palate	Smooth and rich dark malt in mouth, creamy malt, chocolate and hops in big finish

Comments	Splendid dark porter: 'black velvet', says the brewer. Micro-brewery is behind the Cask & Feather pub and also sells to free trade.

Mitchells of Lancaster
- 🖃 **11 Moor Lane, Lancaster LA1 1QB.**
- ① **0524 63773.**
- 🏛 **Yes.**
- ⚶ **by arrangement.**
- *i* **Independent**

DARK MILD
OG 1033° ABV 3.3%
Ingredients: Maris Otter and Pipkin pale malts, crystal malt, torrefied wheat and black invert sugar. 80-90 units of colour. Challenger, Goldings and Progress hops: 90% whole, 10% pellets.

TASTING NOTES
Nose	Malt and delicate toffee aromas
Palate	Creamy malt in mouth, light dry finish with hint of coffee
Comments	Mellow mild with fine creamy malt appeal.

BEST BITTER
OG 1035° ABV 3.5%
Ingredients: Maris Otter and Pipkin pale malts, torrefied wheat and invert sugar. 11-13 units of colour. Challenger, Goldings and Progress hops, 90% whole, 10% pellets.

TASTING NOTES
Nose	Hop resins and malt aromas
Palate	Rich malt and nut in mouth, quenching dry, nutty finish
Comments	Pale gold, refreshing brew.

OLDE PRIORY PORTER
OG 1035° ABV 3.3%
Ingredients: Maris Otter and Pipkin pale malts, crystal malt, torrefied wheat, black invert sugar, roasted malt extract. 120 units of colour. Challenger, Goldings and Progress hops, 90% whole, 10% pellets.

TASTING NOTES

Nose	Dark bitter malt and hops aromas
Palate	Bitter-sweet malt and hops in mouth, hops, bitter chocolate and coffee in finish
Comments	Jet-black, bitter-sweet, creamy yet hoppy beer.

FORTRESS
OG 1042° ABV 4.2%

Ingredients: Maris Otter and Pipkin pale malts, crystal malt, torrefied wheat and invert sugar. 32-36 units of colour. Challenger, Godlings and Progress hops, 90% whole, 10% pellets.

TASTING NOTES

Nose	Big malt and hops aromas
Palate	Malt and nuts dominate mouth, long finish with hops and dark fruit
Comments	Rich, full-bodied fruity ale.

OLDE CLOG
OG 1045° ABV 4.2%

Ingredients: Maris Otter and Pipkin pale malts, crystal malt, torrefied wheat, invert sugar, roasted malt extract. 120 units of colour. Challenger, Goldings and Progress hops, 90% whole, 10% pellets.

TASTING NOTES

Nose	Rich dark malt and hops aromas
Palate	Creamy, chewy malt in mouth, big finish with hops, vanilla and fruit notes
Comments	Dark bitter-sweet beer with great roasted malt and hops character.

ESB
OG 1050° ABV 5%

Ingredients: Maris Otter and Pipkin pale malts, crystal malt, torrefied wheat, invert sugar. 40-44 units of colour. Challenger, Goldings and Progress hops, 90% whole, 10% pellets.

TASTING NOTES

Nose	Powerful smack of malt, hops and fruit
Palate	Big malt and fruit in mouth, deep finish with hops and ripe fruit

Comments   Mellow strong ale of great depth and complexity. Mitchells also brews a winter beer Single Malt (ABV 7.2%).

Moorhouses Brewery (Burnley) Ltd

⌕ **4 Moorhouse Street, Burnley BB11 5EN.**
① **0282 422864/416004.**
🏛 **No.**
⚢ **by arrangement.**
i **Independent**

BLACK CAT MILD
OG 1034˚ ABV 3.4%
Ingredients: Halcyon pale malt (60%), chocolate malt (10%), invert sugar (17%), flaked maize (13%). Fuggles whole hops.

TASTING NOTES
Nose   Roasted grain and nut aromas
Palate   Chocolate notes in mouth, sweet but dry finish
Comments   Dark mild with roast malt character.

PREMIER BITTER
OG 1036˚ ABV 3.6%
Ingredients: Halcyon pale malt (80%), crystal (5%), invert sugar (10%), flaked maize (5%). Fuggles whole hops.

TASTING NOTES
Nose   Good malt and hops bouquet
Palate   Delicate balance of malt and hops in mouth, hops and hint of nut in long finish
Comments   Fine-tasting bitter, winner of two Brewex silver medals.

PENDLE WITCHES BREW
OG 1050˚ ABV 5.2%
Ingredients: Halcyon pale malt (80%), crystal malt (5%), invert sugar (10%), flaked maize (5%). Fuggles whole hops.

TASTING NOTES
Nose   Massive attack of rich malt and hops

Palate	Bitter-sweet malt and hops in mouth, deep, dry finish with good hop character and vanilla notes
Comments	Deceptively pale strong bitter; leave your broomstick at home.

OWD ALE
OG 1060° ABV 6.2%
Ingredients: Halcyon pale malt (71%), crystal malt (6%), flaked maize (6.5%), invert sugar (14%), caramel (0.5%). Fuggles whole hops.

TASTING NOTES

Nose	Delicate aromas of honey and fruit
Palate	Full malt in mouth, long, dry finish with rich fruit and hops
Comments	Ripe, warming and rounded winter brew.

Preston Brewing Company Ltd
⌨ **Atlas Brewery, Brieryfield Road, Preston PR1 8SR.**
① **0772 883055.**
🏛 **No.**
👥 **Yes.**
i **Independent**

PRIDE ALE
OG 1036° ABV 3.8%
Ingredients: Maris Otter pale malt, crystal malt, torrefied wheat. 10 units of colour. Challenger, Fuggles, Northdown and Target whole hops. 25-30 units of bitterness.

TASTING NOTES

Nose	Delicate aromas of malt and hops
Palate	Hops dominate the mouth with malt notes, smooth, creamy finish
Comments	Pale, smooth-drinking bitter with good hop appeal. Pride Dark Mild (ABV 3.6%) is an almost identical brew with the addition of chocolate malt and hops in different proportions.

ATLAS REALLY STRONG EXPORT
OG 1060˚ ABV 6.5%

Ingredients: Maris Otter pale malt, crystal malt, chocolate malt, torrefied wheat. 60 units of colour. Challenger, Fuggles, Northdown and Target whole hops. 30-40 units of bitterness.

TASTING NOTES

Nose	Rich bouquet of malt, fruit and hops
Palate	Nutty malt and bitter hops in mouth, medium dry finish with good hops and dark fruit notes
Comments	Ruby ale with fine balance of crystal malt and hops.

Oak Brewing Company Ltd

⌨ **Phoenix Brewery, Green Lane, Heywood OL10 2EP.**
☏ **0706 627009.**
🏛 **No.**
👥 **by arrangement.**
i **Independent**

OAK BEST BITTER
OG 1038˚

Ingredients: pale malt, crystal malt, black malt, Challenger, East Kent Goldings and Whitbread Goldings Variety hop pellets; dry hopped.

TASTING NOTES

Nose	Tangy bouquet of hops and malt
Palate	Fine balance of malt and hops in mouth, tart, bitter-sweet finish
Comments	Clean tasting and refreshing bitter.

OLD OAK ALE
OG 1044˚

Ingredients: pale malt, crystal malt, black malt. Challenger, East Kent Goldings and Whitbread Goldings Variety hop pellets; dry hopped.

TASTING NOTES

Nose	Rich malt aroma with hops and light fruit
Palate	Full malt in mouth with bitter hops edge, long dry finish with hops and fruit character

Comments   Delectable premium bitter with excellent hop balance.

DOUBLE DAGGER
OG 1050˚
Ingredients: pale malt, crystal malt, black malt. Challenger, East Kent Goldings and Whitbread Goldings Variety hop pellets.

TASTING NOTES
Nose   Pronounced ripe malt and fruit aromas
Palate   Great depth of malt in mouth offset by dry finish with flinty hops and sharp fruit notes
Comments   Complex, tart and fruity strong ale.

WOBBLY BOB
OG 1060˚
Ingredients: pale malt, crystal malt, black malt. Challenger, East Kent Goldings and Whitbread Goldings Variety hop pellets.

TASTING NOTES
Nose   Stunning bouquet of hop resins and ripe fruit
Palate   Enormous vinous malt and fruit in mouth, robust dry finish with bursts of hops and fruit
Comments   Strong ale of great character and complexity. Also brews a Porter, with Humbug at Christmas.

Frederic Robinson Ltd
⌧ **Unicorn Brewery, Stockport SK1 1JJ.**
① **061-480 6571.**
🏛 **Yes.**
朲 **by arrangement.**
i **Independent**

BEST MILD
OG 1032° ABV 3.3%
Ingredients: Halcyon and Pipkin pale malts. crystal malt, small percentage of flaked maize and torrefied wheat, caramel for colour adjustment. Goldings whole hops and small percentage of Northdown; dry hopped in cask with Goldings pellets.

TASTING NOTES

Nose	Light nut and malt aromas
Palate	Nutty malt in mouth, quenching balance of hops in finish
Comments	Excellent quaffing light mild; caramel is added for Dark Mild.

BITTER
OG 1035° ABV 3.5%
Ingredients: Halcyon and Pipkin pale malts, crystal malt, small percentage of flaked maize and torrefied wheat, caramel for colour adjustment. Goldings whole hops and small percentage of Northdown; dry hopped in cask with Goldings pellets.

TASTING NOTES

Nose	Delicate hop resin aroma
Palate	Light balance of malt and hops in mouth, bitter-sweet finish
Comments	Light session bitter, sold in only a handful of outlets.

HARTLEYS XB
OG 1040° ABV 4%
Ingredients: mild ale malt, crystal malt, small percentage flaked maize and invert sugar. Goldings and Styrian Goldings whole hops.

TASTING NOTES

Nose	Pronounced malt aroma with some fruit notes
Palate	Rounded malt in mouth, long, dry, slightly acidic finish with fruit notes
Comments	Pale, tart beer brewed for Hartley's pubs in Cumbria following closure of the brewery

BEST BITTER
OG 1041˚ ABV 4.2%
Ingredients: Halcyon and Pipkin pale malts, crystal malt, small percentage of flaked maize and torrefied wheat, caramel for colour adjustment. Goldings whole hops and small percentage of Northdown; dry hopped in cask with Goldings pellets.

TASTING NOTES

Nose	Rich and complex aromas of Goldings hops, malt and tart fruit
Palate	Superb mouth-feel of rich malt and hops, long, dry finish with citric fruit notes
Comments	Magnificent pale, tart and quenching complex brew; one for the desert island.

OLD TOM
OG 1080˚ ABV 8.5%
Ingredients: Halcyon and Pipkin pale malts, crystal malt, small percentage of flaked maize and torrefied wheat, caramel for colour adjustment. Goldings whole hops and small percentage of Northdown; dry hopped in cask with Goldings pellets.

TASTING NOTES

Nose	Heady, vinous aromas of dark fruit
Palate	Booming balance of ripe malt and peppery hops; deep port wine finish with bitter hops balance
Comments	Dark, rich and warming superior barley wine.

▬▬▬▬▬▬▬▬

Tetley Walker Ltd

- ⌨ **The Brewery, Dallam Lane, Warrington WA2 7NU.**
- ① **0925 31231**
- 🏛 **Yes.**
- 🚶 **by arrangement.**
- *i* **Subsidiary of Carlsberg-Tetley. Tetley Mild and Bitter brewed at Warrington are attempted replicas of the Leeds' brews though the Cheshire version of Tetley Bitter lacks the finesse of the original. Peter Walker brands are brewed for pubs in the Merseyside area. The company now brews beers for the Greenall pub company.**

TETLEY DARK MILD
OG 1032˚ ABV 2.9%
Ingredients: pale malt, crystal malt, micronised wheat, dark liquid sugar, caramel. Northdown whole hops; dry hopped.

TASTING NOTES

Nose	Light malt and nut aromas
Palate	Chewy malt in mouth, sweet finish with hint of hop
Comments	Pleasant, nutty dark mild.

WALKER MILD
OG 1032˚ ABV 2.9%
Ingredients: pale malt, crystal malt, dark liquid sugar, caramel. Northdown whole hops; dry hopped.

TASTING NOTES

Nose	Delicate malt and hint of hop
Palate	Dark chewy malt in mouth, good bitterness and fruit hints in the finish
Comments	Complex brew with good hop and light fruit.

WALKER BEST BITTER
OG 1033˚ ABV 3.3%
Ingredients: pale malt, crystal malt, micronised wheat, liquid sugar. Northdown whole hops; dry hopped.

TASTING NOTES

Nose	Light hop notes
Palate	Refreshing balance of malt and hops with dry finish and hops and light fruit notes
Comments	Quenching, well-balanced session ale.

WALKER BEST BITTER
OG 1036˚ ABV 3.3%
Ingredients: pale malt, micronised wheat, dark liquid sugar. Northdown whole hops; dry hops.

TASTING NOTES

Nose	Tangy hop resins and malt aromas
Palate	Sharp balance of malt and hops, dry finish with hops and citric fruit
Comments	Flinty, refreshing brew.

WALKER WINTER WARMER
OG 1060˚ ABV 5.9%
Ingredients: pale malt, crystal malt, micronised wheat, liquid sugar, dark liquid sugar. Northdown whole hops; dry hopped.

TASTING NOTES
Nose	Rich, winey malt and hops
Palate	Massive dark fruit and hops in mouth, ripe fruity finish
Comments	Powerful ruby ale with fine fruit character.

GREENALLS CASK MILD
OG 1033˚ ABV 3.1%
Ingredients: white malt, crystal malt, torrefied wheat, maltose sugar, caramel. 105 units of colour. Fuggles and Goldings whole hops; dry hopped. 17 units of bitterness.

TASTING NOTES
Nose	Chocolate and roast malt aroma with light hops
Palate	Dark roasted malt in mouth, bitter-sweet finish
Comments	Lightly hopped mild with pronounced dark malt notes.

GREENALLS CASK BITTER
OG 1036˚ ABV 3.8%
Ingredients: white malt, torrefied wheat, maltose sugar. 21 units of colour. Fuggles and Goldings whole hops; dry hopped. 27 units of bitterness.

TASTING NOTES
Nose	Gentle Fuggles hop notes
Palate	Light malt and hops in mouth, smooth finish with light hops, vanilla and delicate fruit
Comments	Smooth, undemanding beer.

THOMAS GREENALL'S ORIGINAL BITTER
OG 1045˚ ABV 4.4%
Ingredients: Maris Otter pale malt, crystal malt, maltose syrup. 30 units of colour. Fuggles and Goldings whole hops. 33 units of bitterness.

TASTING NOTES

Nose	Complex aromas of fruit, hops and malt
Palate	Rich winey fruit in mouth, deep, bitter-sweet finish with ripe fruit and hops
Comments	Fine premium bitter with rich fruit character. Tetley-Walker is also to brew Davenports and Shipstones beers from two more defunct breweries.

Daniel Thwaites PLC

⌧ **PO Box 50, Star Brewery, Blackburn BB1 5BU.**
☎ **0254 54431.**
🏛 **Yes.**
👤 **Yes.**
i **Independent**

THWAITES

MILD
OG 1031° ABV 3%
Ingredients: pale malt, crystal malt (85%), copper sugar (15%). Fuggles, East Kent Goldings and Goldings blend whole hops.

TASTING NOTES

Nose	Pleasing aromas of light malt and nuts
Palate	Malt in mouth, short dry finish
Comments	Easy-drinking smooth dark mild.

BEST MILD
OG 1034° ABV 3.2%
Ingredients: pale malt, crystal malt (85%), copper sugar (15%). Fuggles, East Kent Goldings and high alpha Goldings blend whole hops.

TASTING NOTES

Nose	Rich malt and light nut aromas
Palate	Mellow malt giving way to deep finish with good hop notes and chewy nut
Comments	Superb dark mild of great depth.

BITTER
OG 1036° ABV 3.5%
Ingredients: pale malt (85%), copper sugar (15%). Fuggles, East Kent Goldings and blend of various high alpha whole hops.

TASTING NOTES

Nose	Delicate aromas of malt with hop notes developing
Palate	Mellow creamy malt in mouth with good hop edge; deep bitter-sweet finish with hint of nuts
Comments	Fine amber ale, the archetypal north-west bitter with creamy, mellow malt offset by good hopping. Daniel's Hammer (OG 1050˚) is a Xmas brew.

Weetwood Ales Ltd

✉ **The Brewery, Weetwood Grange, Weetwood, Tarporley CW6 0NQ.**
① **0829 52377.**
🏛 **Yes.**
🚶 **by arrangement.**
𝑖 **Independent**

WEETWOOD BEST CASK BITTER
OG 1039.5˚ ABV 3.8%
Ingredients: Maris Otter pale malt (90%), crystal malt (5%), wheat malt (5%), chocolate malt (0.5%). 20 units of colour. Challenger and Goldings whole hops. 33 units of bitterness.

TASTING NOTES

Nose	Delicate floral hops aroma
Palate	Clean hops and malt in mouth, rounded bitter-sweet finish
Comments	Fine well-rounded beer with great hops appeal.

West Coast Brewing Co Ltd

⌧ **Justin Close, Chorlton-on-Medlock, Manchester M13 9UX.**
☎ **061-273 6366.**
🏛 **Yes (in hotel).**
⋔ **by arrangement.**
i **Independent**

DARK MILD
OG 1032° ABV 3%
Ingredients: pale malt (95%), roasted barley (5%), roasted malt (5%). 100 units of colour. Fuggles, Goldings and New Zealand hop pellets; dry hopped. 18 units of bitterness.

TASTING NOTES
Nose	Dominant Fuggles dry hop aromas with rich dark malt
Palate	Full malt and hops in mouth, fruity finish with roasted grain
Comments	Dark, rich mild with fine roasted grain character.

KANGAROO XXXX PALE ALE
OG 1038° ABV 3.8%
Ingredients: 100% Maris Otter pale malt. 10 units of colour. 100% Pride of Ringwood Australian hop pellets; dry hopped. 40 units of bitterness.

TASTING NOTES
Nose	Intense aromatic hops aroma
Palate	Full bitter hops in mouth, long hoppy finish with some citric fruit notes
Comments	Pale beer with massive hop character, splendid antidote to certain Australian brews.

YAKIMA GRANDE PORTER
OG 1050° ABV 5.5%
Ingredients: Maris Otter pale malt (80%), malted wheat, roast malt, roast barley, chocolate malt. 100 units of colour. American Yakima and New Zealand hop pellets. 20 units of bitterness.

TASTING NOTES

Nose	Fruit, coffee and roasted malt
Palate	Full malt and fruit in mouth, roasted grain and hops finish
Comments	Succulent dark porter with massive malt appeal.

DOBBIN'S GINGER BEER
OG 1050° ABV 6%

Ingredients: Maris Otter pale malt (80%), sugar syrup (20%). 6 units of colour. New Zealand hop pellets. Boiled with dry ground ginger; sliced fresh ginger added to casks. 20 units of bitterness.

TASTING NOTES

Nose	Powerful aroma of ginger
Palate	Light, dry gingery mouth-feel, refreshing spicy finish
Comments	Cloudy pale, wonderfully aromatic and refreshing ale.

OLD SOPORIFIC BARLEY WINE
OG 1086° ABV 10%

Ingredients: Maris Otter pale malt (70%), crystal malt (6%), black malt (0.1%). 24 units of colour. New Zealand hop pellets, dry hopped with East Kent Goldings. 50 units of bitterness.

TASTING NOTES

Nose	Massive ripe fruit and floral hops
Palate	Vinous in mouth, aromatic hops and malt in finish
Comments	Alcoholic marmalade with hops.

Yates Brewery

🖃 **Ghyll Farm, Westnewton, Aspatria CA5 3NX.**
① **06973 21081.**
🏛 **No.**
🚶 **No.**
i **Independent**

YATES BITTER
OG 1035° ABV 3.9%
Ingredients: not revealed. 14 units of colour. 35 units of
bitterness.

TASTING NOTES

Nose	Spicy aromas of hops and tart fruit
Palate	Tangy balance of malt and hops; deep finish with good hop bitterness and light fruit
Comments	Fine straw-coloured bitter, exceptionally dry and well-attenuated.

YATES PREMIUM
OG 1048° ABV 5.2%
Ingredients: not revealed. 12 units of colour. 28 units of
bitterness.

TASTING NOTES

Nose	Rich malt and hops with some citric fruit notes
Palate	Mellow malt in mouth, deep finish with good hops, fruit and vanilla notes
Comments	Straw-coloured bitter of some complexity and depth. Best Cellar (ABV 5.3%) is a rich, warming, copper-coloured winter brew.

LATE ENTRY

▬▬▬▬▬▬▬▬▬▬▬▬▬▬▬▬

Little Avenham Brewery
▱ **30 Avenham Street, Preston PR1 2BN.**
☎ **07725 1380.**
**Brewing Pickled Priest (ABV 3.5%), Clog Dancer (4%),
Torchlight Bitter (5%), Pierrepoint's Last Drop (7%) and
Hedge Row Bitter seasonal beer (4%).**

ISLE OF MAN

The small island midway between England and Ireland has a way of life reminiscent of the mainland in the 1950s though it is sadly up to date in the way of brewery closures.

The old, slightly ramshackle Castletown Brewery produced superb beers that disappeared following its merger with the larger Okells Brewery of Douglas in 1986. Renamed Isle of Man Breweries, it plans to close its impressive plant and move to smaller premises and may, fingers crossed, bring back Castletown Bitter.

Variety has been vastly improved by the arrival of Bushy, owned by the energetic Martin Brunnschweiler, who brews some admired ales and a genuine lager.

Okells and Bushy are aided by the Manx Pure Beer Act which allows only malt, hops, yeast, water and minute amounts of brewing sugar. Mainland brewers please copy!

■■■■■■■■■

Bushy's Brewery

▣ **Mount Murray Brewing Co Ltd, Mount Murray, Braddan IoM.**
① **0624 661244/675139.**
🏛 **Yes.**
🏃 **Yes.**
i **Independent**

BUSHY'S DARK MILD
OG 1035˚ ABV 3.6%
Ingredients: Pipkin pale malt (82.6%), crystal malt (13.2%), chocolate (4.2%). Challenger and Fuggles hop pellets, late copper hopped.

TASTING NOTES
Nose	Dark malt aroma
Palate	Chocolate and liquorice in mouth with some hop notes in finish
Comments	Dark ruby beer with a creamy head and good malt flavours.

BUSHY'S BITTER
OG 1038˚ ABV 4%
Ingredients: 100% pale, crystal and chocolate malt. Challenger, Fuggles and Goldings hop pellets; dry hopped with Fuggles.

TASTING NOTES
Nose	Aromatic dry hop aromas with delicate fruit hints
Palate	Bitter-sweet malt and hops in mouth, light, quenching fruit and hops in finish
Comments	Fine, refreshing session bitter.

OLD BUSHY TAIL
OG 1045˚ ABV 4%
Ingredients: 100% pale, crystal and chocolate malt. Challenger, Fuggles and Goldings hop pellets; dry hopped with Fuggles.

TASTING NOTES
Nose	Sweet malt and powerful hop aromas
Palate	Full and slightly vinous flavours, deep finish with malt, fruit and hops

Comments	Dark and spicy ale; a version called Piston Bitter is produced when the TT races are held.

CELEBRATION ALE
OG 1060˚ ABV 6.2%
Ingredients: 100% pale, crystal and chocolate malts. Challenger, Fuggles and Goldings hop pellets; dry hopped with Fuggles.

TASTING NOTES

Nose	Ripe dark fruit aroma
Palate	Rich malt and fruit in mouth, long vinous and estery finish
Comments	Xmas ale of great complexity, conditioned for three months and sold only in half pints.

Isle of Man Breweries Ltd
⌨ **Falcon Brewery, Douglas IoM.**
① **0624 661140.**
🏛 **Yes.**
🕺 **by arrangement.**
i **Independent. The company is planning to move to new premises**

OKELLS MILD
OG 1034.5˚ ABV 3.5%
Ingredients: Golden Promise or Triumph pale malts (95%), black invert sugar, caramel for colour. Fuggles whole hops plus either Bramling Cross, Northern Brewer or Target.

TASTING NOTES

Nose	Light malt and delicate fruit aromas
Palate	Creamy malt in mouth, light sweet finish with hint of hops and orange fruit
Comments	Easy drinking dark mild, the only Manx beer to use sugar.

OKELLS BITTER
OG 1035.8˚ ABV 3.8%
Ingredients: Golden Promise or Triumph pale malt, crystal malt. Fuggles and Goldings whole hops plus either Bramling Cross, Northern Brewer or Target.

TASTING NOTES

Nose	Rich bouquet of malt and hops
Palate	Full and rounded mellow malt in mouth with bitter-sweet finish and light fruit notes
Comments	Smooth, creamy, easy drinking bitter.

CHANNEL ISLANDS

A major breakthrough has taken place since the last edition: Ann Street Brewery on Jersey has started to produce cask ale after decades of determinedly keg-only brewing. Guernsey retains its two small breweries — the larger owned by Ann Street — producing cask beers of impressive quality, aided by the fact that duty is payable on quantity and not gravity. There is still a demand from older locals for malty dark milds.

Ann Street Brewery Co Ltd
- 🖃 **57 Ann Street, St Helier, Jersey CI.**
- ① **0534 31561.**
- 🏛 **Yes.**
- ⚘ **Yes.**
- *i* **Independent**

OLD JERSEY ALE
OG 1035˚ ABV 3.6%
Ingredients: Pipkin pale malt (95%), chocolate malt (2.5%), wheat malt (1%), sugars (1.5%). 40 units of colour. Challenger, Fuggles, East Kent Goldings and German Hallertau whole hops and pellets. Dry hopped. 33 units of bitterness.

TASTING NOTES
Nose	Rich hops aroma with malty undertones
Palate	Malt and hint of chocolate in mouth, pronounced hop in finish
Comments	Well-balanced session bitter with refreshing malt and hops character.

WINTER ALE
OG 1068˚ ABV 7.5%
Ingredients: Pipkin pale malt (94%), chocolate malt (2%), wheat malt (1.5%), sugars (2.5%). 87.5 units of colour. Challenger, Fuggles, East Kent Goldings and Hallertau whole and pellet hops. 50.2 units of bitterness.

TASTING NOTES
Nose	Rich fruit and hops aroma
Palate	Ripe malt and fruit in mouth, big bittersweet finish with great hops presence
Comments	Ruby-dark strong ale, vinous, hoppy and warming.

Guernsey Brewery Company (1920) Ltd

☞ **South Esplanade, St Peter Port, Guernsey Cl.**
① **0481 720143.**
🏛 **Yes.**
👭 **Yes.**
i **Subsidiary of Ann Street Brewery Company, Jersey.**

LBA MILD
OG 1038˚ ABV 3.7%
Ingredients: malt (98%), flaked barley (1.5%), wheat malt, caramel for colour. Bavarian, Fuggles and Northern Brewer whole and pellet hops; dry hopped with East Kent Goldings.

TASTING NOTES
Nose	Light malt and hops aromas
Palate	Sweet malt and toffee in mouth, dry, bitter-sweet finish
Comments	Full dark mild.

REAL DRAUGHT BITTER
OG 1046˚ ABV 4.1%
Ingredients: malt (98%), flaked barley (1.5%), wheat malt, caramel for colour. Fuggles, Hallertau and Whitbread Goldings Variety whole and pellet hops, dry hopped with East Kent Goldings.

TASTING NOTES
Nose	Rich malt, fruit and hops bouquet
Palate	Rounded balance of malt and hops with long dry finish and fruit notes
Comments	Distinguished amber ale.

R W Randall Ltd

☞ **Vauxlaurens Brewery, St Julian's Avenue, Guernsey Cl.**
① **0481 720134.**
🏛 **Yes.**
👭 **by arrangement.**
i **Independent**

BEST MILD
OG 1033˙
Ingredients: pale malt (93%), wheat malt (3%), sugars (4%). Fuggles whole hops and hop oil.

TASTING NOTES

Nose	Malt, hops and light fruit aromas
Palate	Mellow, rounded malt in mouth with hint of toffee; short dry finish
Comments	Smooth, sweetish, easy drinking dark mild.

BEST BITTER
OG 1046˙
Ingredients: pale malt (94%), wheat malt (3%), sugar and colour. Fuggles and Hallertau whole hops and hop oil.

TASTING NOTES

Nose	Rich, tangy hops aroma with fruit notes developing
Palate	Full malt in mouth with hop edge, long, delicate bitter-sweet finish
Comments	Refreshing, full-bodied bitter.

NORTHERN IRELAND

Northern Ireland is the subject of two disparate beer styles.

Stout and the unremarkable keg beers of the Republic are imported while the Belfast outpost of the Bass empire concentrates on English versions of keg and lager, though it does supply considerable quantities of Worthington White Shield.

Scottish and Newcastle is test-marketing cask ale in the province. Hilden is the only local supplier of the real thing and the arrival of S&N has encouraged the small company to look at the range it produces.

Hilden Brewery

- **Hilden House, Grand Street, Hilden, Lisburn.**
- **0846 663863.**
- *i* **Independent**
- **Yes.**
- **by arrangement.**

HILDEN ALE
OG 1039˚
Ingredients: pale malt, crystal malt. Goldings and Hallertau hops.

TASTING NOTES

Nose	Fragrant Goldings hops bouquet
Palate	Full hop flavours in mouth, dry finish with good hops character
Comments	Fine, quenching golden bitter. Hilden has launched a Porter (OG 1040˚) using pale, crystal and black malts.

Index